thought, in belief, or in action, will be laid aside, and whatever is seen to be called for by this faith, again whether in thought, in belief, or in action, will be accepted and submitted to."

The author presents a brilliant summary of significant trends in Bible study in the past century, and discusses the historical continuity of the Bible, its inner continuity of faith, and the significance of God's self-revelation in Jesus Christ. He then explains in detail the principle of freedom in Biblical interpretation, and applies it to both Old and New Testaments and to the forms of the Church.

This book should be eagerly read by every inquiring Bible student and teacher. It is an extremely provocative expression of clear, vital Christian thought.

THE AUTHOR

Edwin Lewis is well known in many denominations in all parts of the country. Born in England, he was educated in Canada and the United States, receiving his A.B. from New York State Teachers College, and B.D. and Th.D. from Drew University. After instructing in English at New York State College, and in Theology and Greek at Drew University, Dr. Lewis became Professor of Systematic Theology at Drew in 1918. He retired from this position in 1951, and became visiting Professor of Theology at Temple University. Dr. Lewis has lectured at numerous universities and seminaries, including schools in Japan, Korea, China, and India. Among his many published works are *A Christian Manifesto*, *The Faith We Declare*, and *The Practice of the Christian Life*. Dr. Lewis was also joint editor of and contributor to *The Abingdon Bible Commentary*. At present he is living in Madison, New Jersey.

THE BIBLICAL FAITH
AND
CHRISTIAN FREEDOM

Books by Edwin Lewis
Published by The Westminster Press

THE BIBLICAL FAITH AND CHRISTIAN FREEDOM
THE PRACTICE OF THE CHRISTIAN LIFE

THE BIBLICAL FAITH AND CHRISTIAN FREEDOM

The Southwestern Lectures for 1952

by EDWIN LEWIS

Philadelphia
THE WESTMINSTER PRESS

To

Arlo Ayres Brown

President of Drew University
1929–1948

Wise Administrator
Loyal Colleague
Faithful Friend

CONTENTS

Foreword   9

    I. The Point of View   11
   II. The Question of Biblical Interpretation   15
  III. The Emancipation of the Word of God   31
  IV. The Central Issue   48
   V. The Integration with History   63
  VI. The Inner Continuity   81
 VII. The Word as a Person   98
VIII. Free Faith and the Old Testament   115
  IX. An Old Testament Interpretation   127
   X. The Synoptic Gospels   146
  XI. Free Faith and the Gospels   155
 XII. The Epistles and Criticism   166
XIII. New Testament Expositions of the Faith   184
XIV. Free Faith and the Church   205

FOREWORD

WHAT have historical, literary, and other forms of modern Biblical criticism done for the common belief that the Bible gives to men the veritable Word of God? If, after such criticism has done its work, it is still possible to speak of " the Word of God," may we also still use, with complete justification, the concept of revelation? Since the Bible covers a long period of history, and is characterized by many differences, how are we to understand the relation between the changing historical situation, the process of revelation, the increasing and deepening response to revelation, and those features of the Biblical record with which criticism is chiefly concerned?

These are among the questions that I attempt to answer in this book. The book comprises The Southwestern Lectures for 1952, given on a special Foundation at Southwestern University, Georgetown, Texas. The invitation to give the lectures came to me from President William C. Finch, formerly a graduate student of mine at Drew University. It was a pleasure to observe the many signs of his successful leadership of a growing institution, and to renew the happy associations of an earlier day.

At the special request of the Editor, who had heard it given as an address, the third chapter of this book was printed under the same title in *Religion in Life*.

EDWIN LEWIS.

Madison, New Jersey

I

THE POINT OF VIEW

Criticism has made impossible all those conceptions of the Bible which depend upon the identity of the *words* of the Bible with God's own "word." There are good reasons why we may still use the time-honored form, "The Bible is the Word of God," but we cannot use it in any purely literalistic sense. We can say that but for the word of God there would be no Bible, which carries the implication that the Bible and the word of God are inseparable, but this inseparability does not involve co-identity. What it does involve is that a process of divine self-disclosure was at work in history, of which the Bible is the outcome. Under this view, everything in the Bible has significance, but the significance is twofold: there is the significance which any given part may have in itself, as legend, superstition, narrative, genealogy, poetry, history, and the like; and there is the significance which it may have as witnessing to something other than itself. The importance lies at the point of this second kind of significance, which is exceedingly variable. Israel's escape from Egypt is significant in itself as a historical happening: it has a much profounder significance for what it may disclose about the purpose of Israel's God as this came to be apprehended by faith.

Under this view, it is preferable to say that the Bible is a body of witness, and that the reference of the witness is to God — his reality, his nature, his character, his purpose for men. The witnessing is one thing; what is witnessed to is another. Sometimes the witness is direct and intentional; very often it is indirect and unaware. The witness roots in "mighty acts," taken to be acts of God, by which God seeks to disclose himself. But such a divine self-disclosure, while made *possible* by the "acts," becomes a *reality* only as there is a human response, and such response is of faith. God is disclosed through "the wonderful works" which he has done. There is a variation, however, in the degree and kind of the divine self-disclosure. God's "acts" must be interpreted as to what they signify, and this interpretation is conditioned by a wide range of human factors. Similar human factors enter into the expression, the dissemination, and the preservation of the interpretation.

God necessarily initiates the process of his own self-disclosure. Only God knows God, and only God can make God known. The intent of the disclosure is a human response: God would enter into fellowship with his creature man, to make out of the creature a son. The response is subject to contingencies: this is an important consideration in explaining why revelation must be "progressive." In so far as there is response, there is an experience frequently described today as "a divine-human encounter," which really means the same as the older "certainty of God." Implicit in such an experience is the impulse to bear witness to it. The fact of this witness becomes one more of the instrumentalities of the continuing divine initiative. The more that men witness to God, the more God has to work with.

The tendency to characterize God is an accompaniment of the experience. The importance of the characterization is so great that it must be regarded as an element of the revelation: God would disclose to men not only *that* he is but *what* he is. Variation in the human situation, however, has for consequence variation in the characterizations — a fact which in due time will seem to make necessary an *absolute self-characterization* on the part of God. "The Word-become-flesh" will be such an absolute divine self-characterization. Herein will be the correction, the completion, the clarification, and the possible unification of all other divine characterizations as men have been led to make them. The ways of relating God to life will also differ, and a similar corrective and illumination is therefore indicated. The logic of *any* belief in divine revelation is that there shall be *complete* revelation. The Bible provides the evidence that the movement is toward both a final and unmistakable divine self-disclosure and a related disclosure of God's will for the life and activity of men.

The "Word-become-flesh" carries this twofold significance. God's word about himself is also God's word about mankind, which is why his ultimate self-disclosure is made in human terms. Faith is essential to response to the Incarnate Word, as it was to any earlier and limited form of the word. Differences also occur in the characterization of the Incarnate Word himself and in the understanding of his significance for human life. These differences are present in the New Testament, just as differences in the characterization of God and of his will for men are present in the Old Testament. They are implicit not only in the fact of human freedom but in the fact of temperamental and intellectual variations among men. A common faith is compatible with many differences. Since, however, the faith has to do with the finality of God's self-disclosure in the Incarnate Word, where this faith is actually present, differences in the characterizations and in the related forms of behavior become secondary, but always with the understanding that these deviations are open to revision.

The principle in the case is perfectly clear, namely, faith in Jesus Christ as God's final self-disclosure, his Living Word, will involve that whatever is seen to be incompatible with this faith, whether in thought, in belief, or in action, will be laid aside, and that whatever is seen to be called for by this faith, again whether in thought, in belief, or in action, will be accepted and submitted to. This is no guarantee of a flat universal uniformity, since human freedom and human differences, both the intrinsic and the acquired, constitute an obstacle to such uniformity. It is, however, a guarantee of at least the possibility of a complete domination of the Living Word, *as conceived and understood,* in the given life. It is that domination that truly matters. It is that domination that God seeks. It is in the degree of that domination that the whole intent of the divine self-revealing process, continuous from its rudimentary beginnings to its consummation in the Living Word, approaches fufillment.

Clearly, therefore, it is the very nature of the Biblical faith to make for freedom. Where that faith becomes the response to God's Living Word in Christ, freedom is most fully possessed. This freedom is especially manifest in relation to forms of expression and the creation and use of instrumentalities. Faith tends to express itself in two ways: in language and in procedures. It is the very nature of language to be fluid, and therefore changeable, especially where a faith is involved. Procedures are the various means devised to serve faith, to nurture faith, to propagate faith, and to build faith increasingly into life. These procedures are — or should be — as fluid as language. What faith is free to devise, faith is equally free to modify, to abandon, or to replace. The effectiveness of the procedure for its purpose is the test. The courage to apply this test is the best evidence that faith is indeed faith, self-evidencing, self-sufficient, and therefore free — free to devise forms and procedures, free to use them, free to change them.

What is written hereafter is written from this point of view, and is an attempt to expound and justify it.

CHAPTER II

THE QUESTION OF BIBLICAL INTERPRETATION

The Bible is the most important possession of the Christian Church, more important even than all its vast material resources combined — its funds, its endowments, its lands, its churches, its educational and philanthropic institutions, and its business enterprises. We make this high claim for the Bible on the ground that it is the original and supreme witness to that truth of God of which these material resources are but the instrumentalities. The Bible sets forth both the historical reasons for the Christian faith and the origin, growth, and clarification of those truths with which the Christian faith is primarily concerned.

The preacher, as the interpreter of the Bible, is the most important figure in the Christian church. We make that high claim for him on the ground that it is his specific responsibility to keep the Christian faith continually before the mind of the church in such wise as to move the heart of the church, inform its understanding, and motivate its will, and beyond that and through that to keep the Christian faith continually before the world.

The preacher-interpreter and the Bible are therefore not to be separated. The most important possession of the church and the most important figure in the church are mutualities. The human situation being what it is, the one calls for the other. The message implies the messenger, and the messenger implies the message. It is axiomatic that the preacher must be steeped in the Bible to be really a preacher. He must know what the Bible *contains,* but he must also know the *meaning* of what it contains. The first is a matter of the assiduous application of the learning process; the second is a matter of prolonged cogitation, of deep wrestlings of the spirit, of patient searching for the key to the treasures which the Book enshrines. Biblical preaching is Biblical knowledge set on fire. It is quite possible to " know the Bible," as the saying goes, and yet not to know it. It is quite possible to have the Bible at one's fingertips, and still miss the *real* meaning of what one can so glibly quote. A string of verses quoted from Ezekiel, Daniel, Matt., ch. 24, and The Revelation of John may appear to be impressively Biblical, while actually being used to support a complete misrepresentation of what the Bible is fundamentally *about*. Through that living whole which is the Bible runs the deep integrating movement of divine self-revelation, and it is possible to be familiar with the whole and still not detect the inner uniting movement. It is this inner movement that constitutes the ultimate reason for the existence of the Bible itself. One could conceivably give *memoriter* and in chronological sequence the names and dates of the numerous rulers of the Northern Kingdom for the two hundred years from Jeroboam I to Hoshea, and never comprehend what God was *saying about himself* by means of the tragic history! All the parts of the Bible have their own necessity, but that necessity is relative to the purpose and meaning of the whole. He who would possess the true principle of interpretation must therefore possess the true principle of discrimination. To put Rom. 8:35–39 on the same level *as declarative of God* with Eccl. 3:19–22, or John 3:16 with I Sam. 15:1–3, is somewhere to be caught in complete confusion respecting the nature and the purpose of the Bible. The interpreter is helpless unless he can recognize the necessity of distinguishing between the Word of God and those words of men, which in varying degrees and varying forms bear witness to the Word of God. He still has the problem of determining which is which, but in making this distinction he is at least on the way. His call is to be so completely dominated by the Word of God as he comes to apprehend it that, in the striking metaphor of Jeremiah, it becomes as it were a burning fire shut up in his bones, by reason of which he cannot forbear (Jer. 20:9).

Assigning this responsibility to the preacher is not meant to imply that it is his alone. This, however, is the much too common assumption, and it has been a grievous weakness in the Church of Christ. Any kind of Christian witnessing is Christian preaching, and a nonwitnessing Christian is an essential self-contradiction. The Christian faith is interpreted in the degree to which any given life manifestly embodies it. The one certain fact is that the impact of the Word of God upon the world is not limited to verbal utterance. Much less is it limited to designated ecclesiastical status. The supposition that one does not preach, or better, that one does not interpret, unless one is talking, is a fallacy that has lived an opulent life on nonexistent resources. The inescapable impression one derives from The Acts of the Apostles is that every Christian regarded himself as a witness. His use of formal address may have been limited, but his whole attitude to life was such as to leave no doubt in the mind of others that he had committed himself to "the Way" (Acts 18:26; 19:9, 23; 24:14; cf. 8:1–4; 4:13).

Nobody questions the propriety and even the necessity of "difference of function" and "division of labor" within the Church. This goes with organization, and organization is a concomitant of the life. Men "set aside" to "preach the Word" in the formal sense may not be of the "being" (*esse*) of the Church, but they are certainly of its well-being (*bene esse*). So far as Christian witnessing in its truest and most essential meaning is concerned, there is nothing that one Christian, *whatever his office,* may do that may not be done by any other Christian. There are "official duties" which custom and organization limit to designated persons, and nothing that is said here is to be construed as making light of the relevant offices. The office can be defended on sound practical, historical, and psychological grounds. Nevertheless, the New Testament principle of the priesthood and prophetic function of all believers, recovered in early Protestantism — although, one fears, not too long retained by it except in theory — carries with it the most radical implication. If by reason of his participation in the absolute, final, and universal priesthood of Christ, a priesthood carrying its own affiliated prophetic function, every Christian, as "a man in Christ," is a priest, then every Christian is a preacher. Being a priest, he is also a witness — a prophetic witness. He is even, in his own degree, an apostle — "one sent forth" (cf. the "seventy others" of Luke 10:1f., as distinguished from "the twelve" of Matt. 10:1–23). The cause of Jesus Christ is in the keeping of the unnamed "seventies" as much as in that of the immortal "twelves"; as much in the keeping of the humblest layman who bears his name as in that of the proudest of berobed, bemitered, and behatted of elevated ecclesiastics.

These may be regarded as so many obvious commonplaces. For all that, there are, as Paul would say, "differences of preachers." The Church as "the body of Christ," and therefore as "many-functioned," calls for and even requires "diversities of ministrations" (I Cor. 1:4, 5). All prophecy is not the same prophecy, even though its ultimate reference may be to the same Word of God. The priesthood of all believers does not preclude the designation of "official" priests, and the preaching obligation resting upon all men of faith does not preclude the designation of "official" preachers. That the reality of the Christian faith, its power, its significance, its effectiveness for its avowed purpose of human redemption *depend* upon designated officials and could not otherwise be attested in human experience is nothing but a theory cherished by the ecclesiastical mind, and the theory has often enough been disproved by simple and undeniable facts. More than once Paul speaks of "the church that is in thy house" (see Rom. 16:5; Col. 4:15; Philemon 2). This *could* mean the Christian community of a given locality meeting in a given house. But it could also mean that the given family, or even only a part of it, was regarded as a "church." This is surely the acme of simplicity: perchance the father of the family is the priest and prophet of the family, presiding at the family altar, administering the family sacraments, notably "the breaking of bread," and serving as the family instructor — "the prophet" — in the things of the Spirit. This would be a "church" indeed — an *ecclesia* without ecclesiasticism! Would that the world were full of such churches!

One would not be ungracious here. Clearly enough, the identification of ecclesiastical mechanics with essential Christian truth and life appears proper enough to minds of a certain type. To minds of a different type, the identification is a simple incredibility. Years ago, Harald Höffding pointed out the religious significance of varying psychological "types." God has more than one mold in which to form minds. We can only suppose that there are natural-born religious institutionalists as there are natural-born religious libertarians. To one man, a rock is "an idea"; to another, a rock is palpable, undeniable, stubborn, objective, coercive "reality": not a shadowy "in here," but a most evident "out there." Philosophical realists and philosophical idealists are produced, not in the classroom by a skillful teacher, but "in Being's flood, in Action's stream," and on "the roaring loom of Time." It is there that minds are turned forth, "sufficiently impressed." Say what we will, there is a predestination in respect of religious preference. Undoubtedly, ritualists may be made, but the truly contented "made" ritualist was a ritualist at heart before the making began. One man wants his religion set to gorgeous pageantry: he must worship God "in the beauty of holy array." Another wants it in unadorned simplicity: he is content with the austere Doric, and is glad to leave to others the involutions and gyrations of the Romanesque. The author's own "bent" will appear as this book proceeds. With every wish to be catholic, he cannot suppress his conviction that the Christian faith in its essence needs no adventitious supports to give it credence. It can be stripped down to its stark and unadorned simplicity without any loss. Appropriate instrumentalities — yes! It can use them; it may even need them. Only, the instrumentalities are not the realities. Historically, the Christian faith has made more room for the *precisionist,* who wants every step of the way plainly marked lest he go astray, than it has for the *freedomist,* who would rather risk losing his way than be deprived of the right of finding it for himself. But that only means that historically the Christian faith has not been wholly true to its own principle. The principle of faith is — *faith!* And the first child of faith is — *freedom!* The Epistle to the Galatians is a Protestant manifesto! Luther reveled in it. So did John Wesley. So should we.

We return from the seeming digression to say that the priest, using the term now in its more technical sense, is necessarily also a preacher; but his preaching is greatly simplified for him by the very nature of his office. He preaches in the routine discharge of his responsibilities. His service of the altar — to use the comprehensive phrase — is his preaching. In the act of repeating his ancient ritual, and performing his traditional ceremonies, he is bearing witness to the Christian faith. He does not need to be too deeply concerned about questions of " interpretation." He may, in fact, find himself embarrassed if this concern seems to interest him too greatly! On occasion he may " preach " in the more formal sense, but speaking generally it suffices for the priest — whether he be Roman Catholic, Greek Orthodox, or Protestant — that he discharge the offices according to the prescribed intent. The value of this is not here being questioned. In the very form his service takes, the priest speaks for God. Therein he lifts up Christ from the earth. Therein he makes his *confessio fidei.* He finds his vocation in being an instrument — " a channel of grace." His vestments, his intonations, his genuflections, his processions, his prayers, his rites — all speak in being what they are. His own relation to them may seem to be at times curiously impersonal. He is the unquestioning representative of a body of truth that has created these fixed forms of self-expression. In repeating the forms he is proclaiming the truth.

The preacher who is officially designated as such is precluded from this impersonality of attitude. His preaching lays upon him an exacting burden. His very freedom from dependence upon ceremonials and externalities increases his obligation. His appeal is not primarily to the eye or to the aesthetic sense. His appeal is rather to the mind and the conscience and the will. He cannot exhaust his preaching and interpretive function as the great majority of Christians may, simply by " faithful living." The Church sets him aside to be a prophet of the things of God in Christ. It is assumed not only that he will *speak* but that he will be *listened to,* and that what he speaks about will be matters of supreme importance. This assumption of importance will also hold of the office of the priest, but the logic of the assumption will not be the same in each case.

For the preacher is not merely to speak as though his speaking were one more formal rite among many others. The last thing Christian preaching dares to be is the mechanical repetition of something mechanically possessed. A preacher-interpreter is not a phonograph, impersonally droning out an impersonal record. If this is all that he is, then the spirit of Jeremiah is not in him, and much less is the spirit of Paul. There is in his bones no burning fire. He would better by far be content to be a priest pure and simple and serve at the altar, than to presume to fill the office of a prophetic interpreter of the Word of God as though it were just one more in a round of priestly functions. What in the Calvinist tradition is known as " the sacrament of preaching," the breaking of the bread of God's Living Word for the spiritual nurture of God's people, is a valid and beautiful conception; but one may believe that and still stress the fact, as is being done here, that preaching is a function of the prophet rather than of the priest. When a priest preaches, he is by that much less of a priest and more of a prophet. The preacher's immediate concern is not with truth embodied in a stately ceremonial or represented in a series of impressive symbols. His concern is rather with *truth made alive in new ways in human speech here and now.*

The preacher is talking to people face to face. He cannot count on the same commonness of attitude that is usually manifested toward ceremonial or symbol. The priest hypnotizes the critical mind; the prophet arouses it because he appeals to it. Arrestingly to preach is a much more demanding activity than impressively to lead a ritual. The very fact that people are being addressed means that they are being challenged to attend, challenged to think, challenged to weigh and to consider and to decide. It is quite possible that something will be said that will give rise to a doubt or arouse resentment or even create opposition. There is a sense in which the preacher is " on his own." He has, indeed, his own peculiar supports, but they are for the most part invisibilities, lying deep within the recesses of his own soul. The preacher must be prepared to make his points. He is an interpreter, and interpretation involves a degree of subjectivism. All interpretation is not the same interpretation. The preacher must know where he is going. He must look to his fences. It is his task so to declare the Word of God as it has been given to him to see it that it will accomplish its purpose in a situation that is highly complex just because it is composed of persons differing from each other in many ways.

These differences will extend into the areas of needs, motives, and purposes. It is hardly an exaggeration to say that a ceremonial ritual or symbol ignores the presence of differences in the worshipers. It says the same thing in the same way, irrespective of time, place, and persons. The value of this is not for a moment being underestimated. The priest is a guarantee of continuity. He makes for a desirable stability. The unification of sentiment that is often achieved by the unvarying repetition of the familiar is psychologically defensible, even if nothing more. But a frequent by-product of the priest's methodological approach may very well be that on a given occasion some great area of need represented in the worshiper is left untouched, no opportunity being given for its recognition. In respect of the use of the *timely*, the prophet has the advantage of the priest. He has it because of the necessary freedom of pattern which preaching provides. It does not say the same thing in the same way regardless. In a sense it does, indeed, say the same thing, since its concern is always with the Word of God, whose self-identity is not destroyed but only expressed through its inexhaustible nuances, its applicability in some aspect of it to every human situation, no matter what it may be — the lad on the eve of leaving home, the bride on the eve of her marriage, the industrialist on the eve of a crucial decision, the statesman on the eve of affixing or refusing to affix his signature to a document that may prove epochal, the community on the eve of an election concerning an issue that touches its deepest interests, and the like. Preaching involves bringing the self-identical Word of God to bear on one life at one point and on another life at a different point in one and the same hour and by virtue of one and the same varied presentation.

Herein is the preacher-interpreter's "burden." He has to think of the people before him as the priest never does. He has to be concerned that what he says shall be an instrument laid in the hand of the Holy Spirit. Not that the priest knows nothing of this concern: even to suggest this lack would be as unkind as it would be untrue. There is, however, a sense in which the priest can *assume* the efficacy of his offices as the preacher can never assume the efficacy of his preaching. It was not Savonarola the priest who shook Florence, but Savonarola turned preacher-prophet; and he shook Florence because he had himself already been shaken of the Word of God, and " could not forbear." Indeed, did not Savonarola turn from the altar to the pulpit — one speaks relatively — not only because he was driven by some deep need in himself, but also because the most splendid ceremonial failed to awaken Florence from its moral slumber. In the prophet-interpreter, the Word of God possesses itself of a living personality, throws itself into living thoughts in a living mind, utters itself through a living voice, and seeks thereby to evoke a response in other living souls. *Ex opere operato* — automatic effectiveness — may be claimed for a ceremonial, but not for a proclamation.

It is therefore no light thing to be " set aside " as " a preacher of the Word," and to accept the responsibility of being an interpreter of God to men. All the meaning of human existence is focused in that divine Word. Yet the meaning as it stands clothed in a body of ancient writings — the Bible — is not self-evident. One thinks of a *simile* of Jesus, and says, " The Word of God is like unto a treasure hidden in a field." It is there, but not lying around in plain sight. It is there, but only for the finding, and he who would find must " dig." The *meaning* of the Bible waits to be released: this is what Biblical interpretation really is. One searches long in some Biblical books for a few pearls! They are much more "field " than " treasure," much more " record " than " revelation," much more " words of men" than " Word of God." We equate " the Word of God " and " revelation," but revelation is not in the mere fact of the Biblical writings. No mere writing is, *as writing*, revelation. Revelation is *the reason for* the writing, but this requires that we move *from the writing to its reason*. Revelation is revelation in the extent that it reveals. It is a small matter that we claim to " believe in " revelation, unless revelation has passed over "from Biblical attestation" into "personal experience."

The Bible — whose "interpretation" is the chief concern of the preacher as a preacher — sufficiently authenticates that there was once a "divine-human encounter" — for that matter, that there were many such encounters. Revelation is at the point of encounter. But for such encountering, there would not have been the Bible that we know. The Biblical testimony provides for the *possibility* of the encountering being continued, but the possibility becomes an *actuality* only on conditions. The chief condition is that the God said to be encountered is accepted as a Living Reality, and this acceptance is an act of faith. The encounter was of faith in the first place, and it must be of faith still. This fact will be dealt with more fully at a later time. It is stated here because without faith there can be no proper interpretation of the Bible. He who does not know God on his own account cannot speak to others about God with any authority or with any persuasiveness. The Bible is the Book of God. To expound the Bible is to expound the truth of God. He cannot expound that truth who does not know it for himself. This knowledge comes of faith; it is nurtured by faith; it is deepened by faith. Faith, however, is an intensely personal activity. There is no such thing as faith by proxy. The only faith through which God becomes real to a man is the man's own faith. It may be that the Biblical doctrine of "election" means that it was necessary for his more ultimate purpose that *God thrust himself on the attention of certain men whether or no,* and that their faith was their acceptance of the invasion and their response to it; and that their attestation of their own experience became God's deliberately devised instrument through which the self-revelation he had thus initiated might be continued to others, but with more respect to personal freedom. This is a searching question in itself, and much too complex for consideration here. What must suffice to say is that the Bible witnesses to the reality of God in human experience, and to a God of a certain kind, and that through the Bible witness it is possible for the self-revealed God to perpetuate the significance of his own self-revelation, and to bring it to the fulfillment of its purpose. God made himself known to a few that he might make himself

known to all. He spoke once that he might be heard again —
and again — and again. The intent of his speaking was that he
might at last be *known for what he is*. This final "is-ness"
meets us in Jesus Christ, the Word-come-alive. This being the
ultimate self-disclosure, it is this that men need to possess. It
is simple truth that the God disclosed in the Bible is as available today as he ever was; as accessible as he ever was; as
truly holy love as he ever was; as equal to the human situation
as he ever was; as deeply concerned with men as he ever was.

We have said that both the preacher-prophet and the priest
are interpreters, but that the preacher-prophet is an interpreter
who ranges more widely than does the priest. The broad field
of the preacher-prophet's interpretation is the Bible, which he
treats as the Word of God, but which he treats with discrimination. His concern is to bring the God of the Bible into the
very center of the life of today. But what manner of God is
this God of the Bible? We say, "The Bible is the Word of
God." We say, "The message of the Bible is a message about
God." We say, "When we preach the Bible, we preach God
and his truth." This sounds very simple, but actually it is not
simple. "You have nothing to do but to preach the Bible."
Certainly, but meaning what? Or, "You have nothing to do but
to preach the gospel." One agrees, but still asks what is meant.
Or, "You have nothing to do but to preach Christ." Again one
agrees, but what is it to preach Christ? Can the gospel be truly
preached except as the gospel is truly grasped and experi-
enced? Can Christ be truly preached except as Christ is for
the preacher — whether he be a "designated" preacher or
a faithful Christian lay witness — the all-comprehensive reality
he is set forth as being in the final faith of the New Testament?
"As ye go, preach, saying, The kingdom of heaven is at hand"
(Matt. 10:7). What was that "kingdom" that the disciples were
to preach, and how were they to preach it? "Go ye into all the
world, and preach the gospel to the whole creation" (Mark
16:15). What was the disciples' understanding of this gospel,
and how did they come by it? "They ceased not to teach and
to preach Jesus as the Christ" (Acts 5:42). Since the word
"Christ" was the equivalent of "Messiah," what content was
put into the word in that early Christian teaching and preach-

ing? " They therefore that were scattered abroad went about preaching the word " (Acts 8:4). What was this " word "? Was it the same as " the Way " of Acts 19:9, 23; the same as the " Christ crucified " of I Cor. 1:23–25; the same as " the word of good tidings " of I Peter 1:25; the same as " the testimony of Jesus Christ " of Rev. 1:2? If the answer is, " No," then it is implied that the original Christian preaching — the *kerygma* or " heralding " — had no common aim and purpose, no unvarying focal point. If the answer is, " Yes," then it is important, even imperative, to determine what that is in which consists the unity which underlies the variety of expression.

One would like to describe this as a Biblico-theological undertaking, except that the term is awkward and ponderous, and to some might even prove to be a discouragement to further reading. But the unhappy term might at least serve to indicate that critical judgment, scholarly equipment, a feeling for relationships, and some sense of coherence are as essential to the interpreter of the Bible as are personal experience of God in Christ and that spiritual intuition which comes only of prolonged meditation. Christian preaching, interpretive and prophetic as it must be, has to do with God and his relations to men, but preaching on this high theme is properly Christian only as it is Biblically based. What, however, is Biblically based preaching? Is preaching Biblically based just because it begins with a text? Are there not in the Bible great numbers of verses, great numbers of longer passages, great numbers of incidents, which can easily be used to support a message running directly athwart what the Bible as a whole *means?* Preaching may be Biblically based, and yet be very far from being Biblical — much more from being Christian. The very Bible to which preaching assigns a commanding importance, and which in turn assigns a commanding importance to preaching, presents the interpreter with its own problems at the very threshold.

It must be said that this is no less true of the Bible in its use as " a manual of devotion." What has been said above has admittedly more specific reference to the public proclamation of the message of the Bible, but it is certainly not to be limited to that. The Christian Church greatly needs to be told the truth about the Bible! If the so-called " humble layman " is to ascertain the truth that is *in* the Bible, he must be informed in respect of what the Bible *is*. Often he is not. The wise dissemination of what has been brought to light by a constructively critical study of the Bible would have done much to prevent that crass literalism which has been the plague of Protestantism. Uncounted numbers of pious people have been allowed to rest in a view of the Bible for which there was no proper support. That there is in the Bible many a truth whose impact on the soul may be felt — and often is felt — in spite of the most wrongheaded notions about the book itself, is gladly to be admitted; but this does not change the fact that the wrongheaded notions may often lead to a perversion of the truth, and to a failure to apprehend it in some of its aspects. There are, indeed, problems that arise directly from the fact that the Bible contains definite declarations concerning God, his nature, his ways, and his purpose that are at sharp variation with other declarations on the same themes. There is nothing irreverent about subjecting such declarations to critical scrutiny. The interpreter who is first of all a Christian will save himself from wandering down many a blind alley in which he may otherwise lose his way! It is the refusal to use critical judgment that is irreverent, not the informed use of it. We must examine Biblical attestation to ascertain if it really is Biblical attestation. Such an examination calls for a certain point of view. The Bible itself provides the point of view from which alone the Bible *in its totality* may be rightly considered, rightly used, and rightly interpreted. The discovery and statement of this point of view is the chief concern of this book.

This point of view is a creation of faith, and a faith similar to that which created it is the condition to its apprehension and use. There is that in the Bible which never discloses itself to the rigidly rationalistic. Faith is not a mere passive acceptance of a verbal statement. If that is all that it is, then faith is a shackle to bind the soul. But this is the one thing that a true faith is not, especially that faith which the Bible ultimately represents. Faith is not a chain, but a wing. It does not bind; it sets free. If it is simply faith in a book — " the Book, the whole Book, and nothing but the Book " — then it does not set free, but binds. But then, that is not faith at all — at least, not true faith. "Faith in the Bible" is, in truth, a most un-happy phrase, indicating a most unhappy attitude. It is an atti-tude that transforms men into Grand Inquisitors, unimagina-tive dogmaticians, self-appointed guardians of a treasure that cannot be stolen, jealous possessors of a key that fits no lock. The Bible is two things: It is a book, and it is a book that bears witness to God. It is the witness that counts; it is the witness that needs to be ascertained; and it is the witness to which faith is a response. As a book, the Bible is the outcome of a complicated historical, social, and literary process, and the more we know about this process, the more we are impressed with the persistent vitality of that inner core of reality which gave the process both its unity and its reason. A divine-human relation, bespeaking revelation on the one hand, and a faith-response on the other hand, was manifestly at the center of the process. Lacking this central determinative reality, the Bible remains simply a book, a collection of writings, "an ancient library." A library it is, but a library whose coherence is due, not to the fact that a binder may have put it between two covers, but to the fact of an inner principle. What appears manifold is in reality unitary. Christian preaching is concerned primarily with the elucidation of this unifying actuality, which is nothing less than a divine self-disclosure made "by divers portions and in divers manners," and moving forward to a point of all-interpretative climax in a "Son . . . the very image of his substance," by whom was made "purification of sins" (Heb. 1:1–4). The unifying central, persisting actuality, compacted of "revelation-faith-response," is not always imme-diately apparent, at least not at the given time and place. The Bible is subject to the law of perspective: what we see depends on where we stand. It is only when the continuing center comes to its final clarification and fulfillment that we may stand where God intends that we shall. Only then does the long process become indubitably clear. The process had its own irregularities, sometimes seeming to be arrested, some-times even to be reversed. Yet in "the fulness of the time" came the ultimate clarification. It is in this ultimate clarifica-tion that Christian faith is anchored, and what is the theme of Christian preaching if not the Christian faith? To discover this point of reference, to make it one's own, to have no least doubt respecting it, to see its manifold relationships, to have some comprehension of its bearing on the long and slow process of which it came, to grasp its significance for the whole round of existence, human and divine — all this is a demand on the Christian prophet. It is equally the requirement of any Christian witness, in such measure as may be. It constitutes the creative power in the life and activity of the Christian Church. And it is the leaven which in the purpose of God is destined to permeate and transform the life of the world.

The so-called *authority* of the Bible therefore comes to light. Its authority is in that faith which created it, and to which it bears witness, especially that faith in its final Christ-centered flowering. Christian faith, Christian authority, Christian interpretation — these may be spoken of separately, but they are not in themselves separable. They constitute one unbreakable threefold cord. The Bible has a certain subsidiary authority, especially in matters of history. Archaeology is continually proving the truth of many of its historical statements and allusions. Where Old Testament records cross those of other peoples, the result is frequently Old Testament confirmation. Yet complete historical dependability is by no means the supreme Biblical consideration. There are good reasons for believing that Israel was once in bondage in Egypt; that it escaped; and that in due time it again returned to the ancestral land of Canaan. But much more important than the time of these events, the circumstances of the escape, the route which was followed, the details of the conquest, and the like, is the belief of Israel that the entire episode was under the control of its God, Yahweh, and that through it he was revealing both himself and his purpose to the people whom he had chosen. The deepest significance of the episode is not in its ethnographical concomitants, but in the religious interpretation attached to it by faith. Anyone must feel a grave doubt about the statement in Num. 2:32, 33, that within a year after the departure from Egypt the number of Israelite *males over twenty years of age capable of bearing arms* (ch. 1:1–3) was 603,550, excluding the Levites. This would imply a total population of well over 2,000,000. That Moses could have handled such a vast multitude, feeding, instructing, disciplining, and protecting them during forty years of wandering in the wilderness is simply incredible, and we gain nothing by refusing to say so. The ways of God are passing strange at times, but they must still be reasonable! The accuracy or otherwise of these numbers just does not matter; it certainly does not either validate or invalidate the major Biblical *theme.* On the other hand, three Old Testament books that we *know* are largely unhistorical, Esther, Jonah, and Daniel, have a significance for *the purpose of the Bible* that is certainly no less, and some would say greater, than that of what is generally recognized as being the finest piece of objective historical writing in the Old Testament, namely, II Sam., chs. 9 to 20.

He who accepts the Bible witness to God, and its ultimate clarification in and through Jesus Christ, knows very well that the acceptance involves an initial act of surrender on his own part. A religious truth is not the same as a historical truth or as a scientific truth, and it is not to be attested or verified in the same way. The authority of the Word of God is not the authority of a table of logarithms. Faith is not logic, although there is a logic of faith. Unimpeachable objective tests for the religiously authoritative are simply not possible. He who depends on such alleged supports is building his house upon the sand. The man of faith literally " takes his soul in his hand." A dogmatic externality is wholly alien to Christianity, whose essence is inwardness. The Bible witness to God is authoritative for any man only in so far as he is willing to have it so, and even then he must distinguish it from the highly complex and intensely human milieu within which it is set. Faith is the soul's free act — in a sense, its supremely free act. Of the free act of faith comes another freedom — freedom from reliance on all adventitious supports. When the Bible has spoken to me, and I have responded to its message concerning God, *I can dispense with it.* But although I can then dispense with it, I shall not do so. Rather, I shall then better know how to use it; and in knowing how to use it I shall know how to interpret it to others in such wise that they too will know how to use it.

CHAPTER III

THE EMANCIPATION OF THE WORD OF GOD

O̲ NE of the speakers at the 1948 Amsterdam Assembly, describing the spiritual situation in Germany since the
collapse of Nazism, said: " Jesus Christ, the Word made flesh,
was recognized and acclaimed afresh as the sole Word of God.
And one of the strongest Bible movements in the history of
the Church has taken place during the last few years in the
evangelical Church through its new understanding of the Old
and New Testaments" (*Man's Disorder and God's Design,*
Vol. I, p. 101. Harper & Brothers, 1949).

Christ as " the sole Word of God "; in consequence, " a new
understanding of the Bible " — this fairly describes " the new
Biblicism "; but the difference from the old Biblicism is nothing less than radical. The old Biblicism shackled the revelation; the new Biblicism would set it free. The old Biblicism
was concerned to take the Bible " as is." The new Biblicism is
critical, discriminating, unafraid. The old Biblicism yielded a
static authoritarianism. The new Biblicism promises to issue
in the creation of a dynamic spiritual freedom. Inwardness,
certitude, compulsion — these are the authenticating attendants of the Word of God, provided that the Word that controls
is truly God's Word and not the words of men. The Word was
inseparable from the Spirit in its primal self-communication;
he must continue to be inseparable from the Word in its continuing apprehension, renewal, proclamation, and application.
" Ye shall know the Word, and the Word shall make you free."

The Protestant Reformation had its origin in the recovery
of the Word of God as centered in Jesus Christ. But Lutheran-
ism quickly departed from the epochal insight of Luther, and
Calvinism followed suit. It is difficult to see how Calvin could

have written some of his Biblical expositions if he really committed himself to his own principle of *testimonium internum Spiritus Sancti*. The radicalism of Luther could be maintained only on Luther's presuppositions, and these all too quickly disappeared. The question of authority raised its head. Rupert E. Davies, in *The Problem of Authority in the Continental Reformers,* concludes that neither Luther nor Zwingli nor Calvin ever quite freed himself from " the medieval error that the source of authority is necessarily to be found in some place wholly outside the individual." It is certainly true that this " error " returned with full force upon their followers. The courage to hold oneself free of external constraints in matters that have to do with the soul and its destiny is not easily acquired, nor is it easily kept. It was much easier to be a third century Christian, secure in a *regula fidei,* believing oneself incorporated into a closely knit organization which already could challenge the civil power than it was to be a primitive Christian, when there were no written documents to speak of (apart from the Old Testament), no imposing organization, but only a body of testimony calling for response and strangely authenticating itself when the response was made. The true Protestant is a primitive Christian — and he must maintain his " freedom " in the face of the " authoritarianism " of Rome.

But this is no simple matter. The narrow gate quickly proved itself too narrow. Protestantism could not maintain its own principle. Over against hierarchical infallibility it set Biblical infallibility. The slogan was, " The Book, the whole Book, and nothing but the Book." Bibliolatry was born.

Not many people, says Troeltsch, are so constituted as to be able to dispense with objective standards. That may be so, but it remains that externality began to bear its inevitable fruitage in the checking of creative spontaneity. Divine authority was invoked on behalf of folklore, legends, superstitions, numbers, genealogies, and the like. Vindictive sentiments uttered by men, and vicious actions performed by men, were ascribed to the leading of God, and then defended with a dialectical subtlety that would have done credit to any scholastic. Theories of plenary inspiration, documentary inerrancy, verbal infallibility — " if we had the original autographs! " — came into being, to plague the Church for generations. The wind was freely sown, and in due time the whirlwind would be reaped for harvest.

That time came with the birth in the nineteenth century of the new natural science and the new historical criticism. Protestantism found itself in a quandary. Inevitably there were serious divisions. Even in the early years of the century, a rationalistic tendency began to make itself felt. Already Lessing had edited the *Wolfenbüttel Fragments* of Reimarus, with their acute attempt to undermine the credibility of the Gospel narratives, especially in respect of the miracles and the resurrection. Later, this work of Reimarus was to afford Schweitzer the starting point for his epochal investigation. Paulus of Heidelberg and many others continued the attempt, but it was David Friedrich Strauss, in his "first" and "second" Life of Jesus, who made it clear to everyone that a life-and-death struggle was on. Strauss was deeply influenced by Hegel, which partly explains why A. M. Fairbairn said of him that he was "neither historian nor critic, but a speculative philosopher," and why he described the *Life* as "a pure creation of the philosophical imagination." The furor created by the book was itself significant: even the politicians took note of it. Its devastating effect was undeniable, in spite of Strauss's numerous efforts to soften it. The "first" *Life* was published in 1835. This was the work translated into English by George Eliot in 1864, a fact which enormously increased its influence. Something comparable to the Strauss rationalism and anti-supernaturalism is evidenced in Renan's *Life of Jesus*, published in 1863, amazingly readable, but frequently approaching pure bathos. In 1865, in England, Sir John Robert Seeley published *Ecce Homo*. Seeley was by profession a historian, and later wrote an important book, *Natural Religion*. He brought to his Life of Christ a sanity and objectivity not found in the German rationalists. He undertook to give an account of Christ that would be intrinsically credible, and the book, disturbing as it was to many devout churchmen, is still worth reading for its spirit, its reverence, its balance, its stress on the genuine humanness of Jesus, and its recognition of the large place occupied in his thought by the idea of the Kingdom.

Meanwhile, what had been done with certain parts of the New Testament was being matched in the field of Old Testament criticism. Reimarus had his counterpart in the French physician, Jean Astruc, a Roman Catholic, who called attention to certain features of the Pentateuch which suggested variety of authorship. Various scholars worked with the clue, which eventuated, in the third quarter of the nineteenth century, in what is known as the Graf-Wellhausen documentary theory of the Pentateuch. Other parts of the Old Testament were subjected to similar scientific criticism, and the general result was that Protestantism seemed to be confronted with the loss of its foundations. The spread of the new conception of the creative and natural processes served to deepen the despair which had seized so many minds.

There were, of course, able scholars, working in both the Old Testament and the New Testament, who were not deceived by merely a priori criticism, and who believed that whatever was proved to be true in the new science and the new criticism was to be humbly accepted and the Bible understood accordingly. They did their work, however, in an unfriendly situation. In 1853, Frederick Denison Maurice, then professor of divinity in King's College, London, published a volume of *Theological Essays* which led to his deposition as a " heretic." One of the charges brought against Maurice was based on his denial that " eternal " in the New Testament necessarily meant " everlasting." The idea, he held, was qualitative rather than durational. In 1860 seven scholars published the sensational *Essays and Reviews*. This was quickly followed by a discussion of the Hexateuch on highly critical lines by John William Colenso, an Anglican bishop in South Africa. At about the same time something more definitely constructive was attempted by a group of young Oxford scholars led by Charles Gore. The result of their efforts was the epochal *Lux Mundi,* a bold effort to capture the new positions in both natural science and Biblical criticism for an elucidation of the Christian faith. Both the *Essays and Reviews* group and the *Lux*

Mundi group met severe criticism, and Colenso barely escaped deposition. Even Benjamin Jowett, the great Master of Balliol and the translator of Plato, did not escape the storm. He was the personal friend of some of the authors of *Essays and Reviews,* and he was known to champion the cause of Free Churchmen at Oxford. Jowett promoted the Biblical critical movement, in particular with a volume on *The Epistles of St. Paul* and with an essay on *The Interpretation of Scripture.* As a consequence, he was for a while forbidden the University pulpit, and was threatened with the withholding of his salary as professor of Greek! As was to be expected, Matthew Arnold, true to his devotion to " sweetness and light," and determined that at all costs " culture must prevail," offered his solution of the problem in *Literature and Dogma.* His thesis was simple enough: realize that the Bible is a body of ancient literature concerned with the promotion of righteousness, and controversy will vanish. Yet it was a niece of Matthew Arnold, Mrs. Humphry Ward, who in 1888 published the novel *Robert Elsmere.* It was in no sense a great book, but it created a sensation, partly because of the family out of which it came. The book described how a young clergyman was torn from his traditional moorings by the new knowledge and the new criticism, and came to rest in a position that combined the rationalism of Strauss and his successors with the noble humanitarianism of Seeley.

There were great numbers, however, who clung stubbornly to their Biblicism. They were the people who could find complete satisfaction in the rolling eloquence of Canon Liddon's Bampton Lectures on " The Divinity of Our Lord " or in the quiet persuasiveness of F. W. Farrar's *Life of Christ,* which left in the mind of the reader no haunting sense of doubt because there had been none in the mind of the writer. It would be ungracious, however, not to mention the fact that Farrar revealed a sturdy independence in his *Eternal Hope,* both in the theme of the book itself and in the way he faced the storm the book evoked. Perhaps nothing dramatizes more completely the tenacity of the prevailing Biblicism than the volume of Edmund Gosse, *Father and Son.* In it the famous essayist and critic tells the story of his relations with his father, Philip Henry Gosse. The elder Gosse was a natural scientist, a member of learned societies, and a recognized authority on marine life. But he was a complete Biblical infallibilist, a leader of a small Bible sect in the south of England. He attempted to train his young son in the same tradition, and with apparent success until the son, in his teens, left home. Then the inevitable tension began to manifest itself. The visits of father and son became increasingly painful affairs. The last letter printed by Gosse in the book is one he received from his father after such a visit, and one reads it with sadness. A man of personal charm and culture might have been held to the Christian faith instead of becoming a virtual skeptic, had he received wiser training.

How widespread was the attitude of the elder Gosse is evident from the treatment accorded to eminent Biblical scholars in the closing decades of the nineteenth century and the opening years of the twentieth. W. Robertson Smith was removed in 1881 from the chair of Old Testament at Aberdeen, Scotland; on the American continent, Henry Preserved Smith at Lane Seminary, George C. Workman at Toronto, Charles A. Briggs at Union Seminary, and Henry H. Mitchell at the Boston University School of Theology, were all subjected to humiliating experiences. Mitchell's book *For the Benefit of My Creditors* is enough to make the heavens weep — as doubtless it did! Similar ecclesiastical excoriation, not unsupported by a fearful laity, was poured on the notable English Wesleyan Methodist Biblical scholar and theologian Joseph Agar Beet, in his case for nothing more serious than his challenging, in the spirit of Maurice and Farrar, the accuracy of the ordinary understanding of the New Testament teaching concerning the duration of future punishment. And there are those who still remember how leaders of the same Church proposed to treat George Jackson for his alleged "advanced" views. It was indeed a spectacle that sons of John Wesley were prepared to repudiate a man who could head a great and successful mission in Edinburgh and who could write a book entitled *The Fact of Conversion.*

Easily the most dramatic and widely publicized "trial" of

an Old Testament scholar was that of W. Robertson Smith. The story might well be read in connection with that of the youthful McLeod Campbell, who some fifty years before had been driven from the ministry of the Church of Scotland for preaching that God's love embraced all mankind! The trial of Smith could have split the Free Church of Scotland, had the victim himself but given the word. Smith was young, but he was the outstanding Old Testament scholar of his Church. He had, however, challenged traditional conceptions, as anyone will realize who knows his *Old Testament in the Jewish Church* and his *Prophets of Israel.* The trial was in process for some two years. How sharp was the division may be seen from the fact that at one point a motion that would have greatly modified the charges was lost by only a single vote, 321 to 320. The final vote to remove Smith from his chair was taken at the Assembly of 1881, and stood 394 to 231 for removal. One of Smith's strongest supporters throughout the whole trial was A. B. Bruce, who was to write books which would be read by almost every Protestant minister throughout the world, such as *The Theology of Paul, Apologetics, The Humiliation of Christ,* and *The Training of the Twelve.* After the final vote was taken, and before the sentence was pronounced, Bruce obtained the floor, and made a noble speech in behalf of his friend. He ended by saying: "I cannot sit down without expressing my sorrow and shame at what is about to be done. I never expected to see the day when such a spectacle could be witnessed in our Church. . . . We humbly think [our Mother Church] is doing a great wrong, but we count surely on a reaction and a noble repentance in which she will cancel the ostracism which she is about to exercise against her ablest servant and devoted son" (Quoted from *William Robertson Smith,* by Black and Chrystal, p. 439; publ. by A. & C. Black, 1912). What Bruce anticipated more than came to pass. Another young Smith, this time George Adam, was given temporary charge of W. R. Smith's classes during the period of temporary suspension. He later became professor of Old Testament in the Free Church College (now Trinity), at Glasgow, and in 1910 became principal of that very University of Aberdeen whose classrooms had once been denied to his namesake. No man did more than George Adam Smith to spread abroad the true understanding of the Old Testament. He gave, in 1899, the Yale Lectures on " Modern Criticism and the Preaching of the Old Testament," and while the lectures evoked some threats in Scotland, Smith's principles found increasing acceptance there. Yet his " critical " views were substantially those of the man his Church had removed! Indeed, the views were those that came to prevail in the Church at large, although the character of the obstacles to be overcome may be further inferred from the fact that even so reverenced a figure as that of Mr. Gladstone was moved to enter the lists on the side of tradition with a volume, *The Impregnable Rock of Holy Scripture*. This was at the turn of the century, but more than a decade earlier Gladstone had written, " The Old Testament . . . is now far more than the New the battleground of belief," and in a letter to Lord Acton in 1889 he declared that " the Old Testament destructives now have possession of the public ear."

The opening years of this century reveal a condition which makes the emergence of the so-called Modernist-Fundamentalist controversy entirely understandable. There were men of great competence who may be said to have sought to carry on the spirit of the authors of *Lux Mundi*. They were found in Great Britain, in Europe, and on the American continent. It would be invidious to select names, but one whose own mind and outlook were being formed in those days may perhaps be allowed to acknowledge a lasting debt to such men as James Denney, R. W. Rogers, A. S. Peake, William Sanday, A. E. Garvie, P. T. Forsyth, H. Wheeler Robinson, A. M. Fairbairn, Milton S. Terry, Adolf Deissmann, James Hope Moulton, Auguste Sabatier, H. J. Holtzmann, B. Weiss, A. B. Davidson, and James Moffatt. In the first decade of the century or so, these men, and many like them, were active, some as Old Testament scholars, some as New Testament scholars, some as theologians. In the main, these men were constructive and open-minded, sympathetic as respects the function of literary and historical criticism, but loyal to what could in any proper sense be regarded as the essential features of the Christian faith, one of which was most certainly not a static literal Biblicism.

But this was only a part of the story. In Germany, Franz Delitzsch was waging the Babel-Bible battle, and virtually denying any unique revelation in the Old Testament. Wrede, in *The Messiah-Secret in the Gospels,* was declaring that it was impossible to construct, from our available sources, a critically tenable account of the life of Jesus. Harnack, in the famous Berlin Lectures of 1899 on " The Essence of Christianity," was revealing the ultimate logic of his Ritschlianism in the reduction of Christianity to little more than a statement of principles already present in the Hebrew prophets: " Not the Son, but the Father alone," said Harnack, " belongs to the gospel as Jesus proclaimed it." Kaltoff was declaring that Christianity originated as a purely social and economic movement, and that a particular person named Jesus had little enough to do with it. Paul Schmiedel was propagating his theory that there were nine " foundation " passages in the Gospels for a scientific life of Jesus, and these were passages which affirmed his fallibility, his ignorance, or some other limitation. Anything not compatible with these " nine " was to be ruled out. Arthur Drews was broaching his " myth theory " of the origin of the Gospel Portrait, and was finding support from J. M. Robertson in England and from W. B. Smith, a mathematician at Tulane University in America. W. Bousset, in a volume entitled *Jesus,* eliminated from the Gospels everything which suggested that there was anything unusual in the *person* of the Master. More fantastic still was the view that Jesus was an unstable psychotic, an interesting fact considering the attitude to Jesus of contemporary psychiatrists. The " insanity " theory evoked a reply from an American scholar, Walter Bundy, in *The Psychic Health of Jesus,* as the " myth " theory evoked the " reply " of T. J. Thorburn, *The Mythical Interpretation of the Gospels,* of which James Denney said that if such a book had to be written at all, this was the way to do it. The *Encyclopaedia Biblica* was popularizing a destructive radicalism, and T. K. Cheyne, one of the editors of the *Biblica,* boldly and baldly put the case in *Bible Problems and Their Solution.* Kirsopp Lake was demolishing the evidence for the resurrection, and J. M. Thompson, dean of theology at Magdalen College, Oxford, would soon do the same with the evidences for the miracles. Percy Gardner's *Historic View of the New Testament* was disturbing even to those who appreciated Gardner's interpretive skill. The popular young minister of the City Temple, London, Reginald J. Campbell, advocated, in *The New Theology*, a type of mystical pantheism which brought him into an open antagonism with a fellow Congregationalist, P. T. Forsyth. Campbell later left the Congregational ministry, in due time repudiated *The New Theology*, and sought and received ordination in the Anglican Church; in that Church he came to a position of great influence as a teacher of a markedly conservative view of Christianity, as may be seen in his volume *Christian Faith in Modern Light*.

It was another Congregational minister, Richard Roberts — later, like R. J. Campbell, to return to a much more conservative position — who wrote the article, "Jesus or Christ? An Appeal for Consistency," which led to the famous *Hibbert Journal* supplement of 1909, in which some eighteen scholars dealt with the pros and cons of Roberts' question. Add to all this the fact that the Bross Prize for 1905 was awarded to James Orr for his volume *The Problem of the Old Testament*, a vigorous attack on the entire critical position, and the prevailing confusion is apparent. And Orr was a colleague of George Adam Smith!

This is in no sense an adequate account, but it may serve to suggest the situation. Nor must it be supposed that the Roman Catholic Church was unaffected by the new criticism. Sufficient evidence of this is provided in Paul Sabatier's Jowett Lectures for 1908, entitled "Modernism." Sabatier describes the liberalizing movement within the Roman Catholic Church which Pope Pius X labeled "modernism," and which the pope claimed to analyze in detail in the Syllabus *Lamentabili*, dated July 3, 1907. The Syllabus enumerated sixty-five false propositions held to be current, the second one named being that which claimed that the Church's interpretation of the sacred books must be regarded as open to revision or modification. All the propositions are declared "condemned and proscribed." This was followed a little later the same year by the lengthy encyclical letter *Pascendi Gregis,* the text of which may be read in Sabatier. This encyclical was chiefly instrumental in creating the movement known as Neo-Thomism, since it prescribed that the writings of Thomas should be the basis of theological study in the Church, especially in seminaries and religious houses.

The encyclical undoubtedly had special reference to Abbé Loisy, who for some years had been under suspicion. Indeed, Friedrich Heiler describes Loisy in a recent monograph as *Der Vater des Katholischen Modernismus.* Loisy had replied to Harnack's *Essence of Christianity* with a little book entitled *The Gospel and the Church,* which largely separated Catholic dogma from any direct and intimate relation with the original gospel. Rome hardly possessed a more illustrious, but at the same time more radical and aggressive, New Testament scholar than Loisy. He was subjected to progressive humiliations, and these issued finally in excommunication. He has told the story in a book which is almost frightening in its exposé of dictatorial methods, entitled *My Duel with the Vatican,* a good introduction to his later volumes of *Memoires.* An almost similar fate, for a largely similar reason, befell the Jesuit priest in England, Father George Tyrrell, one of the great Christian souls of our time. And if there are those who still covet the " security " offered by Rome, let them read the *Marching Orders* of William L. Sullivan, who tells there of his Odyssey from Romanism to Unitarianism, the journey being marked on the way by a series of *Letters to His Holiness.*

What was indicated in all this was the necessity of a reconsideration of the whole idea of revelation. The great Biblical scholars had naturally been chiefly interested in questions connected with the text of the Bible, as is evident from W. F. Howard's fascinating Tipple Lectures for 1947, " The Romance of New Testament Scholarship." The great theologians were concerned chiefly with the creedal question. The appearance in 1913 of A. S. Peake's courageous book, *The Bible, Its Origin, Its Significance, Its Abiding Worth,* combined both interests in a way truly remarkable. Peake's chapter on " The Problem

of Biblical Theology " will always be worth reading, and,
Methodist though he was, he could write in the preface of the
book that he was " conscious of a special debt to the writings
of Robertson Smith for the general view of what the Bible is."
The blast, however, that shook alike the foundations of liberal
New Testament scholarship, conservative theology, and static
Biblicism, was let loose in 1906 by a brilliant young scholar of
Alsace-Lorraine. Until then few had heard of him. Today the
whole world knows him as Albert Schweitzer. In that year he
published a book, *Von Reimarus zu Wrede,* soon to be known
by its English title, *The Quest of the Historical Jesus.* Schweitzer subjected to a searching examination what New Testament
criticism throughout the nineteenth century had offered as a
credible portrait of Jesus. He declared that the whole portrayal
was false and misleading. There was never such a Jesus as was
presented: he was a pure fiction. Schweitzer's own conception
of the historical Jesus and of his significance may have been —
it was! — far from satisfactory, but his researches did at least
one thing — they showed that it was impossible to force Jesus
into ready-made categories. He fitted into no established pattern. Schweitzer's insistence on the " eschatological " element
in the thought of Jesus both about himself and about the Kingdom had already been anticipated by Baldensperger, Johannes
Weiss, and Loisy; it would be repeated in Tyrrell and many
others; and it would blossom in the " realized eschatology " of
C. H. Dodd and others of like mind in our own day. Its immediate significance was to restore the centrality of the mysterious Jesus to his own gospel. It restored, too, the transcendent
character of the Kingdom. Neither Jesus nor the Kingdom was
to be accounted for according to some smoothly working rational process. The unexpected, the unpredictable, the cata-
clysmic — these are inescapable features of the Gospels. The
very things which the critics had been trying to get rid of as
" unhistorical " were precisely what had created the " history."
The dramatic career of Schweitzer has perhaps served to throw
the significance of his New Testament work somewhat out of
perspective, but its epochal character is undeniable.

Within a few years the blast let loose by Schweitzer was

followed by another. This time it originated with a young Swiss pastor, Karl Barth, who in 1919 published the first edition of *Der Römerbrief,* a commentary on Romans. It was an altogether new kind of commentary, both in its method and in its disclosure of "the strange new world within the Bible." This "disclosure" was to become increasingly the characteristic of Barth's work. He challenged the Church to face the fact of an "absolute revelation of God," to be taken just as it was, and to be taken with complete seriousness. The exaggerations and aberrations of Barth, and of the "dialectical" and "crisis" theology in general, must never be allowed to detract from the fact that he did more than any other one man to connect the Bible again with a specific revealing activity on the part of God, climaxed in Jesus Christ as the "Word-made-flesh," in and by whom God at once judged the world as lost in sin and of his unmerited grace offered it salvation. The Bible was not the story of man's search for God, but of God's search for man. The rapid spread of the so-called "Barthian movement" is ample evidence to the sense of futility that had been created by radical naturalism, humanistic liberalism, and theological compromise.

Back of Barth could be seen the towering figure of the melancholy Dane, Søren Kierkegaard. Many of Kierkegaard's contemporaries in the Danish Church of the middle of the last century had been strongly influenced by Hegel. One result of that influence was the endangering of the "crisis" note in Christianity. Every Christian verity, including the incarnation itself, was held to be explicable in terms of an inevitable impersonal dialectic. When the metaphysical distinction between God and man is broken down — and Hegelianism at least implies this — Christianity loses its radical character. Kierkegaard saw this happening, even in so able a theologian as Martensen. He was led to reaffirm this distinction; to confront the Hegelian "both-and" with an uncompromising "either-or"; to proclaim the complete helplessness of man to throw a bridge across the gulf that separates the creature from the Creator; to assert that if the gulf were ever to be bridged, it would have to be from the divine side; and to announce as the central theme of Scripture the fact that in the "existential moment" God did actually cross the gulf, and that he had done this supremely in and as Jesus Christ who, Man of Sorrows as he was, was literally God incognito among men. Salvation came of faith that Jesus Christ was indeed this and no other.

This emphasis on Christ as the sacrificial and redeeming irruption of God into our human history — the *totaliter aliter* become *totaliter ejus generis* without ceasing to be *aliter,* which is John's "Word-become-flesh" — is what Barth sought to recover. This meant nothing else than divine revelation — revelation absolute. Here was a specific, concrete self-disclosure on the part of God, philosophically inexplicable, Scripturally attested, apprehensible only to faith, but undeniably so to him who "believed." *Sola fide.* The Reformation principle, which is to say the original Christian principle, was again laid bare. The Bible was no longer a book to be apologized for. The Church was built on the Word of God; the Church lived by the Word of God; the Church's one testimony must be to the Word of God. Revelation is central.

But we must not be misled here. Barth and those who came to conceive of revelation as he did had no least thought of reviving a static Biblicism. Because the vital connection between revelation and the Bible has been freshly realized, to the great quickening of Christian hearts and minds, does not mean that all the results of patient Biblical criticism are now to be ignored, and that we are again where we were before Reimarus and Astruc initiated the critical movement. The critical movement has issued in our time in the emancipation of the Word of God from identification with the words of men, and there will be no return to the bondage. Rudolf Bultmann, for example, is sympathetic to Barthianism. Yet he holds an extremely critical view of the Gospels, and indeed of the Scriptures as a whole, as is apparent in his *Theology of the New Testament.* The one certain thing about the new Biblicism is that it is not a revamped fundamentalism. If anyone supposes it is, let him read the symposium *Revelation,* edited by John Baillie and Hugh Martin; H. Wheeler Robinson, *Redemption and Revelation;* Cunliffe-Jones, *The Authority of the Biblical*

Revelation; H. H. Rowley, *The Relevance of the Bible;* E. P. Dickie, *Revelation and Response;* Paul Minear, *Eyes of Faith;* C. H. Dodd, *The Gospel and History;* Vincent Taylor, *Jesus and His Sacrifice; The Message of Jesus Christ,* by Martin Dibelius, especially the " Explanation " in Part II; and D. M. Baillie, *God Was in Christ.* Probably not one of these writers would wish to be called a Barthian; but not one of them would disagree with the substance of what Barth wrote in *The Word of God and the Word of Man.* The last thing that these men could desire as a result of the recovery of the Bible witness of God would be a return to the blind credulity of unimaginative verbalism. The religion of the Bible is a religion of revelation, but the revelation is not to be mechanically equated with the total Biblical language. The " Word " is to be reached through the " words." What is unfortunately being called " faith in the Bible," can only mean *confidence* that the Bible witnesses to God and his Word: the " faith " that saves and transforms and empowers is *faith in him to whom the Bible witnesses.*

For " we have this treasure in earthen vessels." This, indeed, is the burden of what is known as form criticism, the claim that the first disciples and teachers threw into " forms " determined by the occasion the message of Jesus and the faith that had come of their experience of him. This means that only occasionally may we suppose that we have the *ipsissima verba* of Jesus. The supreme example of a devised " form " for the embodiment and proclamation of that Living Word of God which is Christ is the Fourth Gospel itself. The Fourth Gospel is the most profoundly Christian book ever written; yet we do not know who wrote it; we do not know when it was written; we do not know that any one of its long discourses or its extended metaphors or its carefully worked out analogies was ever spoken *verbatim* by Jesus — indeed, considering the radical vocabulary differences of the Fourth Gospel from the vocabulary of the Synoptics, it is highly probable that it was not. Nevertheless, the Fourth Gospel confronts us with the Living Word; it witnesses to an Act of God in which God himself was finally because redemptively disclosed; this Act was Christ, the climax of numerous lesser acts of God: yet while lesser, still his acts, still disclosing his character, still making known his will and purpose, still apprehended by men in varying degrees as the Holy Spirit could teach them, and still attested by men in word and action according to their individual powers. When the lesser acts are read in the light of the supreme and final Act, and when the Old Testament record arising because of these lesser acts is read in the light of the New Testament record arising because of his supreme and final Act — when this is done, then we see in what sense the very faith that brings us under the judging and redeeming power of the acts of God which are his Word, his Self-revelation and Self-communication also sets us free from bondage to the letter. The words of men — these are instrumental; that to which they are instrumental is the Word of God.

No one of our contemporaries is more clear at this point than Emil Brunner. In his most important book, *The Mediator,* Brunner equates the Word of God with the revelation of God. The *form* of this Word is divine action in history evoking a faith-response in men. Herein is " the divine-human encounter." In the book of that title, Brunner left it uncertain whether the issue of this encounter included the apprehension of truth; the certainty *that* God is seemed not to be carried over into a certainty as to *what* God is. In a later volume, *Revelation and Reason,* this uncertainty is removed. The truth of revelation is distinguished from the truth of reason; but it is held that " revelation and reason possess one common element: they both claim truth " (p. 362). God makes himself known by events — but what do the events *mean?* That is to say, what *truth* do they convey? The prophet had this truth made known to him by the Holy Spirit, and as he saw it, so he proclaimed it. But no man can ever speak the Word of God in its purity and completeness. Always the Word is limited and obscured by the human personality. The prophet and the Word are never the same. The Word is complete, final, and absolute only as it is " made flesh." Christ is the Word of God come alive. He does not merely *proclaim* the Word that has been given to him: he is himself the Word. The Gospels describe him and bear witness to him, but the Gospels are not the Word. Unless the

Gospels lead us to the Living Word which is the only reason why they came into being, they remain the questionable words of men. It is that Living Word to which faith is the response. It is by that Living Word that the Church is created, nurtured, and empowered. To make known the Living Word to other men, and to seek to bring the world under its judging and redeeming power, is the task alike of the individual Christian and of the Church.

This is the new Biblicism. That it brings its own problems is evident. The Amsterdam appointment of a Commission to consider these problems, and in due time prepare a pronouncement, is itself suggestive of the implications that go with the accepted distinction between God's self-disclosure and the witness to it in Scripture. For example, if Jesus Christ is himself the Living Word of God, significant primarily as God's supremely revealing and redeeming Act, Act and Actor as co-identities, so that " saving faith " is faith that this precisely is what Christ is and what he means — if this is so, and if the Gospels are so many witnesses to him as thus understood, is it possible to see the Gospels any longer as other than " instrumental "? In that case, what happens to the supposition that the heart of the Gospel is in Jesus' " words " and " teaching," which we certainly do not have in their entirety, nor as they fell from his lips. Perhaps the new Biblicism will compel the reconsideration of the whole Christological question, and by consequence of the whole soteriological question, as it has done already with the whole question of revelation. Perhaps the emancipation of the Word of God will have for corollary the emancipation of the Christian mind. The emancipated mind, however, will still be bound: but it will find its bondage not in blind submission to the Bible in its verbal totality, but to a Living Reality which faith generates out of that totality as faith was responsible for its presence there in the first place. Willing bondage to such a Reality is a bondage in which is true freedom. In what follows an attempt is made to show what that Biblical faith is which issues in Christian freedom, and what that Christian freedom is which springs of Biblical faith.

CHAPTER IV

THE CENTRAL ISSUE

WHENEVER the Bible is considered with respect to its
ultimate significance, that significance must be held
to be in its witness to God. The nature, reality, dependability,
and finality of this witness provide the central issue. All else
is subservient to this. All else finds its value in its bearing on
this. The Bible has significance in other respects than this central and dominating one, but this is what ultimately matters.
According as this is discounted, the Bible loses its unique character. It becomes, as has so often been contended, simply a
body of ancient literature. Matthew Arnold's proposed alternative — *literature* or *dogma* — did not touch bottom, nor did it
fairly represent the situation. The Bible is *not* " dogma," and it
is " literature." But it is not *merely* literature, one more of " the
great classics," to be treated as such. It is a literature — and in
many ways a very great literature — through which runs a witness to God, which is not only the *reason* for the literature but
is a witness whose truth or falsity is a matter of the deepest
concern to every human soul.

There is a God of the Bible. He is not easily arrived at, as we
shall see. The range of description is very wide, and the determinative conception which holds throughout all the variety
is one upon which we must ourselves decide. But we may at
least inquire, even this early, respecting the *intent* of the
varied description. Is it the intent of the Bible to describe that
God who is the God of all creation? Is the God of the Bible that
God in whose image man exists, so that between man and this
God there is already an initial bond other than the mere
Creator-creature bond? Is the God of the Bible that God ac-

cording to whose nature, character, and purpose all else is to be looked at, and, so far as may be, understood? Is he the God before whom every other " god," no matter by how many believed in and by how many worshiped, must finally pass away?

If this is the God he is, then he will not be the final point of arrival of rational reflection. He will not be the " discovered " God but the " self-disclosed " God. In that case, he will be the God with whom — and it is said here with the deepest reverence — rational reflection must *begin.* God as a reflective conclusion is God made in the image of man — and the images that man makes he may also destroy. It is true that the self-disclosed God must be conceived, but the conceiving process *begins* with the self-disclosure. The conceiving process will be subject to human conditioning, but what it *deals with* will be a " given." Revelation means " givenness " of a distinctive kind, or it means nothing. The slogan of a former day, " Revelation is discovery," was a self-contradiction. Revelation is not discovery, but *acceptance.* It involves a " confrontation " to which the confronted soul may yield, or from which the confronted soul may turn away. The great Bible question is, " Canst thou by searching find out God? " and the answer is, " No! " There is a God who is man's magnified self-projection on the backdrop of the vast stage of existence, but this is not the God of the Bible. The Bible deals not with a God whom men " found " for themselves and of themselves, but with a God who through great tribulation " found " men, and who found men by disclosing himself to them.

Not that the self-disclosure left men without an option. God can never be so manifest, so palpable, so unmistakably " here and now," that the human recognition of him and submission to him becomes an utter inevitability. The price paid for being a man is the possession of the right to vote — and to *vote against God.* The same Bible that witnesses to God and to his self-disclosure also witnesses to his frustration at the hands of men. The God of the Bible rides in no car of Juggernaut. He seeks not to overwhelm but to persuade. He calls, knowing that he may not be heeded. He engages in " mighty acts," knowing that the intent of the " acts " may be entirely missed.

All this because the God of the Bible is not merely one more object in a world of objects unmistakably there, irresistibly coercive, a common element in the apprehension of all rational creatures, so that not to apprehend him is to be self-declared as defective in rationality. He is not this to us, and he was not this to the men of the Bible.

This is not to say that men may not, from accepted premises, follow through a dialectical process to a certain ultimate *Idea* which they equate with God. They have done this, and they will continue to do this, as is their right. But this is not how the God of the Bible came into possession of men's souls. This God is not the conclusion of a carefully constructed syllogism, a conclusion dialectically inescapable, logically impeccable. The God of the Bible is a self-disclosed Living Reality, but self-disclosed in such wise as to confront men with *a free option* that the purely dialectical process never knows. Logic imprisons the mind; marks its course; compels the movement. But not faith. Faith is a free act. It is an act under a certain constraint, but the constraint is not irresistible: it leaves a margin for the exercise of freedom. The divine self-disclosure comes to completion only as it evokes a response, and this response is faith. The God of the Bible is a self-revealing God, but human faith is the factor by which alone the revelation is known to be such and by which alone its purpose is fulfilled. Revelation is revelation only as it reveals, and the measure of revelation is according to the measure of faith.

When, therefore, it is declared that the central issue in respect of the ultimate significance of the Bible is that of its witness to God, the question at once becomes whether we are to treat this witness as representing so much reflection, rational or otherwise, on the part of men, or whether we are to treat it as the issue of a specific activity on the part of God — in a word, of his self-revelation. So far as the Bible is concerned, this is the question of questions. One who accepts the witness as resting on revelation is not thereby precluded from supposing that the men of the Bible reflected on the revelation and on all the vast implications which they began to see went with it, nor is one precluded from such reflection on one's own

account. The very fact that man is made in the image of God
means that he has certain capacities. One of these is his power
of rational reflection. This power, so far from dispensing with
the necessity of faith, is a presupposition of its exercise. Only a
rational being is capable of faith; his faith is therefore the act
of a rational being, and his faith is therefore not only not to
be kept severely out of the reach of his reason, but could not
be so kept even if he should wish. An utterly irrational faith,
if such there could be, would not be faith at all: it would be
credulity and superstition. That with which faith has to do is
to be vitally and constructively related to the whole of life;
its implications are to be made explicit with a remorseless
fidelity; its application to every aspect of experience is to be
faithfully pondered and fearlessly accepted; and all these are
rational functions. A man of faith is not a man who has airily
dismissed his mind. Instead, he is a man who has recognized
what manner of creature he is — an intelligence in whom is the
necessity for an invisible but dominating center around which
the orbit of his life is to swing; a center which he cannot
"find" but which he may "accept" when it is presented to
him; and a center concerning whose actual reality he may be,
if not absolutely *certain,* at least absolutely *satisfied.*

Every man is constituted relative to this activity: his very
nature calls for it and justifies it. Only thus does he find
"wholeness," and cease to be something less than he is meant
to be. He is the one being to whom it belongs to center his life
in God, as God is the one Being to whom it belongs to disclose
to a man in "Whom" and in "What" the man's life is to be
centered. Herein is a human necessity, and herein is a divine
necessity, and the two necessities cohere under the principle
of mutuality. No man can center his life in a God of whom he
has no awareness; nor can there be such awareness save on the
initiative of God himself. The God to whose voice we can listen is the God who so made us that we might hear. In vain is
the rope thrown to the drowning man who has no hand where-
with to grasp it. The God who throws the rope made the hand.
The God who made man is the God who made man salvable.
But the hand may refuse the rope. The wanderer may refuse

the guide. The existential man may spurn the existential moment. Faith is a possibility inherent in the very nature of man, but that nature comes to its fruition only as the possibility passes over into an actuality. Whether or not it shall do that even God cannot determine. Without faith there is no salvation and faith is a free option.

God may initiate, but man must complete. God may touch the bush into burning, but Moses must turn aside, and Moses must take off his shoes. God may speak in "the sound of a gentle stillness," but Elijah must mark the contrast between the earthquake which says nothing and the stillness which is pregnant with meaningful sound. God may throng the surrounding mountains with "horses and chariots of fire," heralds of victory, but the prophet's servant sees them not until his eyes are "opened" as are those of the prophet himself. God may have his permanent abode in his great House in Jerusalem, and the seraphim and the altar and the live coals may be there continually, but whether Isaiah shall exclaim, while all others around him keep silence, "Mine eyes have seen the King," depends on some deep response being made in Isaiah's own soul. The prophets continued to be read, equally with "The Law of Holiness," in that priest-dominated Jerusalem of the fourth century B.C. which Ezra and Nehemiah had called into being, and if ever God spoke to men it was in and through these prophets. But what matters that prophets be heard, even that God speaks through them, if none listen. There had been no book of Jonah, so audacious in its universality, so devastating in its rebuke to the self-esteem and the deadly complacency of a people who called itself the chosen of God — there had been no such book if through all the frightful lethargy of that period one man — one lone man — had not really listened to the voice of God in the prophets, and knew, yes, *knew,* that God "chose" Israel because he would save Nineveh, even Nineveh, arrogant, despotic, destructive, hated Nineveh, with its one hundred and twenty thousand babies — "and also much cattle." It is God's prerogative to perform "mighty acts." It is man's prerogative to see God in the "acts." But such seeing is of faith, and where there is no faith, the "act" bespeaks no God.

Because the Bible is the book of God, it is therefore also the book of faith, and it is the one because it is the other. All else in the Bible is so much support for this central reality, so much commentary on it, so much varying expression of it, so much effort to tie it into the stream of life. We have a freedom as respects all this support, all this commentary, all this expression, as we have not a freedom as respects what is so manifestly central. Because we share the Biblical faith does not require that we surrender our critical judgment respecting the historical, ceremonial, social, and literary milieu in which the faith is set. The history of the people of Israel would be but the history of one more ancient people were it not for that "revelation-faith mutuality" which underlies, permeates, colors, and controls it. But for this mutuality, the articulation of this history with history in general would be but one more example of the same general laws which are operative in the history of any other people. But for this mutuality, the Biblical description of the religious life of Israel would simply provide so much more data for the student of the history of religion or of the so-called science of comparative religion. And as to the relation of the New Testament to the Old, it would on the proposed basis be explicable in terms of the influence of a dominant personality, one who took his religious heritage, rethought it, set it free from certain confining traditions, revitalized it with new insights of his own, and touched it with the promise of universality. Such universality, however, would not also be the promise of permanence, since what originates exclusively with man it belongs to man to improve, and even to destroy and replace.

The central issue as respects the Bible being in its witness to God, what authority it has will lie in this witness. The authority of the witness — and even this authority is reached only when the witness is clarified — by no means extends to all the concomitants. Do I surrender to the Bible witness to God? In the measure in which I construe that witness, I do. Do I therefore surrender to everything that was said and done and believed by those who created this witness? I do not. Even divine revelation cannot authenticate what is palpably human vagary. The stock gibe of the skeptic concerning the great ages assigned to the so-called patriarchs has nothing whatever to do with the Biblical witness to God. If Jacob did not actually live to the age of one hundred and forty-seven years (Gen. 47:28), then his experience at Beth-el (ch. 28:10 ff.) and at the ford of the Jabbok (ch. 32:22 ff.) is of no significance! One marvels at the mind that can be content to dismiss the Bible on such a *non sequitur*. It became an indestructible conviction of the people of Israel that their long journey from Egypt to Canaan was under the control of their God, that it revealed both what manner of God he was and what his purpose with them was, and that it set the pattern for their future history. In what sense is that conviction invalidated by the fact that in the accounts of the journey as they have come down to us in the Bible are numerous inconsistencies, interpolations from a later time, and even outright impossibilities? According to Ex. 12:37–42, the number of Israelites who left Egypt the night of the first "passover" was 600,000 men on foot besides children (and, presumably, women and aged men) and "a mixed multitude," the constituents of which we can only surmise. In addition were flocks and herds and all the equipment. In Num. 1:46 this figure is in substance repeated, but it does not include the tribe of Levi, and it is limited to men above twenty years of age and capable of bearing arms. If to this are added all the persons under twenty, all the women, and all the aged men, we have a prodigious total. It was simply impossible, as remarked in an earlier chapter, for so great a multitude to leave a given spot in a single night, or to be handled and fed and instructed by a few leaders (see Ex. 18:13 ff.), or to be addressed by a single person at one time (ch. 32:25 f.), or, still later, for an even greater multitude to cross the Jordan into Canaan as a compact body at a given spot ("right against Jericho" — Josh. 3:16) in what was apparently a single day. This is nothing but the unrestrained imagination of later scribes, and one speaks of it at all only because so many still think it affects "the central issue," when in truth it does nothing of the kind.

A similar difficulty confronts us in the elaborate instructions concerning worship, reported in Ex., chs. 35 to 40, especially those having to do with the structure and furnishing of "the tent of meeting." When we remember that these instructions were ostensibly given to a people largely nomad, and living under conditions of extreme austerity, we cannot resist the conclusion that these instructions represent a " reading back " into history by interested persons — in particular, priests — of a later time. We must pronounce a like judgment on the ethical code and the numerous agricultural instructions contained in the short form of " The Book of the Covenant " in Ex. 21:1 to 23:19. The great bulk of the cultus instructions and of the instructions concerning conduct are simply not germane to the wilderness period.

This sort of questionable historicity is common enough in the Old Testament. Anyone who reads The Book of Joshua, for example, would suppose that the " conquest " of Canaan was rapid, and that it was virtually complete before the death of Joshua. Not only is this incredible on the face of it, but it is entirely at variance with the testimony of The Book of Judges, and with much in The First Book of Samuel. Judges tells the story of a people engaged through many long years in the attempt to establish themselves in a land that was not rightfully theirs, and meeting with only indifferent success. A like sense of sharp contrast is yielded by a comparison of the books of Chronicles with the books of Samuel and of Kings. In the earlier books there is some approach to historical objectivity, but in the later books (Chronicles, finally compiled about 300 B.C.) history is very definitely written to support a point of view. This point of view was largely that which characterized " the priestly party." Indeed, the extent to which priestism colors Old Testament history is a question that will never be completely answered, and its influence is not entirely wanting, as we shall see, in the New Testament. It was certainly not wanting from the way in which some of the simplicities of the New Testament were very quickly interpreted in the Church. Especially did the Chronicler idealize the character of David. By every indication, the real David is the David of the books of Samuel. Here is the man of flesh and blood; the man of many romances; the man who for a while was the acknowledged leader of a band of freebooters (I Sam.

22:1, 2; 27:8 ff.); the man of great loyalties and great generosities; the man strangely compacted of the high and the low, who could sin greatly and achieve greatly; and yet withal the man in whose character and whose realm men of a later day saw an adumbration of that King and Kingdom for which the ages waited.

This is not to imply that there is in the Bible no good history. Much of the history in the Old Testament can be verified from independent sources — from archaeology, from monuments, from the archives of other nations. Speaking of "the early source of Samuel" in contrast to later sources, Robert H. Pfeiffer says, "Once freed from later additions . . . [this source] is the outstanding prose writing and historical masterpiece of the Old Testament" (*Introduction to the Old Testament,* Harper & Brothers, revised ed., 1948, p. 356). The historical dependability of much of the story narrated in The Acts of the Apostles has long been recognized by scholars. Sir William M. Ramsay's researches at this point are more than convincing. But dependability on the part of Biblical history is not uniform, and we have no reason to expect it to be. In this respect, it is like all other ancient history. It picks and chooses. It preserves folklore and legend equally with demonstrable fact. Its writers are not free from bias. It rarely gives a photographic panorama, and this is true even of the accounts of the life of Jesus. Often what is preserved is that which interested parties were determined should be preserved, and we need not doubt that much passed into oblivion for partisan reasons. At the same time, Biblical history often preserves the stark actuality, shameful though it may be, because there were those who were not afraid to put the truth on record. The account of the reign of Manasseh (II Kings 21:1–16) is credible on the face of it: no Hebrew historian would have been at the pains to "invent" such a reign, any more than a Christian historian would have "invented" the shameful story of Ananias and Sapphira (Acts 5:10, 11), or the declarations of gross infidelity as set forth in "the seven letters" of John (Rev., chs. 2; 3). There is on occasion a frankness about both the Old Testament and the New that is nothing less than startling; for example, prophetic descriptions of the moral chaos rampant among a so-called people of God (Isa. 1:2–15; Jer. 8:4–22; Ezek. 8:5–18; Hosea, ch. 4; Amos 2:6–8; 6:1–6; Micah 2:1–11). And what shall we say of the dreadful implications concerning the behavior of so-called Christians in Corinth as we read these implications out of Paul's first letter (I Cor., chs. 5 to 8; 11:17–21)?

Historical dislocations, historical uncertainties, historical confusions, even deliberate historical perversions, combined with history of unimpeachable authenticity; unsocial attitudes, restricted sympathies, irreligious sentiments, ethical aberrations; and running through it all a story of the commerce of God with the souls of men — a commerce initiated by God, and designed to promote more and more fully the self-disclosure of God, yet a commerce whose effectiveness was in proportion to the human response: this in large part is the Old Testament. This is very far from being a fair description of the New Testament: the admitted continuity of the New Testament with the Old must not be allowed to conceal the fact of their profound differences and of the ultimate reason for these differences. Nevertheless, even the New Testament sets the problem of distinguishing between substance and form, between what the book is *about* and how it *deals* with what it is about. Not the dealing, but what is dealt with, constitutes the finality in the New Testament. Not the argument in Rom., chs. 5 to 8, but what the argument aims to set forth, is what chiefly matters. Not the analogy in Hebrews between the Levitical sacrifices and the work of Christ is the centrality, the more so as the analogy breaks down at certain crucial points, but the great truth which the analogy is intended to illustrate — this is central, and it would still be central even if the analogy were not used.

The justifiable distinction between substance and form bears on the New Testament at many points. The distinction will be returned to at a later time. For the present it must suffice to suggest that the distinction relieves much of the difficulty connected with the long list of " woes " recorded in Matt., ch. 23; with such parables as those of the equal pay for unequal work

(Matt. 20:1–16) and of the dishonest steward who benefited by adding to his dishonesty (Luke 16:1–9); with the claim that "about three thousand souls" were converted under Peter's preaching on the Day of Pentecost (Acts 2:41; cf. 4:4); with the bitter description of some of his fellow Christians contained in The Epistle of Jude; and with the cryptic and even bizarre symbolism which characterizes The Revelation of John. When one considers the dreadful conclusions that have been drawn from Paul's words, "Through the one man's disobedience the many were made sinners" (Rom. 5:19), and the very high degree of probability that Paul would be deeply shocked if he could know of these conclusions, one might very well wish that Paul had never written them, or that he had expressed himself in a less ambiguous way. One ventures a similar wish concerning the foreknowing, foreordaining, and calling passage in Rom. 8:29, 30. The passage has created endless perplexity for those who took it at what seems to be its face value, and it has caused much obloquy to fall upon those who did not, that is, upon those who sought to "interpret" the passage agreeably to the universality of the grace of God, which is the very heart of the Christ-revelation. Many people have taken great comfort from Paul's advice to Timothy, "Be no longer a drinker of water, but use a little wine for thy stomach's sake and thine often infirmities" (I Tim. 5:23), and many have been sincerely troubled, even dismayed by it. The bearing of the advice on what is here being called "the central issue" in respect of the significance of the Bible is remote indeed, perchance even nonexistent. Both groups were equally justified in their attitudes so long as they were assuming that every statement of Paul was "plenarily inspired," "verbally infallible," and in consequence "divinely authoritative." Paul did, indeed, utter many opinions of dubious Christian value — for example, on women speaking in the churches (I Cor. 14:34–36); on marriage, virginity, and celibacy (I Cor. 7:25–40); and on the veiling of women and the shearing of their hair (I Cor. 11:2–16). It seems likely that these opinions were offered in view of the prevailing social situation; but the transforming of contemporary pragmatisms into Christian principles of universal and permanent validity is just one more illustration of the dire consequences of misunderstanding "the central issue" respecting the Bible.

Much more of a similar nature could be added to what has now been written, if that were necessary. A false view of the significance of the Bible makes for perplexity and confusion. A proper view discloses how much of the medium in which the Word of God is preserved and by which it is conveyed is simply so much explainable verbal wrapping. It remains, however, that substance and form alike make up the Bible as we have it. The only Bible we know is the Bible that is characterized by all these obviously human elements. We have to take it as it is, study it as it is, understand it as it is, and interpret it as it is. We might undertake to rewrite it, edit it, rearrange it, according to the findings of historical and literary criticism, but even if we did that — or could do that — we should still be confronted with the question of what this "revised" Bible is *about*. In any changed form we might be able to give the Bible, we should still have a body of writing whose essential significance would be in its witness to God, and in the declared origin of that witness in some divine initiative to which there had been human yielding in varying degrees. We should still have to inquire concerning the reasons for the belief that the witness did have this origin. We should still have to inquire into the variations in the witness, these arising, at least in part, in variations in the human understanding of the God to whom the witness is borne. We should still have to inquire whether, since the variations are manifestly there, it is possible to find a point of absolute finality in respect of the nature, character, and purpose of God with reference to which the variations are to be so treated that a consistent witness is secured to one and the same God.

Once again, therefore, the declaration is made that the central Biblical issue is God. Since God alone knows God, the Biblical witness to God will be valid according as it springs from a divine self-disclosure. In the Bible the witness to God is rooted, not in his general cosmic activity, but in what are regarded as special acts of God — his "wonderful works" which he has done; in what certain men took these acts to signify; and in what the assent to this signification meant to those who were first led to see it (the "Spirit" being their Teacher) and to those who accepted their word. Up to this point, however, we are still dependent on human testimony. The links in the chain of testimony may be seen to hang together, *but to what is the chain itself ultimately attached?* An unattached chain, no matter how strong the links, will make nothing secure. When it is declared that God acts, and that his acts mean thus and thus, there is still a distinction to be made between the act and the Actor. The two stand over against each other, and the extent to which the act discloses the Actor is always in question for any who will have it so.

Is there any way of breaking out of this circle? The Bible declares such a way. It is at the point where the distinction between the act and the Actor is no longer operative. At such a point, God is absolutely self-disclosed. Here we meet him in his living actuality. Here we know what he is. The point is where the Creator appears as an intrinsic part of his own creation. Very God presents himself as Very Man, with all that that means for the divine and with all that that means for the human. Into the stream of the historical comes the overhistorical. The Eternal is born and lives and dies as a man. No longer is it necessary to move precariously and uncertainly from the act to the Actor, saying, "Because God does *this*, he must be *that*." Rather we can say, "Here the Act and the Actor are identities. This is not simply something that God *does:* this is what God *is*." The succession of "mighty acts" of a veiled God, evoking the response of faith, is consummated in the "Mighty Fact" of a God unveiled, at once faith's confirmation and its all-sufficient justification.

This point is known as the incarnation of the Eternal Son of the Eternal Father. It constitutes Immanuel, "God with us." God is not with us by proxy, but in person, because, although the Father "sends" the Son and the Son "comes" in obedience to the Father's will, the Father and the Son are two eternal inseparables. The Word, in whom is the possibility of creation in all its parts, but who is ever himself distinct from creation, here "becomes flesh," becomes a man like unto us, a Man to love us and to be loved by us forever. The Word — the Son — is that in God in whose image man is made. Herein every man is kin to God. But at last One appears who is not simply in the image of the Word. Instead, he is the Word himself. What every man *signifies*, this Man *is*. He who takes the incarnation of God in Christ as literally that is declaring himself confronted with God in his living actuality. Eternity accommodates itself to time; time opens to receive eternity. Logic rebels at the paradox, but faith, affirming the paradox, transcends it by embracing it. The metaphysically incomprehensible passes over into the evangelically credible. What *cannot* be not only *is*, but *must be*. The "must" lies on God if he would redeem his creatures, and on his creatures if they would be redeemed. Briefly, in Jesus Christ as the Word-become-flesh, the divine-become-human, God stands for evermore sacrificially and redemptively self-defined and self-disclosed.

This is the essence of the Christian gospel. Consequently it is the presupposition of the Gospels. The Gospels are a historical but fragmentary and incomplete account of the form under which the Son of God appeared among us. The account is therefore secondary and derived — as secondary and derived in relation to the perfect self-disclosure of God in Christ as the Old Testament is secondary and derived in relation to the imperfect self-disclosure of God in mighty acts and wonderful works. What is primary as respects the Gospels, and indeed, as respects the testimony of the entire New Testament, is that divine-human conjunction of which Jesus Christ is the living form.

God in his complete and final self-disclosure at this point is God as he is in himself and as he always has been and always will be. That the incarnation involved a disruption of the normal mode of his existence is a truth — often enough strenuously objected to even by men of Christian faith — to be concerned with later. But God in his essential selfhood changes not. God-in-Christ is the God of Israel. He is the God of the "mighty acts." He is the God of the revelation. He is the God who confirms Israel's faith, while just as certainly correcting or supplementing the forms in which Israel describes him and the activities and purposes Israel assigned to him. Nothing that is said about God elsewhere in the Bible, or throughout all religious history everywhere and of every kind, including Christian history, has final validity save as it is manifestly compatible with such a God as God showed himself to be by his entry into our human lot in the person of his Son, Jesus Christ our Lord.

The all-determinative approach, therefore, to the question of God, the central issue as respects the significance of the Bible, is provided by Jesus Christ understood in the way now described. According to how he is understood, so God will be understood. "The Christian understanding of God" will be according to the Christian understanding of God's self-disclosure in Christ. What Christ is to faith, God will be to faith. The Old Testament may be described as a God-centered book, and the New Testament as a Christ-centered book, but there is no proper opposition here, no gulf keeping the two books apart. The Bible is not two books, but one book, one Word of God, because the God who is central in the Old Testament is the God whose complete self-disclosure is Jesus Christ. The two books, for that matter the many books, are made one book by a central theme. The central theme is God, but it is in Jesus Christ his Incarnate Son that God is known as he would have us know him. The God of the Old Testament and the God of the New Testament is therefore one and the same God, but what manner of God he is is fully known only through his unveiling in our human form. God-in-Christ — this is what the Bible is ultimately *about*. This is the great interpretive fact. By this all is to be measured. According to this there will be rejection, and according to this there will be acceptance. When God at last tells us about himself, then and not till then shall we know how true or how false is that which men have told us about him. Jesus Christ is God telling us about himself, and all other alleged words of God must submit to the scrutiny of this one Word, this Word come alive in the fashion of our mortal flesh.

All Biblical interpretation must therefore be according to the God-interpretation, and all God-interpretation must be according to the Christ-interpretation. Here we take our stand. We can do no other. May God help us!

CHAPTER V

THE INTEGRATION WITH HISTORY

THE Bible is the book of God and the book of faith, but it is also a book of history. The history is not only in what is narrated but in that immensely larger area of the stage of human activity within which what is narrated takes place and by which it is so deeply affected. The history of the people of Israel is very much more than just that, as the early history of the Christian Church is very much more than just that. This more specific history does not consist in a self-contained corridor, bounded on either side by an impenetrable "curtain," running through history in general. There are, in fact, no such things as self-contained historical corridors. There is an organicism of history as truly as there is an organicism of the natural environment of history. History is a vast fabric, and its countless strands run not only lengthwise but crosswise. The "here" is implicated with the "there," the "now" with the "then." Localized action has universalized reverberations. A shot is fired, and it is heard around the world, and the embattled farmers have changed the course of history. Jealous brothers sell one of their number into slavery, and not even Thomas Mann could tell the whole story of "Joseph in Egypt." A man is seduced to treachery by a face and form surpassing fair, and there follows a ten-year war, and the "lofty towers of Ilium" fall before the flames, and blind Homer tells the story in immortal lines, lines that still echo in the classrooms of civilizations, to form growing tastes and to thrust back mental horizons — as may they ever do! A foolish Jewish king breaks faith with his overlord, and soon his capital is in ruins, his people are exiles in a strange land, and there, " by the canals of Babylon," many an ancient dream is buried forever, and new dreams arise to take their place — dreams of a Suffering Servant by whose stripes healing will come to an afflicted world, dreams of a Holy City "undimmed by human tears." Uncounted centuries of varied history, passing over into Roman conquest, Roman power, Roman glory, Roman law, precipitate at the point of "a strange Man on a cross," and the cross which is the issue of such vast complexities is destined to become creative of complexities still more vast, reaching out into every least corner of the life of men, to redeem and to transform. Shortsighted men may mark out a preserve, erect around it a high wall, and think to live in lordly isolation, but history operates according to its own immutable law: "By my God do I leap over a wall."

Because, therefore, the Bible is concerned with a historical movement surcharged with a peculiar significance does not mean that this movement is unaffected by what may be happening elsewhere at any given time. The mutuality may not immediately manifest itself, but it is at work none the less. It is proper enough to speak, with Daniel Ropes, of "sacred history," but not if what is meant thereby is a segment of history which proceeds on its way with no least reference to the laws of interrelation and interdependence. Time and again, what was to happen to Israel would be determined by events and decisions elsewhere with which Israel had nothing to do. They were decisions and events depending on nearby or distant contemporaries. The rise of world powers — Assyria, Babylon, Media, Persia, and the like — their ambitions and their rivalries, are factors of enormous significance not only in the history of Israel but, by consequence, in the history of divine revelation — to use the phrase; just as Roman policy profoundly affected Christian life and procedure as this is reflected in the New Testament and in later writings and institutions.

It is difficult to believe that there was once a time when men could suppose that because Israel was "a chosen people" it carried an intrinsic immunity against all outside influences; or that because Jesus was "the Son of God become man" he was exempt, except on such occasions as he chose to represent them, from all the distinctive human characteristics. The supposition was the purest apriorism, and it could not have endured even a casual reading of the Scriptures by a mind bold enough to lay the apriorism aside. In actual fact, one of the most palpable features of the Bible is the way in which it reflects and responds to the contemporary. A list of the various countries and peoples, and of the conspicuous figures among them, referred to in the Bible would occupy many pages; and when it comes to forms of expressions — and even to "thought forms " — contemporary influences are even more manifest. Was it not from certain fantastic features of Babylonian sculpture and architecture that Ezekiel derived the raw material of the complex vision that he describes in his opening chapter? What history lay back of Jacob's well near Samaria, and back of the pool of Bethesda, and back of Jewish shepherd customs and domestic habits and religious festivals, and back of the attitude to leprosy, and back of scribism and Pharisaism? And how much of what Jesus said and did would either not have been said or done at all or would have been said or done differently from what it was, but for these features of his immediate time and place? Paul gives us an amazing piece of autobiography in II Cor. 11:23–27, the details of which are almost entirely unknown to us. How profoundly did these experiences affect his apostleship — yes, and even his "interpretations" of the gospel of Christ? What was there about Bithynia — its geography, its climate, its people, its means of travel and of communication — which persuaded Paul to turn back, a decision resulting in, humanly speaking, the epochal vision at Troas, the crossing of the Aegean Sea to Macedonia, and all the story, involving so large a part of the New Testament and of later Christianity, that was to follow? These are all so many commonplaces, or may be regarded as such, yet often enough a so-called commonplace turns out to be a nexus around which swings the destiny of mankind.

The very first mention of Abram sets him at the crossroads of the ancient world, and the fact was nothing less than predictive of what was to be the fate of his posterity. It would be no exaggeration to say that the Bible, considered merely as a historical record, describes the history of Israel under the metaphor of a ganglion. A thousand lines cross and recross at this continuing center, and while the ganglion resolutely preserves its identity, the identity is preserved through panoramic change. Sometimes the change is due to surrender to externality, and sometimes it is due to stubborn resistance to it, since even resistance may modify that which resists. What would Israel have been but for the Euphrates Valley and all the teeming civilizations that it from time to time supported? Take Babylon and Nineveh out of the Old Testament, and great is the gap — as great as the gap left in the New Testament if Rome be taken out. Whatever significance we eventually assign to the history and experience of Israel, and to the history and experience of the Early Church, it was a history and an experience which, springing though it did from a deeply hidden source, was yet conditioned in incalculable ways by the general social, political, and cultural milieu. Whatever God may have been doing with and through a particular people, he did with that people relative to that situation in which it found itself. While the life of this people was profoundly affected by what it came to believe about its God, and while the origin and the nature of this belief is a question by itself, the most passionate belief could not release such a people from the play of historical contingencies or create for it the luxury of complete isolation. There were, indeed, occasions when Israel fought for this isolation — an aspect of the conviction that Yahweh was "a jealous God" who demands all or nothing — just as throughout Christian history there have been groups who saw in a like isolation the sure condition to salvation, quite ignoring Jesus' metaphors of the leaven, of the salt, of the city on the hill, and of the lamp set on the stand. Nevertheless, always at last someone arose to remind the isolationists that their status as "a chosen people of God" or as "a Christian brotherhood," was endangered by this very isolation. Not to share is to lose. Not to look without is to lose the power to look within. Not to maintain communication along the line of the horizontal is to lose the zest for communication along the line of the vertical.

It is not the purpose of this book to go into the details of Biblical history. The main center of interest is the Biblical meaning, and the possible bearing of this meaning on the understanding of life. Perfect knowledge of the history is no necessary guarantee of constructive insight into the meaning. Since, however, the meaning is given through the historical movement, and is integrated therewith, a brief reminder of the more conspicuous epochs that mark the history may serve a purpose.

(1) Not particularly important for our purpose is the pre-Abramic period, which is largely a period of folklore and legend. (2) From the migration of Abram to the settlement of the clan in Southern Canaan is more substantially historical, and the period is characterized by deep religious and ethical insights. (3) From the migration to Egypt to the call of Moses and the Exodus and the Wilderness period, events occur — in particular the revelation of God as "Yahweh," the escape at the Red Sea, and the promulgation of the Sinaitic covenant — which were to have a profound effect upon the future faith and thought of Israel. (4) The conquest of Canaan and the anarchistic period of the Judges is religiously barren, perhaps understandably so when one considers the conditions. (5) With the founding of the monarchy and the work of Saul, David, and Solomon, there comes some clarification and purification of the religious tradition, and a greater emphasis on religious institutions. (6) The division of the kingdom that followed the reign of Solomon gave rise to widespread moral confusion, especially in the North, to a Baalism not only popular, but officially approved, and to a progressive weakening of the Mosaic and Davidic traditions. (7) Prophetic influence became marked with the reign of Hezekiah in the Southern Kingdom (Judah), Isaiah being the mentor of Hezekiah, and this influence, sharply directed as it often was against a corrupting priestism, was a significant factor until the fall of Jerusalem in 586 B.C. (8) The period of the Exile saw the continuation of prophetic influence, but it also saw a widespread pessimism, reflected in many of the psalms, the collapse of national hopes as fostered by memories of the reign of David, and a great

strengthening of priestly and legalistic conceptions, destined to check religious spontaneity. (9) The beginning of the return from Exile (538 B.C.), the years of uncertainty and confusion that followed, led eventually, with the reformation effected by Ezra and Nehemiah on the basis of the Code of Holiness, to the creation of Judaism properly so called. (10) The Egyptian, Syrian, and Roman dominations respectively saw the production of much of the Psalter, the emergence of late prophetic voices, the increase in legalistic niceties, and the priesthood in virtual control of the life of the people. (11) The birth of Christianity in the Herodian (and Roman) period effected a crisis in Judaism, a crisis reflected throughout the New Testament.

This is but the briefest survey, but the propriety of recognizing these broad divisions is apparent when it is realized how vitally the various historical, social, and political transitions bore upon the contemporary religious insights, experiences, and pronouncements. The single case of apocalypticism which, appearing sporadically in the prophets, came to such unrestrained and abundant expression in the second and first centuries B.C., is a striking illustration of the effect on the conception of God, of his ways and purposes, of the moral order itself, exerted by calamity, disappointed hopes, natural disaster, ruthless oppression through which a grim faith held that "the day of the Lord" would yet come to punish evil and reward righteousness.

We must realize that Abram, crucial man as he was in the plan and purpose of God, was still a Semitic nomad, still the exponent of Semitic customs, still conscious of his racial heritage, still supposing that he must offer up to his God in a blood sacrifice the very best that he had. The significance of Abram for the ultimate Christian faith could never have been detected by any forward look at the time, any more than the form and visage and capacities of a man could have been predicted from the primeval brute. The comprehension of Abram's significance for the complex web of history, political, social, religious, comes only of the backward look; wherefore the implication stands, child of audacious faith, that there was purpose working through Abram's posterity, to come to ultimate fulfillment when God, in "the fulness of the time," should send forth his Son to become the progenitor of a new Israel, but this time an Israel not after the flesh but after the Spirit.

Few men would be willing to undertake to separate the legendary from the historical in the period beginning with the journey of Jacob and his family from Canaan to the land of Goshen in Egypt, and ending with the resettlement of his descendants in Canaan under Joshua some four hundred years later. That there is genuine history there can hardly be denied: it is required to make intelligible some of the basic concomitants of the Old Testament religious faith, conceptions, and institutions. A great leader providentially prepared, spared, and called; an indispensable deliverance inexplicable on purely naturalistic suppositions; a God giving himself a new name, "Yahweh," not because he was a new God lacking known antecedents, but because the older names by which he was known — El, Elohim, El Shaddai, El-Elyon — were not adequate to describe him; the apprehension of the new name as indicative not merely of God's everlastingness, but of his utter dependability, of his stability in the fulfillment of his promise and in the pursuit of his purpose, of the unchangeableness of his moral character; the establishment of a covenant between this Yahweh and the people he had chosen for his own; and the vast vicissitudes attending the relation of God and people: if the substance of these experiences, events, decisions, disclosures, waverings, and beliefs cannot reasonably be assigned to the period immediately following the threshold of Biblical history, then we can make little enough of the most familiar and the most truly characteristic features of the later Biblical story and of the religious faith and practices that attend it. Belief in God's "mighty acts" and in their function as revelation is Biblically foundational. The call of Abram was a mighty act; the birth of Isaac was a mighty act; the rescue of Isaac at the last moment was a mighty act. Mighty acts too were the escape from Egypt, the sweeping back of the Red Sea, the theophany at Sinai and the covenant that was its issue, the survival of the wilderness wandering, the final arrival at the plains of Moab, with the Land of Promise at last in plain sight. These events were destined to be included in the stuff out of which an increasing comprehension of the character of God and the ways of God was to be acquired, forms of divine activity which time and insight and faith and the Spirit's illumination would weld increasingly into God's " Word." Yet they were events made possible by the situation as it was, as all events must be. What if it be so that but for the Code of Hammurabi there had been no Ten Commandments of Moses? — the Commandments are no less of God, and their authority is no less of God. That whatever self-disclosure of God there may be will occur, not *apart from* the historical and social conditions then prevailing, but *by means of* them, should be a natural expectation, and the facts support the expectation.

The Book of Judges must always be a problem for the interpreter, unless he sees it for what it is. The book reeks with a brutal frankness. Nowhere does it idealize the people of Israel. Instead, it describes them as the half-barbarians we should expect them to be: fickle, ruthless, unscrupulous, primitive in the proper sense. Any constructive influence from the Moses and Joshua traditions is little enough. It is a bloody book, full of assassinations and treacheries and repulsive deeds. Samson is a Hebrew Paul Bunyan! The most impressive character in the book is Gideon, but although he began his career by boldly smashing the idolatrous altar in his father's yard, he celebrated his victories by erecting a similar altar on his own account (Judg. 8:22–27). Yet for all that, embedded in the book (ch. 2:11–22) is a moral judgment which is a true "Word of God."

Many of the characteristics reflected in The Book of Judges continued into the period that followed. The corruption of the worship of Yahweh; the low morals that would suggest that there had never been such a man as Moses with his austere legislation, except that a Samuel appears, or an Elijah, or a Rechab and his family (Jer., ch. 35; cf. I Kings 10:15), and these would seem to call for a Moses to account for them; the necessary intermingling with the Canaanitish tribes (since Israel was not *always* at war with its neighbors) and the radical change in many of the ideas and customs of Israel which the intermingling involved — all this, and much more of a similar nature, must be recognized as simply implicit in the historical situation. The fact of God's purpose with the growing nation, and of here and there a deepening apprehension of that purpose and a faith-response to it, did not mean that sociological laws, economic laws, and the laws that operate in the formation of patterns of behavior were held in suspense. If the people of Israel were to live in Canaan, and create there a settled life for themselves, it would require that in many ways they should become Canaanites. There is nothing modern about the principle of "the melting pot." The principle has been an attendant upon human history from the beginning. God did not dispense with it for the benefit of "a chosen people," even though in time the people themselves attempted to do so. On the contrary, the principle is of his own ordaining.

If, therefore, the settlement in Canaan was due, as Israel more and more came to believe, to a providential leading stemming out from the Abramic and Mosaic covenants, then we can hardly escape the conclusion that the same "providence" was prepared to see the people subjected to the social, political, and moral hazards that life in Canaan would involve. God has "deposited" among this people a certain tradition about their origin, their early forebears, their relation to himself as Yahweh, their peculiar function in the world, and their national destiny. It is to this as to an inner control that he must trust. Its persistence, its clarification, its deepening hold — it is on this that he must depend. Humanly speaking, the prospects that the frail reed would endure were sometimes incredibly slight. It is only as we see that human freedom was mysteriously subject to a pervasive necessitatedness, and that necessitatedness was operating amid conditions of human freedom, that we can see the reason for what we know actually took place.

The whole story of the preparation for the Hebrew monarchy, its founding, and its checkered career, can be read, if one so wishes, as a piece of simple political history. The two traditions about Samuel's attitude to the people's demand for a king; the adulation Saul received for his victories; the increasingly strained relations between Saul and Samuel; the appearance of David as a threat to Saul's domination; the mingled shine and shadow in David's own reign; the brilliant career of Solomon, and its tragic issue in the division of the realm — all this follows a perfectly understandable political pattern. Here we see the interplay of human motives in the development of a national structure. Much of it could be matched in national developments elsewhere. This is how history moves along. The intensely human quality of the books of Samuel and of the Kings is there for anyone to see. *The Bible Is Human* is the title of Wallis' challenging book: certainly it is not nonhuman! The attempt of a later generation to surmount David's crown with a halo, and to modify his kingly shrewdness with saintly piety, is not to be wholly discounted when its purpose is considered, yet we are not deceived thereby. David was still not a' Christian man born out of due time! Doubtless, too, our imagination is captured by the splendor of the reign of Solomon, and by the magnificence of the "house" that he built for Yahweh. What this "house" was to mean for the people of Israel for centuries to come need not be emphasized. Yet did not Solomon, pliant in the hands of his "foreign wives," permit the presence within this very "house" of Yahweh of alien altars, dramatic evidence at once of the status of the religion of Yahweh and of the subtle influence of political and social considerations!

And yet this is not all the story. It is not all the story now any more than it is to be throughout the sad years of the division. One insists properly enough upon the presence and activity of the usual social factors throughout the period of the early monarchy and throughout the period of the North and South division. One cannot ignore the fact that during a period of some twenty years of Northern history, six rulers occupied the throne, of whom four were assassinated, and in each case the assassin took the throne. We cannot brush aside the reign of Ahab, or the infamy of the Phoenician Jezebel, archcorrupter of Israel's Yahwehism. We cannot pass over the situation in Judah, where a high-minded king like Hezekiah could be succeeded by a son like Manasseh, the traditional murderer of no less a man than that Isaiah the prophet who had been the stay of Hezekiah, by whose defiance even Assyria was cowed.

Isaiah! The very mention of his name bespeaks a light " amid the encircling gloom." What has been said about the play of typically human factors in the period covered by the historical books of the Old Testament has nevertheless to be read in the light of another factor. The name of Yahweh, corrupted as it was, allied with a debasing Baalism, invoked in support of practices which it were a shame even to mention — this " name " did not perish. And not only did the name in its original significance not perish: there were always those who were not only aware of this significance and determined to keep it alive, but who also made varying contributions to its deepening. Whatever might be happening to the nation, considered simply as a nation, the treasure that God himself had hidden in it as in a field was so far from being lost that its value steadily increased. Priests there may have been to whom the bull was a sufficiently expressive symbol of Yahweh, but over against such priests were others like Jehoida (II Kings, ch. 11), and perchance Urijah (ch. 16:10 f.), who, with all their limitations, were not wanting in ethical idealism and in loyalty to a high tradition. " False prophets " in their hundreds there may have been — false because they prophesied according to what they knew was desired to be heard, as the four hundred of the Jehoshaphat-Ahab story (I Kings, ch. 22); but over against the many false were the few " to whom God verily whispered in the ear " — the Nathans (II Sam. 12:1 f.), the Gads (ch. 24:11–14), the Ahijahs (I Kings 11:29 f.), the Elijahs, the Elishas, and that one Micaiah who was willing to have his fearless utterance judged by the outcome of the event (ch. 22:24–29). Men of their time though they were, these prophets spoke the Word of God as it was given to them to see it. Saints they might not have been, but men of God they truly were. They were susceptible to the meaning of God's mighty acts. They saw deeper than the surface of things. They knew in themselves the divine-human encounter, and they construed the encounter with some approximation to the God of the burning bush, the God of the

Red Sea deliverance, the God whose voice was heard and whose will was declared amid the thunders and lightnings of Sinai, and the God whose glory hovered above the mercy seat.

Nor shall we forget, as we survey the often depressing history, how magnificently Amos and Hosea, Isaiah and Micah, carried on the Yahweh tradition, deepened it, clarified it, thrust out its scope into something approaching universalism, cleansed it of much of the accumulation of generations of virtual paganism, and began that overwhelming elucidation of the " name " of Yahweh which would come to its grand climacteric in a Life that would be " the Word-become-flesh " and in a Community that would be the Brotherhood of the Redeemed. " Made by their times " were these men, but it is no less true that they helped to make their times, and that they did this by virtue of their experience and understanding and representation of the character and the ways of God. Surely Amos is not altogether to be explained by his shepherding and orcharding, nor by the conditions of the reign of Jeroboam II, even though it was those conditions that evoked his utterances; nor Hosea by his domestic tragedy, greatly although that tragedy loomed in his life; nor Isaiah by his access to the court and by the threats that were implied in the ambitions of Assyria; nor Micah by his apparent occupation as a farmer at a time when wealthy city dwellers were trying to merge the small peasant farms into great holdings and reduce the farming class to a state of virtual peonage.

That these men, and many others like them, lived and worked in these conditions is simple truth; and it is no less true that the conditions exercised a formative influence on their utterances, and even upon their point of view. But this man Amos was no mere echo: he was an original voice, declaring truths that had never been heard before. This man Hosea was no mere pathetic victim of a wife's unfaithfulness and of a desolate hearth: he was the matchless interpreter of a Yahweh " whose compassions fail not," let Israel his chosen bride " play the harlot " as she will; and whether Hosea's mind moved from himself to Yahweh or from Yahweh to himself becomes a question to consider. This man Isaiah was no mere confidant of kings, a statesman who knew how to give bold counsel in a time of national crisis. Once his pride and self-esteem and spiritual complacency had been shattered by an overwhelming consciousness of God. The furnishings of the Temple where he was worshiping took on, as they were intended to do, the significance of a vast symbolism. They spoke to him of God — of God transcendent, of God utterly holy, of God driven by moral concern, and yet withal of God calling for a willing and worthy messenger to declare his will and purpose to a reprobate people. Isaiah never ceased to be dominated by that experience and all its far-flung meaning. It was for him a " mighty act " of God and a " wonderful work," the crux of a divine self-revelation to his inmost soul. It was through *that*, and through that supremely, that he came to " rethink God," that he came to his great doctrine of the inviolability of Zion, and later, when the asserted inviolability was seen by him to be a relative rather than an absolute truth, to the much greater because much profounder doctrine of the " remnant." And as for this man Micah, pupil of Isaiah as he may have been, he was no mere revolutionary peasant, a Hebrew Wat Tyler of the eighth century B.C., jealous of his little ancestral plot, doubly endangered as it was from the Philistines whose borders it almost touched and from the voracious land-grabbers of the city who, already possessing much, craved still more, madly determined to " build up Zion with blood, and Jerusalem with iniquity " (Micah 3:10). He was, indeed, such a peasant, or so it would seem, and he could talk like any Amos. But he looks at the situation that confronts and threatens him and his neighbors, not only as a question in social justice and economics, but also as a question in religious faith. He brings God into the picture. " What doth the Lord require of thee? " What Lord? The Lord Yahweh. Yahweh, whose very " name " is a revelation of his own deepest selfhood. Yahweh, who has committed himself to a covenant, and who includes in that covenant not only a promise to give himself wholly to his people but an expectation also that the people shall give themselves wholly to him, the attestation of that self-giving on the people's part consisting in doing justly, loving mercy, and walking humbly, reverently, and obediently with their God. Is this attestation forthcoming? It is not. Costly religious pageantry is offered as a substitute; and in the absence of the only attestation that really matters, Yahweh regards the pageantry as mocking pretense. And pretense it was, and pretense it still is. " Will Yahweh be pleased with thousands of rams, or with ten thousands of rivers of oil? shall I give my first-born for my transgression, the fruit of my body for the sin of my soul? " The answer is, " No! "

The point need not be labored further, the more so as the principle involved will appear again and again in what is to follow. The necessary articulation of the movement of revelation, to call it that, with the movement of history, and the Bible as the record and description of this mutuality, must be a postulate both of all Biblical comprehension, all Biblical interpretation, and all Biblical translation into life. Any adequate philosophy of the history of Israel will need to recognize that whatever absoluteness may attach to the commerce of God with the souls of men within Israel — and, for that matter, anywhere else — is a correlative of historical contingencies. Sovereignty of purpose — even divine sovereignty — must take note of the unpredictabilities, themselves the evidence of sovereignty, of human motives and relationships. To give these contingencies and unpredictabilities the same " authority," the same " inspiration," the same " infallibility," that is ultimately to be assigned to what the social and historical complexities were seen to be subserving and helping to bring to light, is to be involved in endless confusion. It is to put an intolerable burden on religious faith. It is to mechanize the free. It is to identify the stabilities of the divine with the frailities of the human. It is to be driven into all manner of subterfuges to avoid the plain logic of the asserted premises. The persisting purpose of God — yes. The growing self-disclosure of God — yes. The growing apprehension of God — yes. The growing clarity of the understanding of God — yes. The unmistakable even if variable insinuation of God into the religio-historical process — yes. The more passionate self-commitment to God on the part of men and the more persuasive and convincing descriptions of what God *is*, of what he *purposes*, of what he

would *do for men*, of what he would *endure* for this doing, of
what life ought to be and will be in view of such a God — all
this, yes. But all this is so much precipitate from a variety of
conflicting forces, partly divine, partly human, partly demonic,
and partly so variable and so fluid and so elusive as to baffle
description — this too.

Even amid the immense complications of the life and utterances of Jeremiah, what we chiefly look for is that which made
him the manner of man he was. There might still have been a
man Jeremiah had there been no black shadow cast by an
approaching national calamity which more than any other he
plainly foresaw and predicted and moralized upon; but what
manner of man he would have been, what manner of lovely
songs this natural-born poet of Israel would have sung, had
the lines fallen unto him in a happier time, who shall venture to say? Great was the price paid by the people of Israel
that there might be the Elijah that we know; greater still that
there might be the Hosea that we know; but what was the cost
of the production of a Jeremiah? A nation must be destroyed
that a man might hear and embody and proclaim the Word of
God! Jeremiah, surveying his life, could only declare that "before he came forth from the womb he was sanctified" (Jer.
1:5). He was a predestined child of maternal travail. But he
was more than that: he was the predestined child of the
dreadful travail of his nation. He learned the truth of "the new
covenant" — a truth even yet so rarely grasped — only in circumstances in which the old covenant seemed to have come
into utter collapse, all the ancient agreements nullified, all the
ancient promises vanished like morning dew, all the ancient
hopes rolled in the dust of irrecoverable loss. Was it worth-
while that a nation be shattered in order that a new and revolutionary idea might arise out of the ruins? God seemed to
think so. At least, this is the procedure that God followed —
whether freely or perforce, who shall say? Wherein lies a
parable.

The Exile was a bitter experience, yet it was not unique.
Many a small nation of the ancient world knew what it was to
be transported from its homeland, as a political necessity of

a conquering power. From one point of view, the Exile is but a small incident in the history of the ancient East. Yet who shall say that it is only that? Out of that darkness shone a light, and the light was of God. How much more understandable become some of the psalms when it is realized that they are " exilic " — the utterances of faith or of despair or of hope, conditioned by a situation. The precise " dating " of the psalms is admittedly a problem, but if Ps. 71 be the utterance of an old man of the Exile, its deep significance is greatly augmented. Ezekiel had not been the man we know had he been able to spend his life serving in the Temple at Jerusalem instead of being under necessity to keep faith alive in his people by the canals of Babylon where he " saw visions of God " (Ezek. 1:1) while they hung their silent harps on the willows (Ps. 137:1–4). The bearing of the Exile on the growth of the Code of Holiness, which, as already said, is the presupposition of scribism, of the Reformation effected by Ezra and Nehemiah, and of the narrow nationalism and deadening legalism that followed, is a story in itself. The same Exile that gives us Ezekiel and the Code and the scribe, however, also gives us the Second Isaiah. It determines the form of " the Messianic hope " which he kept alive by moving and eloquent descriptions of " the return " — descriptions very far removed from the actual fact. But this " Evangelist of the Old Testament " was also he whose mind conceived " the Suffering Servant of Yahweh." Out of what a wide range of history, human experience, tragedy, religious ebb and flow, hopes and fears, conquests and defeats, was the conception formed and brought to sharp focus! Similarly, the incredible agonies that preceded and accompanied the Maccabean period, including the studied cruelties of the mad Antiochus IV, were the travail of which was born The Book of Daniel, so bold in its defiance, so audacious in its faith, so confident in its anticipation of a kingdom which, unlike the great world powers of the past, would never pass away, because it would be a gift to men of " the ancient of days " and because it would be ruled by " one like unto a son of man."

The historical integration so evident in the Old Testament is no less apparent through the New, although it must suffice at this point merely to mention it. Neither the events recorded in the New Testament nor the forms in which the New Testament deals with the events are separable from historical considerations, nor are they understandable if these considerations are ignored. It was well enough for Matthew to write that Jesus was born in Bethlehem in order " that it might be fulfilled which was spoken . . . through the prophet." In actual fact, the birth fell at Bethlehem because this was assured by a complication of historical, political, and social factors. Lacking any one of these factors, the birth could very well have occurred at Mary's home in Nazareth. What Paul calls " the fulness of the time " was not a precise date already marked on a pretemporal calendar. The actual time could have been earlier or later, according as certain events did or did not occur. All across the Gospel records lies the shadow of a definite time and place. Some of the most striking parables of Jesus — say the Prodigal Son — presuppose certain distinctive customs in whose light alone the parables are intelligible. The most important writers of the New Testament, the author of the Fourth Gospel, the author of Romans, the author of Hebrews, reveal on almost every page the time in which they live, their own intellectual predilections, the various cultures in which they have been nurtured. Most of the Epistles of Paul are a response to a situation whose immediate causes might or might not have become operative. Consider the single fact that the marvelous epistle to the Colossians was written relative to a " heresy," largely Gnostic, which had crept into the churches in and around Colossae. There had to be Gnosticism in order that there might be The Epistle of Paul to the Colossians! What is that if not unanswerable proof that the Word of God is subject to historical contingencies? It is far too common to suppose that the book of Revelation had no relation to the time in which it was written; that God gave it to John directly in a vision or a series of visions, and that its reference is wholly futuristic. There could hardly be a more melancholy mistake. The writer had saturated himself in the language and symbols of apocalypticism; he was thinking of the situation immediately confronting him and Christ's Church; he was concerned with what is to be done and endured by Christian people *here and now;* and if at times his mind does range the distant future, it is only because he sees that what must be true for *his* time must be true for *every* time — even for ours!

There can be no proper interpretation of the New Testament if these considerations are not continually borne in mind, as will yet be seen. What is immediately at issue is the fact of the explicability of the Scriptural record according to the normal laws of history. This is by no means the *only* issue, but it is an issue that is to be kept alive for its interpretive significance. What seems from one point of view to be so entirely the result of the interplay of normal processes turns out to be at the same time the means of receiving, nurturing, expressing, deepening, and embodying a divine-human relationship of a quite distinctive kind. Within the historical continuity another continuity is being maintained, depending on the historical but far from being wholly explained by it. To detect this other continuity, to find the reason for it, to see what it implies, to find in it its own justification, to mark its increasing dominance over the lives of men, to be aware of its strange persistence even when it is driven underground, to note in what strange and unpredictable ways it receives here a sudden acceleration, there a startling augmentation, until that Living Word appears who is the explanation of all that has gone before — to do this is the obligation on any man who would be the messenger and interpreter of the Word of God to men.

THE INNER CONTINUITY

A T THE expense of some repetition, it needs to be emphasized that within the historical continuity which the Bible so plainly reflects is embedded another continuity. In any organism we distinguish between the organic structure and the organic principle. Neither exists apart from the other. There is a mutuality which bespeaks also a continuity. If by any means the organic principle should change, there would be a corresponding change in the structure. The structure remains continuous because the principle remains continuous.

The analogy with the Bible is a precarious one, and must not be pressed. Only in a very relative sense may the Bible be compared to an organism. Nevertheless, there is propriety in the analogy to the extent that the Bible is characterized by an inner and outer mutuality which bespeaks also an inner and outer continuity. The Bible is *about* something, and this "aboutness" constitutes its "inwardness" and the continuity of this inwardness. But the "aboutness" is set in a framework. This framework constitutes the "outwardness" of the Bible and the continuity of this outwardness. To detect the inner through the outer, the "aboutness" through the "framework," is a condition to proper interpretation.

The self-disclosure of God evoking the response of faith — this is the essence of the inner. In *principle* this nowhere changes and herein lies the inner continuity. The self-revealing God answered to by the faith-responsive man is the creative root whence springs the Bible as a book. To separate these two is to seek to dispense with the root by which alone the Bible is explicable. No revealing God and no believing man, then no

Bible. The Bible is to be regarded accordingly. It is implied that that wherein the Bible is ultimately rooted has an absolute significance for human life. This is itself a faith-judgment, which no dialectical process can ever completely validate. The *act* of faith is a human necessity and so far is self-justified. The *subject* of faith, however, is *held* in faith, which means that faith is faith in faith! This is not a vicious circle. It is simply a recognition of the fact that the Bible presupposes *a continuous venture in self-commitment* on the part of men, and that neither revelation nor faith is possible where there is not this venture. The Bible therefore witnesses to venture, is the creation of venture, finds its unity in venture, and is rendered inwardly continuous by venture. God's self-disclosure was through "mighty acts." Faith was a response to the self-disclosure. In such a response the "mighty act" became a "Word" of God. But the reading of the "act" as a "Word" was not a purely human achievement. The God who disclosed himself in the "act" was not wholly absent from the faith that made the "act" a "Word." The Bible has much to say about the Spirit of God, and while it is impossible to reduce all it says to complete consistency, the *intent* of much that is said about the Spirit is to prevent the supposition that the faith that makes out of the "act" of God a "Word" of God is a merely logical inference, a natural deduction. Faith is never just that. It is, in fact, impossible to make a complete analysis of faith in the sense that every factor is laid out clearly before the mind. There is always present a factor whose actuality is undeniable but which is not susceptible of precise delimitation and precise description. All faith bespeaks some divine "prevenience" and some divine "co-operation." No man can put his finger on this, and no man deny that it is there. He will recognize it as the area of the activity of the Spirit — the Spirit of God, the Holy Spirit, name it how he will; but what will be chiefly significant will be, not the name, but what the name stands for. The constituent elements of that inner continuity discernible in the Bible are "mighty acts" of God, faith-response to these "acts," "acts" transformed into "words" by reason of this response, the activity of the divine Spirit as a factor in the response and in the interpretation which it effects. Always in what might be called "the high moments" interwoven with the Biblical inner continuity these elements are unmistakably present.

The indispensability of the divine Spirit to the experience is a concomitant of the very nature of man. At least we must say that God is spirit, and we can say no less of man. If man is constituted relative to fellowship with God, then there must be some commonness between them. The essential God is never a visibility, and the essential man is never a visibility. The concept of spirit is a difficult one at the best, but it is indispensable if any adequate account is to be given of the deepest experiences of human life. All *vital* encountering of man with man is "in the spirit," and all *vital* encountering of man with God is "in the spirit." For certain purposes we speak of these encounters as "objectivities," but they are objectivities whose significance is in their correspondence to hidden "subjectivities." The actuality of God is not the actuality of the universe, but the actuality of spirit. The actuality of man is not the actuality of body, but the actuality of spirit. Any "help" that man may receive from God is the help of spirit to spirit, and how else may spirit help spirit than by spirit.

Admittedly this point may make for confusion and obscurity, the more so as we are so "incurably realistic," so committed to the finality of the ponderable and the measurable. We want everything "laid out in order on the table," and we forget that the most important and therefore the most valuable things of life do not lend themselves to this treatment. But if we cannot lay out and schematize the great fundamentals, we can at least see them at work. We can see them — or some of them — at work in what is brought to us in the Bible. We can see them at work in what was referred to above as "the high moments" of the Biblical inner continuity. Abram feeling his hand stayed at the crucial moment by the altar on the mountain in Moriah; Moses turning aside at the burning bush; Gideon mysteriously confronted as he secretly threshed his wheat; Nathan realizing that even a king could not do "what he liked"; Solomon's noble prayer at the dedication of the Temple; Elijah recovering his confidence in the cave at Horeb; the unknown prophet at the altar at Beth-el — not forgetting how deplorably he failed; Amos turning from his flocks to declare the universality of Yahweh and his utter righteousness; the devastating insight, " I must bring the harlot home! ", that came to Hosea in respect of the unfaithful Gomer; Micah, overcome by the contrast between the poverty-stricken countryside and the luxurious city that waxed fat thereupon; Isaiah, marking the burnt offerings of rams, and the fat of fed beasts, and the blood of bullocks, and the vain oblations, and the solemn meeting, and the appointed feasts, but knowing in himself the holiness of the sovereign God, impelled to declare that upraised hands that drip with blood remain unseen, and will continue to do so until they are truly cleansed; the mind of Habakkuk flooded with illumination what time he betook himself to his watch tower; the transformation of outlook and mind of the young Josiah as there fell on his ears the solemn adjurations of " the Second Law "; Jeremiah standing at the gate of the Temple as the worshipers pour in, a burning fire still in his bones, and bravely if bitterly inquiring: " Will ye steal, murder, and commit adultery, and swear falsely, and burn incense unto Baal, and walk after other gods . . . , and come and stand before me in this house . . . ? Is this house, which is called by my name, become a den of robbers in your eyes? " (Jer. 7:9–11); the soul of exiled Ezekiel swept again and again with ecstasy whereby he is led to see that nothing important happens save as it is indwelt and animated by the Spirit of God; another exile, his name unknown, cherishing the hope that he may yet see again his native land, but nevertheless giving classic expression, under the form of a " Suffering Servant," to the great truth, interpretive of life's most deeply tragic yet most ennobling aspects, that the way of suffering is the way of redemption, and that one must suffer that others may be redeemed; another unknown author, resident of a city-state whose slogan was exclusiveness because it was also the slogan of its God (so it thought!), coming under compulsion to declare, by startling and dramatic presentation, that Yahweh was no exclusive God, concerned with only a chosen few, but that his purpose of grace extended even to ruthless and pagan powers like Nineveh; still another unknown author weaving around the figure of still another exile a series of fantastic stories and a succession of audacious but illuminating symbols, with the intent to make clear to a desperate people that the Yahweh who had prevailed over wickedness yesterday would prevail over it again *today* and *tomorrow* and *tomorrow,* since no image whose feet were clay could long endure (Dan. 2:31–45).

The story continues, still enshrining the same elements: a half-clad man, preaching passionately in the wilderness of Judea, led by the signs of the time to declare that the Kingdom of God is at hand, and that the great fan that separates the chaff from the wheat is about to swing in terrifying curves: "Wherefore, ye offspring of vipers, repent, if ye would not be cast into the fire"; a maiden of Nazareth stricken "breathless with adoration" as it comes to her that she, even she, of all "the mothers of Israel," is to be that one mother of whom will come "great David's greater Son" to bring to his people the long-promised "consolation"; a Boy undergoing initiation ceremonies in the Temple at Jerusalem, and finding himself strangely possessed of the conviction that henceforth for him "his Father's business" is all that can matter; the Boy arrived at manhood and having it borne in upon him *by the Spirit and from above* that it is by him that the Kingdom of God is to come to men; a group of perplexed men and women gathered for prayer and meditation in "an upper room," and suddenly set on fire by the realization that in a crucified and risen Man the Very God had confronted them in a saving Act; a young persecuting zealot falling to the ground in a terror of blindness only to discover that in his blindness lay the promise of true seeing; that same zealot transformed into "a slave of Jesus Christ," and, as he is urging his fellow Christians to have "the mind that was in Christ," finding his own mind moving from range to higher range until it halts at the audacious thought that One who had been given "a name above every name" because he had been obedient even to the death of a cross, was of native right eternally "in the form of God" and that he had laid aside this right to participate redeemingly in the lot of men (Phil. 2:5–11); and, to add one more to the many parts that served to make up " the inner continuity " of act and faith and Word and enlightenment, that high moment of which we should like to know so much more than we do — the moment when it was given to a man of faith to see that all altars pointed to one Altar, all priests to one Priest, all sacrifices to one Sacrifice, this " Altar-Priest-Sacrifice " being no other than Jesus Christ, by whom was opened " a new and living way " into the Holy Place (Heb. 9:11–28).

" High moments " indeed in the movement of the divine self-disclosure and the faith-response and the inspired interpretation! We do not doubt that the earlier moments and the later moments, exhibiting the same pattern, are all of a piece. Seamless is the robe, woven from the top throughout. These are not so many isolated moments, each standing off by itself, representative and expressive of a divine arbitrariness. The high moments are intrinsic to the methodology of revelation, to call it that. They are conditioned by various factors operating in the persons concerned, in their situations, in their heritage, in their peculiar qualities. But always there is at work that other factor which, elusive as it is, has its own distinctive category, and we have called this the divine Spirit. There is a mutuality of the Spirit of God and the spirit of man. The precise line of demarcation in the experience — revelation, faith-response, apprehended Word — which bespeaks this mutuality it is not possible for us to draw. All we can say is that the human encounter with God or experience of God or certainty of God — let it be called what we will — is divinely initiated. God is in himself unknowable, in himself undiscoverable. If he is known, it is because he makes himself known. If he is discovered, it is because he uncovers himself. He is essentially *absconditus:* if he becomes *revelatus,* it is by his own act.

The Bible confronts us as we are confronted nowhere else with the reality of this give-and-take. " The high moments " are expressive of it in its more dramatic forms. But we shall not find the full significance of the Bible if we limit our attention to the " high moments." There are the " low moments " as well — to call them that — and to a large extent it is in these low moments that we find the reason for the high moments, and their justification. *Even the men who knew the high moments did not always live at that level.* Jacob was not always at Beth-el. Elijah was not always on Mount Carmel: indeed, did he not go from his Carmel exaltation to his juniper-tree depression? (I King 19:4). Isaiah was not always in the Temple, nor Ezekiel always under seizure of the Spirit, nor Habakkuk always at his watch tower, nor Zechariah always talking with an angel (Zech. 4:1). Mary was not always under the shadow of "the angel of the Presence," nor Jesus always on the Mount of Transfiguration, nor Paul always "caught up even to the third heaven" — in fact, he definitely dates the experience to indicate its rarity (II Cor. 12:2) — nor John always "in the Spirit on the Lord's Day." What the high moment did was to leave a memory for the motivation and the inspiration for the much more extended low moments. Many a man has gone forty days and forty nights in the strength of one great spiritual feast. The function of the special is, at least in part, to set the tone for the usual. One ascends the height to survey the territory yet to be traversed and to mark the direction, and then descends to plod steadily on one's way. The high moment is evidence that retains its significance even after it has passed. Revelation is augmented and clarified in the high moment, and the augmentation and clarification carries over into the stuff of life.

This " carry over " is not limited to the person to whom the high moment was granted. It gives him a voice with an authentic note, and his testimony commands attention. They speak for God with most authority to whom God is most real. God whispers in the ear of the few, that the few may proclaim what they heard to the many. " How shall they hear without a preacher? "

" Thou wouldst not *alone* be saved, my father.
   Alone conquer and come to the goal."

He not only would not: he could not. The high moment is truly kept only as its meaning is propagated. The eleventh chapter of Hebrews calls the roll of many who knew for themselves the high moment and who gave it determinative influence in all their life and action. And then the illuminating comment: all this was theirs that it might become ours, and it is only as it becomes ours, that all the reason for its being theirs is fulfilled: " That apart from us they should not be made perfect " (v. 40). The " lost chord " is never truly lost: its reverberations continue into many a remote corner " like the sound of a great Amen." " Ye did not choose me, but I chose you, and appointed you, that ye should go and bear fruit, and that your fruit should abide " (John 15:16). The specific reference is to the disciples of Jesus, but the principle is applicable throughout the Bible. It is stated as early as the covenant with Abram: " In thy seed shall all the nations of the earth be blessed." Divine choice is a fact not to be exscinded from the Biblical record, but the choice is not merely for the sake of the chosen. The choice is a means of securing and accelerating a continuity in which the characteristic concomitants of the choice shall be exhibited. God chooses some that he might thereby call others. The Bible is a book of witness, but included in the witness that it bears is a witness to witnessing. Here we see not only what came to men in certain high moments, but what came to great numbers of other men because those who knew the high moments bore witness to what they knew.

We make a mistake therefore if we limit the scope of revelation and the fruit of it to specified crucial points. There is a revelation of God in what happens to more obscure men who, through the witnessing of more highly favored men, are brought into the knowledge and experience of God for themselves. God may not — he does not — deal with every man in the same way: nevertheless, he seeks to have dealings with every man. If he seems to deal more directly with some, it is to use them as a means for a less direct dealing with others. There is a manifest economy in the strategy of revelation. It is not necessary that every man be a Moses, an Amos, a Jeremiah, a Paul, a John of Ephesus. By every evidence, there is an element of uniqueness about these men, not only about their personalities, but about their function in the process of the divine self-disclosure. Their function is that of the special instrumentality. The Spirit who came into such possession of them could now use them, and did use them, as a means for coming into possession of others. The witnessing of the chosen ones does not make the activity of the Spirit less necessary: what it does is to enlarge the area in which his activity may take place.

The prophetic movement itself is a dramatic illustration of this. To limit the prophetic movement in Israel to a score or so of known and unknown men is simply to discount what these men were the means of accomplishing. The prophets bore witness to God as God had disclosed himself to them in varying degrees, and in consequence had led them to see what manner of God he was, what manner of demand he laid upon men, and what manner of fellowship he would have with them. The witnessing was not altogether in vain, although the fact that prophet after prophet laid similar charges against the superficialities and fruitlessness of mere priestly religion would indicate that in many ways the prophet was "a voice crying in the wilderness." Yet that prophetism fostered in the nation the growth of religious and ethical life, both individual and social, seems undeniable. Israel was the better for its prophets, even although it killed some and spurned others (Matt. 23:37). That the general life never moved at the level of the prophetic preaching is obvious: there is a pathetic similarity between Amos 5:10–13, 21–24; Isa. 1:10–17; Micah 6:6–8; Zeph. 1:2–6; Jer. 7:1–26; Ezek. 6:1–7; Zech. 7:8–14. All sorts of hindrances conspired to lessen the influence of the prophets — and we shall do well to remember that the activity of the Spirit is conditioned by hindrances just as truly as it is by more positive means. No prophet explains himself: that is, no "true" prophet does. It is "the prophet who prophesies falsely" who carries his sole explanation within himself, he being self-appointed. The true prophet is Spirit-captured, Spirit-possessed, Spirit-driven. Doubtless this raises an interesting psychological problem, but we would better listen to the prophet than simply seek to analyze him! Explanation must always be less important than the thing explained: certainly so when "the thing" explained is the spectacle of a "God-intoxicated" man. The prophetic preaching that was the fruit of the Spirit was not without some fruit on its own account: we shall shortly see the evidence of this in the Psalter. Prophetic preaching served to lay open the souls of the listeners to the divine approach. Doubtless this happened in only a limited degree: there was more than one way of crucifying a prophet, as the history of Israel testifies. Always, however, there were some who, having "come to scoff," yet "stayed to pray" (see I Kings 13:1–10). The charge of drunkenness could give way to the earnest question, "Brethren, what shall we do?" We cannot believe that the tender preaching of Hosea, "O Israel, how shall I cast thee off?" made *no* difference or that the preaching of Isaiah in Jerusalem affected only its "foreign policy" and not its religious life. It was largely through the witnessing of Ezekiel and of the Second Isaiah that there remained among the exiles many who were still able to "sing the Lord's song in a strange land." The God who plants the seed will also nurture it. "For as the rain cometh down and the snow from heaven, and returneth not thither, but watereth the earth, and maketh it bring forth and bud, and giveth seed to the sower and bread to the eater; so shall my word be that goeth forth out of my mouth: it shall not return unto me void, but it shall accomplish that which I please, and it shall prosper in the thing whereto I sent it" (Isa. 55:10, 11). Shall we say that the Bible is the book of God's sowing and harvesting? Even for God the rule holds: "In the morning sow thy seed, and in the evening withhold not thy hand; for thou knowest not which shall prosper, whether this or that, or whether they both shall be alike good" (Eccl. 11:6).

The thesis of the present chapter is nowhere more clearly illustrated than in the Psalter. Here we see the extent to which the revealing activity of the Spirit moved from more specific forms into the daily life and experience of the people. Here and there a given psalm will bespeak a high moment in the writer's relation to God, but the one palpable truth about The Psalms is that it was not limited in its use to the writers but became "a manual of devotion" for the people at large, or as it is sometimes said, "the hymnal of the Second Temple."

There are many questions about The Psalms which are not germane to our immediate purpose. The more recondite questions will be found sufficiently dealt with in Elmer A. Leslie, *The Psalms,* John Paterson, *The Praises of Israel,* and in the valuable discussion in Robert H. Pfeiffer, *Introduction to the Old Testament* (revised ed., Part V, Chapter 1). The psalms may be broadly classified as pre-exilic (a few), exilic, and post-exilic (chiefly). In many cases, the period in which a psalm originated is reflected in the psalm itself — sometimes in the form, sometimes in the purpose, sometimes in the sentiment, sometimes in the implied or stated understanding of God. These variations have their own proper significance, but the deepest significance attaches to what they have in common. Not all the Biblical psalms are found in the Psalter. In Judg., ch. 5, is the ancient song of Deborah, and in II Sam. 23:1–7 what purports to be the last psalm of David. There are psalms in the pre-exilic prophets, such as Hos. 6:1–3; Isa. 2:1–4; ch. 12; Jer. 14:7–9; in the literature of the Exile, such as Isa. 42:10–12; 66:10–14; and in the postexilic literature, such as Jonah 2:2–9; Neh. 1:5–11. The great bulk of the psalms, however, are postexilic, and it was in the late part of the third century B.C. that the Psalter began to come into extensive use. Separate collections were made from time to time, and were added to those already in use, as is indicated by the breaks at the close of Ps. 41; 72; 89; 106. Psalm 150 is a doxology concluding the entire collection.

The immediate concern of the present chapter is to show that there runs throughout the Scriptures a continuity of faith; that crucial moments occur within the continuity; and that these crucial moments not only promoted the continuity but introduced into it a deepening and quickening of the general faith. The character of this general faith is not only seen in the Psalter: the Psalter also greatly nourished it. The Psalter presupposes a heritage of faith, belief, and experience. Only by persons to whom God had already made himself known, either directly or through the testimony of others, could the psalms have been written. They did not come "out of the blue"; they came out of the travail of national and individual experience. The authorship of many of them — in fact, of most of them — is unknown, as it should be: the tradition that ascribes them to specified persons is exceedingly unreliable. Whether or not David wrote Ps. 23 or Ps. 51 has little or nothing to do with its intrinsic worth. It is more than likely that many psalms are of composite authorship in the sense that what one man may have written in the first place was subjected to numerous revisions according as it came increasingly into corporate use, and it is this very fact of corporate use that gave to the psalms their immense significance for the continuity of faith. Each of the five separate collections that make up the Psalter represents, as a modern hymnal does, a high degree of selectivity. Many a man must have been moved to write a psalm which failed of general acceptance. One is intrigued at the suggestion of a possible volume entitled *Lost Psalms Recovered.* There are numerous psalms that expressed satisfaction at the discomfiture of enemies (Ps. 18), but there is scarcely a reference to the joy of a mother at the birth of her child. Yet I Sam. 2:1–10 and Luke 1:46–55 show how the Hebrew mother felt; and one cannot doubt that many such psalms were written which were unable to pass the censorious gaze of the Temple elders! The one hundred and fifty psalms as we have them were doubtless a selection from a much greater number. As one plods wearily through the uninspired mechanisms of Ps. 119, one may be forgiven for confessing that one would gladly barter the entire one hundred and seventy-six verses for a single verse of the quality of Ps. 23:4.

In general, one must suppose that a psalm had to be tested in the crucible of use before it could have any promise of permanence. It had to speak to something in the hearts of men; it had to put into moving language some indubitable human experience; it had to prove itself a " means of grace," a door through which the soul could move into richer pastures; in a word, it had to attest itself able to minister to religious need if it was to survive. Psalm 119 must have " got by " in spite of such tests — although one does well to remember that the period of its labored composition was doubtless that when

Pharisaic legalism was in control, and when such a composition could easily be put into general circulation. Besides, are there not modern hymnals which, competent editors notwithstanding, have their barren stretches? The Psalter as a whole, however, bespeaks not only the activity of the Spirit in the origin of it, but the activity of the Spirit in the use of it. The Psalter was both a body of witness and a means of increasing that to which witness was borne.

Almost every religious mood and aspiration is here reflected. The sentiment is not, however, uniformly lofty. The imprecatory psalms have been a perplexity to many, although there have not been wanting those who used them with great personal satisfaction! The perplexed failed to understand the inevitable human intrusions into the movement of revelation, and the satisfied users failed to understand that what they supposed carried divine authority was in truth nothing but understandable but still deplorable human desire.

> "O daughter of Babylon, that art to be destroyed,
> Happy shall he be, that rewardeth thee
> As thou hast served us.
> Happy shall he be, that taketh and dasheth thy little ones
> Against the rock!" (Ps. 137:8,9).

The sentiment is understandable, but the Christian man would better not repeat it. Evidently the Psalter, although it has high Christian uses, is far from being a wholly Christian book. Very much in it has to be recognized for the relativity that it is. When we remember the Hebrew conviction that Yahweh was "a jealous God," and what that jealousy was supposed to involve, it becomes quite intelligible that the duty of the pious is declared to be "to hate them that hate Yahweh," to "hate them with perfect hatred" (Ps. 139:21, 22). It is equally intelligible that this hatred should sometimes be extended to one's personal enemies for reasons themselves largely personal (Ps. 69:18–28). There certainly is not wanting in the Psalter something of the spirit of self-righteous Pharisaism (Ps. 101), and of an unlovely legalism (Ps. 119:105–112), and of exultation

over the calamities of others (Ps. 58), and of despair at Yahweh's seeming neglect (Ps. 44; 74). In so far as this varied
spirit creates a problem for us, however, it is in part because
we overlook the inevitable human limitations which prevented
the psalmists from making full use of the best that their heritage contained; partly because we overlook the fact that there
was much in their heritage that was far from perfect; partly
because we overlook the fact that the tutelage of the Spirit
is proportioned to the given conditions; but chiefly because we
look back at the Psalter from the standpoint of our own faith
in the Living Word, whereby we subject the Psalter, as we
should, to *drastic Christian criticism.* There is no least reason
why, because the Psalter is a part of the Bible, we should approve all its sentiments, and repeat, unashamed, all its execra-
tions and untamed desires.

The problems of the Psalter are not insoluble. They are, indeed, such as naturally inhere in the process of revelation, and
are to be dealt with according to the principles here being considered. The Psalter affords striking evidence to the ways of
the Spirit in the self-disclosure of God. The Psalter springs
from witness; it is itself witness; it increases the sweep of witness; and in all these ways it serves the " inner continuity " of
faith which is embedded in the " outer continuity " of history.
Central to the Psalter is faith in God, but in God understood
in a certain way and apprehended after a certain form. Even
the psalms which glorify wars of aggression (Ps. 60) express
what is supposed to be the proper function of such a God as
Yahweh is taken to be. The *supposition* is correct enough; it is
the *conception* that is defective. The psalms that deal with nature deal with it as manifesting the power and beneficence of
Israel's God (Ps. 65:104), and here the Christian man feels
more at home. The psalms that express a nostalgia for the ancient days (Ps. 74) do so because God's " mighty acts " seem
to be rather in the past than in the present: nevertheless, he
who *was* dependable is dependable *still,* and will be dependable *tomorrow:* " Lord, thou hast been our dwelling-place in
all generations. . . . Even from everlasting to everlasting,
thou art God " (Ps. 90:1, 2). Where but to such a God should

his people go for help, either as individuals or as a nation (Ps. 27; 80)? Where can trust be placed, if not in him (Ps. 124; 139)? Who but he is worthy of utter adoration (Ps. 84; 122; 145)? What could there be beyond his reach (Ps. 104; 135)? When one considers him in his unstained holiness, and then oneself in one's deep sinfulness, what other mood can there be than that of broken-hearted penitence (Ps. 38; 51; 106)? When trouble seems greater than can be borne, who like Yahweh will be as a "familiar friend" (Ps. 41); who like Yahweh will "command deliverance" and "rise up for our help" (Ps. 44); and in that confidence who can any longer fear (Ps. 73)? In a time when the chosen nation is the sport of the kings of the earth, why should the faithful be afraid, seeing that the God whose word and purposes fail not will yet set his chosen over the nations (Ps. 2), bring his chosen to a permanence like unto his own (Ps. 72), even as he had covenanted with Abram (Ps. 105), and making his chosen indeed "a priest for ever after the order [manner] of Melchizedek" (Ps. 110)?

Who is this God of the Psalter? He stands in the direct lineage of that God who at the burning bush declared himself to be Yahweh. But much has happened in the meantime. Prophet and priest; high man and low man; moving experiences of individuals; shattering experiences of the nation; the growth of the cult and its sacrifices; the growth of the law and its austerities — all have played a part in the process through which Yahweh, by many a devious route and against many a threatening obstacle, has made more and more evident the significance of his "name." The God of the Psalter — not, indeed, at any one point, but as he appears in the totality — is the precipitate of this prolonged, varying, but continuing divine-human interplay. At no time did he leave himself without a witness, faint though the witness often was. Always there were those who had not bowed the knee to Baal. It is God who created and who sustains the heavens and the earth, yet heaven and earth together do not disclose the full range of his power. "Heaven and the heaven of heavens cannot contain thee" (I Kings 8:27). This is the God who centers his deepest concern in man, "a little lower than the angels [or, the gods]" though man may be (Ps. 8:5). It is relative to his purpose with this man that God conducts his universe, controls the direction of history, and discloses himself in providential happenings, "mighty acts," "wonderful works," and secret transactions with men's souls. He "counteth the number of the stars" (Ps. 147:4; cf. Isa. 40:26). In one single psalm he is God the Omnipotent, God the Omnipresent, God the All-Knowing (Ps. 139). He lays all nations under tribute for the outworking of his purposes (Ps. 72; cf. Isa. 45:1–7). Always there is a "far-off divine event" which is as much in the care and keeping of God as were the various little beginnings in the distant past in which that Event was predicted and anticipated (Ps. 72; cf. Jer., ch. 33). Yet this God does not depend on Israel absolutely. In the Psalter, as in the Prophets, the possibility of the rejection of Israel is recognized (Ps. 79; cf. Isa. 5:1–7), but that the purpose for which God called and guided and variously dealt with Israel shall fail — no!

This, not at any one point, but in the by and large, is the God to whom the Psalter bears witness. This is the God in whom the Psalter expresses *confident trust*. This is the God to whom *grateful praise* is due. This is the God against whom *sin* is committed, and to whom *penitence* and the *prayer for pardon* is directed. This is the God to whom it belongs to *cleanse and renew* the sinful soul. This is the God who requires of his people *clean hands* and a *pure heart*. This is the God whose will is given in the *law*, so that delight in the law is delight in the Lawgiver. This is the God to whom men look for *guidance*, and in whom they find *strength*, and who gives *wisdom* to the perplexed. This is the God of the Presence who makes himself felt in the dark valleys, and at whose right hand are "pleasures for evermore."

Even so brief a consideration of the Psalter serves to make clear its bearing on the continuing process of the divine self-disclosure. The Psalter is not sufficiently accounted for by simply referring it to the various men who wrote it. The Psalter bears rich and explicit testimony to a movement to which many men contribute, of which many men are aware, and in which many men participate, yet withal a movement not traceable to any one man, not discerned by any one man, not dependent on any one man. The movement is that of God's increasing entry into the stream of human life. The Psalter not only bears witness to it: it was the means, as it still is, of a far-spreading propagation of that to which it witnesses. *This is a fact greatly to be stressed.* We can only infer the contemporary success of the prophets: the success of the Psalter is written on the face of it. We are to remember that uncounted numbers of the faithful pious were saturated in the Psalter. It was their book of private devotion. It was their book of public worship. Humanly speaking, the Psalter brought into the life of Israel the divine self-disclosure to the prophets to a degree in which it had never been done before. It did it as priestism did not do, and as legalism did not do. The Psalter created the piety and devotion of that little group which William Sanday once called " the seed-plot of Christianity," the faithful and expectant " quiet in the land " of whom, after the flesh, Jesus came, among whom he was reared, by whom he was taught, and from whom he gathered his first followers. One may ponder long the profound significance of these facts.

And yet he who has seen God in the face of Jesus Christ cannot take the Psalter just as it stands, any more than he can take any other book of the Old Testament just as it stands. The Psalter is for Christian use, but the use must be discriminating. The Psalter is to be " interpreted," and the standard for its interpretation is not in the Psalter, but elsewhere.

VII

THE WORD AS A PERSON

CHRISTIAN reflection on the self-revelation of God, on its discernible processes, its varied forms, and its increasingly fruitful experiential consequences, led to the conviction that God was not a mere *Solitary*, an undifferentiated *One*, but that he was in himself a Fellowship, and that it was by virtue of the fact of this Fellowship that he could be Holy Love, or could disclose himself as Holy Love. The complications of this conviction are many, one of them being the formulation of the doctrine of the Trinity. It is not necessary for the purposes of this book to enter into these complications at any great length. One thing that must be stressed, however, is the fact that the New Testament confronts us with the declaration that in Jesus Christ the Word of God took the form of a Living Reality, " bone of our bone, and flesh of our flesh." It could do that because of the very nature of God on the one hand and of man on the other hand. The divine could appear in the human because both the divine and the human were constituted relative to that possibility.

The constituent of God's nature which is the determinative presupposition of the form of his creative activities is given the designation *logos* in the Fourth Gospel. The conception was present in earlier and contemporary philosophical thought, and there is no need to question that John took it over from these sources. The difference is in the use he made of it. No Hellenistic or Judaistic philosopher ever gave to *logos* the significance given to it in the Fourth Gospel. What is distinctive in the Johannine usage is that *logos* " became flesh " in the form of a specific man, Jesus Christ. Without being expressed by the same term, the *idea* is present elsewhere in the New Testament. The *idea* is that a basic reality in the nature of God took "the form of a man"; that this was necessary to the fulfillment of God's ultimate purpose; that it was on God's part a supremely costly act; that by it and in it God is self-disclosed as he is nowhere else and as he could be nowhere else; and that the intent of the act is to "reconcile men to God," that is, lay the foundation for perfect divine-human fellowship. This *idea* meets us not only in John 1:1–16, but also in Phil. 2:5–11; Col. 1:12–20; Heb. 1:1–5. Perhaps the differences of expression will suggest to us that what is chiefly important is not the form of the expression, but the *idea* that is being expressed. The case may be stated thus: There is that in God which, as the ultimate determinant of his nature and of the form of his free activities, constitutes therefore the basis both of his involution in the creative process and of his involution in the self-revealing and redemptive process. This is called variously the *logos;* the Word; an eternal divine "form"; the divine "self-image" which all things reflect and in which they cohere; the "Son" who eternally expresses God's substance. This is what "takes flesh" and becomes Jesus Christ. If this *is* the idea which in these various ways is struggling for expression, then the inexhaustible fruitfulness of the idea for human life and human thought and human experience, and for the whole interpretation of existence, ought at least to call for our serious consideration before we impatiently dismiss it as so much superstition.

Logos immanent and determinative in God; *logos* immanent and determinative in creation; *logos* immanent and determinative in the processes of divine self-revelation, but for more special purposes than in creation at large; *logos* immanent and determinative in man, but in such wise that man is thereby in the image of God; *logos* entering the human lot as Jesus Christ, in whom therefore God is fully self-disclosed, this entry not only crowning creation but crowning also all earlier revelation, and opening for man the way into the Holy of Holies: this is what confronts us. Since the common meaning of *logos* is "word" in the sense of a representation whose reality is in the thing represented, the declaration that Jesus Christ is *logos* become flesh is a way of saying that Jesus Christ is the Living Word of God to men. God here addresses himself to men in the person of his Son, his eternal Son who consented to take his place among the sons of men as one of them, at once divine and human, at once their Lord and their Brother, at once the source of their existence as rational creatures and the means of their becoming a new creation. " Wherefore if any man is in Christ, he is a new creation [or, creature]: the old things are passed away; behold, they are become new " (II Cor. 5:17). " Ye have put off the old man with his doings, and have put on the new man, that is being renewed unto knowledge after the image of him that created him: where there cannot be Greek and Jew, circumcision and uncircumcision, barbarian, Scythian, bondman, freeman; but Christ is all, and in all " (Col. 3:9–11). " For ye are all one man in Christ Jesus. And if ye are Christ's, then are ye Abraham's seed, heirs according to promise " (Gal. 3:28, 29).

The immanence of *logos* in the creative and revealing activities of God is the ground of the fact of meaning. By reason of the kinship of God and man, the meaning which these activities express for God is susceptible of being apprehended by man. God being constituted as he is, it belongs to him to project situations which are for him so many uttered " words," and it belongs to man to read out of these words a degree of meaning. God " speaks "; man " hears " and " interprets." To know that there is meaning, to search for meaning, to ponder meaning, to grow by entering more fully into meaning, and to seek to extend the range of meaning by planning, promoting, and participating in meaningful activities — to do this is the lot of man. He cannot wholly escape it if he would. His nature leaves him no alternative. His nature reflects the nature of God. It is therefore a " word " of God. It says something *for* God, and therefore something *about* God. Man is a revelation of God. His meaning is in his power to lay hold on meaning, and chiefly in this power as it concerns itself with certain " acts " of God conceived as " special " in themselves and therefore as having a " special " meaning deeply important for man himself. It does not follow that he will use this power, because its use involves faith, and faith is always a free option. He may be utterly indifferent to God; he may even be at the pains of denying God; he may deliberately set himself against what is declared to be God's will and purpose; but nothing he can do can "unsay" what is being said by his very nature. Man is what he is, and he cannot change himself into something different. He reveals *logos* significance in the very efforts he might make to deny *logos* indications. A man he is, and a man he must remain: even as a "lost" man — as he may be — he still speaks for God. Into his very constitution has been interwoven an element that is an analogue in him of *logos* in God. His very awareness of meaning is an evidence of his linkage with his Maker, and an indication of where his own deepest significance is to be found.

The meaningful acts of God will increase in meaningfulness according as they more fully disclose *logos* — that is to say, disclose God himself. *Logos* is present in every situation according to the extent of its meaning, but in the nature of the case *logos* is most present in human situations, because it is with human situations that God is ultimately concerned. His concern with other situations is but relative to his human concern. Man's destiny is to find himself confronted with God, and God can confront only a creature whose structure is such that he can recognize the confrontation. What we have considered as the process of revelation is the process of the increasing indwelling of human situations on the part of *logos* — of God — and, as needful correlative, the increasing apprehension of this indwelling and of its significance on the part of man, according to the measure of faith and of the Spirit's illumination. The "mighty acts" of God vary in their "mightiness" according as they vary in the meaning which God intends them to convey. There are those in whom a striking natural phenomenon may evoke a greater conviction of God than is evoked by a deed of sacrificial and self-giving love, yet actually God is self-disclosed in the second as he is not in the first. Unlike Elijah, they find God in the wind, the earthquake, and the fire, but not in the sound of a gentle stillness. They are awed by apocalyptic upheavals, but not by Love hanging helplessly upon a cross.

" The Word [*logos*] became flesh." This is an occurrence within the framework of human history. In the terms of the present discussion, it is the climactic point of the varying course of the divine self-disclosure. What hitherto was partial and provisional is now complete and final. To repeat what has already been said, that which the very structure of the divine on the one hand, and of the human on the other hand, made possible, namely, the personal appearance within the human of that in the divine in whose image the human is constituted, at last becomes an actuality. Herein is the completion of a process that had been embedded in a long historical movement. The completion is both a part of the movement and the final reason for it.

So far, we have considered this question of the Living Word with what some may regard as a certain cool detachment, as though it were simply one more arguable philosophical proposition. For certain purposes, this sort of detachment is justifiable. Christian reflection must not seem to be dogmatic asseveration. There are, however, considerations which give to the Word-become-flesh the aspect of the tragic, whereby emotion is profoundly stirred, and philosophic calm gives way to evangelical fervor. Human sinfulness and God's holy wrath, the human predicament and the Holy Love that would shatter it — these must enter the picture, and as this takes place the colors become bolder and more contrasting, the design becomes more startling, and under deeper consideration the general theme becomes more arresting. The stage of history is transformed into a vast setting for a divine Gethsemane, over it the shadow of a cross, a cross cosmic in its dimensions, eternal in its redeeming promise. It is one thing for situations to be of such a kind that in them and through them the reality of *logos* is so disclosed as that they become so far forth declarative of God. It is another thing for God himself as *logos* to enter so completely into the human that he becomes himself subject to the law of the human, all the way from birth to death. In the self-identity of the Creator with the creature we have divine self-disclosure at the highest possible level and accomplished at the highest possible cost. More than this God could not do on behalf of men. More dramatically than this he could not confront men with the fact of their own infinite worth. Faced by the Living Word and by all that the Living Word represents, the man of faith can but exclaim with tremulous lips, " That I was worth to God, whose wheel the pitcher shaped."

This is faith's reading of Jesus Christ. The question therefore becomes: Is such a reading justifiable? Not, Is such a reading absolutely inevitable? for inevitability here precludes faith. But, Is such a reading one of whose truth a man may be persuaded within himself, with the consequence that he commits himself wholly to it? A faith-persuasion is something less than a logic-persuasion — *and something very much more!* It is Biblical testimony that in Jesus Christ the Very God entered the human lot, both to disclose himself to men in the fullness of his redeeming love and to do for men that which they desperately needed to have done, but which even God could do *only from within the human situation.* Jesus Christ *means —* God! He is divine revelation so complete that the revelation and what is revealed are one and the same. " The Word " is not one thing, and " the flesh " another, so that two things entirely different are brought together in a temporary conjunction, in due time to fall apart again: not that; but each is the other in so intimate a way that the cessation of the one would be the cessation of the other. Jesus Christ is not two, but one. Christianity affirms " The One Christ, indivisibly Son of God and Son of Man." The Word became a man. But for the Word there would have been no such man. To ask, as was recently done in a much-lauded book, " What became of the Man Jesus after the ascension? " is not only to ask a question incredibly naïve: it is to indicate a complete misapprehension of the nature and of the significance of the incarnation. Every man is constituted in the Word (in *logos*), but the Man Jesus was not constituted in the Word: rather, he, living under the conditions of the human as he was, was himself that Word in which all other men were constituted.

It is obvious that all these are so many affirmations of meaning, but affirmations made in faith. If one will have it so, they are interpretations of the significance of Jesus Christ. They do not violate but rather confirm and require the principle that revelation necessarily falls within the area of meaning. Admittedly more than one meaning has been attached to Jesus Christ, but this is the meaning that permeates the New Testament, dominates its life, characterizes its faith, and yields its message.

But here we must make certain distinctions. Our knowledge that this was the meaning which men found in Jesus Christ depends upon testimony, such testimony as meets us in the New Testament and in the fact of the Church. The testimony, however, includes both the faith of men respecting their Lord, and the account of his life, work, teaching, sufferings, death, and resurrection, on the basis of which they came, under the Spirit's tutelage, to their faith. These two sides of the testimony are always to be kept distinct. The faith side is the fundamental one. The account side is secondary. One may accept the account as reasonably reliable, and still not accept the faith. We depend on human testimony — on "the Gospels" — for what knowledge we have of the historical Jesus. On the other hand, no human testimony can validate the faith. The faith that the Word became flesh, and that the form of this divine becoming was Jesus Christ, cannot possibly be validated by any kind of documents or by any kind of objective authority. The documents bear witness to the fact of the faith, but if a person accepts the faith for himself solely on the ground of the documents, then he does not truly accept it, and he does not really know what it is. To say, "I believe that God was sacrificially present and redeemingly active in Jesus Christ, the Eternal Son come in the flesh, because the Bible says so," is to be a very long way indeed from touching bottom. It is to substitute confidence in the Gospels as human documents for faith in the gospel as God's mightiest act. This substitution has always plagued the Church, and it plagues it still. The Gospels are not the gospel: they *assume* the gospel and they *bear witness* to it; but what a given man does about the gospel will depend upon something other than his attitude to the Gospels.

No human testimony can create faith: that is to say, it cannot create that faith to which the New Testament everywhere bears witness. It is quite possible to acknowledge that the New Testament does indeed bear this witness, and still not share the faith. In the purpose and activity of God, his self-revelation in and as Jesus Christ is an absolute: it is by the commitment of faith, personal faith bespeaking personal decision, that it becomes an absolute for any given man.

The absolute of faith, however, is not only a point of arrival through what travail of mind and heart and will may be required to reach it — and this is a variant which no pedagogic methodology or psychological subtlety can ever wholly regularize: not only is it this. It is also a point of departure. It connotes an assurance which persistently maintains itself in the face of many a challenge. He for whom " God is in Christ," all-sufficiently, finally, redeemingly, absolutely, is in possession of a secret of which he cannot be robbed. The familiar lines of F. W. H. Myers still say it as it has rarely been said:

" Whoso hath felt the Spirit of the Highest
    Cannot confound nor doubt him nor deny;
  Yea, with one voice, O world, though thou deniest,
    Stand though on that side, for on this am I.

" Rather the earth shall doubt when her retrieving
    Pours in the rain and rushes from the sod,
  Rather than he for whom the great conceiving
    Stirs in his soul to quicken unto God.

" Ay, and though then thou shouldst strike him from his glory,
    Blind and tormented, maddened and alone,
  E'en on the cross would he maintain his story,
    Yea, and in hell would whisper, 'I have known! ' "

He who has arrived at this point cannot possibly be swept away from it by any critical question connected with the Gospels. The conditions under which the Gospels were compiled, and even the names of the compilers, become for him matters of secondary import. What matters supremely is God as self-revealed in Jesus Christ; the kind of God he therein showed himself to be; the purpose for which he made the self-disclosure; and the meaning for human experience that comes of faith that God is indeed such a God as this. This is the faith because of which the Church came into being; this is the faith that led to the writing of the Gospels; this is the faith that accounts for the rest of the New Testament. Such faith means that the story in The Acts of the Apostles may be subjected to all the canons of historical criticism, with numerous ensuing uncertainties, while yet what undergirds and inspires the story remains untouched. It means too that while there may be questions about the authorship of this epistle or that, about its time and place of composition, about its original destination, even about some of the opinions expressed and some of the advice given, the Epistles, regarded as so many expositions of the faith that Jesus Christ is the Living Word of God addressed to men, of the meaning that he contained in himself, and of the meaning of all that he endured at the hands of men and in fulfillment of the Father's will and purpose, are not thereby robbed of their authenticity. The *intent* of the Epistles and the *witness* of the Epistles, like the intent and the witness of the Gospels, are nowise affected by these merely secondary considerations. Their proper interest for the scholar is gladly admitted, but when the scholar has done his worst — perhaps one should rather say his best! — the faith which the Epistles expounds is still there.

What lies at the center of the Biblical faith at its climactic point in the New Testament witness is, however, not a reality wholly self-contained, but a reality of far-flung and universal relationships. It involves the nature and the purpose of God. It involves the nature and the purpose of creation. It involves the nature and the purpose, the failure and the possible recovery, of man, and therefore his eternal destiny. It involves the movement of history and its meaning. In particular, it involves the history reflected in the Old Testament, and the significance of that inner continuity of revelation-faith-response of which the history is the milieu. And what may seem to the secular mind to be the height of audacity, this Biblical center is here asserted to provide the foundation stone of a philosophic thought structure from whose vast sweep and comprehensive scope nothing can escape.

For what shall we say of God himself, whose final and complete self-disclosure took the form it did in Jesus Christ — eternal Sonship humanly set forth, Very God as Very Man? The effect on the divine of incarnation in the human is something we may shrink from contemplating, except that if we do shrink from it we have not traveled the full orbit of our faith. We have not yet fallen, overwhelmed into adoring silence, like the rapt soul described in Dante's closing stanzas, before the emergence of the lineaments of a human face from the very center of the manifold but unitary splendor which both reveals and conceals the Triune God. No " Christian understanding of God " is wholly Christian, or can be, which does not take its departure from the faith that Jesus Christ was the eternal Son of God in the flesh — the divine filial become the human filial. Anyone may lay down certain a priori philosophical principles that preclude the very possibility of an " event " such as this. For example: " The eternal cannot become historical. Almightiness cannot become frailty. Omniscience cannot become ' learn by experience.' Deity cannot become humanity. What never began to be cannot be born and what cannot be born cannot die." And so forth. Apriorism has its own proper justification as a necessity of rational thought. But apriorism may easily become the most dictatorial and arbitrary of human tendencies. The apriorism that renders unintelligible the richest and deepest of human experiences is thereby rendered suspect. This is certainly so where matters of faith are involved. Man's " cannot " may turn out to be God's "can." This possibility may easily enough be abused, as some of the dogmatic pronouncements of ecclesiasticism bear pathetic witness. But where the concern is with the Biblical faith, its nature, its object, its grounds, its significance, non-Biblical philosophies arrived at with no least reference to this faith and all it implies cannot be allowed to be in all respects determinative. The Christian thinker must still say, as respects his faith and all that it seems to him to mean, " Here I take my stand! " More than once it has turned out that " God made foolish the wisdom of the world " (I Cor. 1:20). It is not the rock upon which faith stands that gives rocklike quality to the faith so much as it is that the rocklike quality of the faith makes the rock truly a rock. The Christian will have *good reasons* for his faith, as, indeed, being a rational creature, he must have. But the reasons are never such as to have in themselves an irresistible coerciveness. The movement from the " good reasons " to the faith is a movement of venture, trust, free commitment. Without these, the " good reasons " remain unproductive. Only by faith can the best of reasons in this regard become the ground of a felt certainty.

1. *The incarnation of the Word discloses what God is in himself.* The disclosure can mean nothing else than that God is Love — we would better say Holy Love, to avoid the danger of mere sentimentalism. It is not that the love of God had not already been disclosed in the processes of revelation. The disclosure had been by " acts " to which faith responded as to acts of love, but the fullness of the love, its deeply sacrificial character, its " agapaic " quality, that is, its utter selflessness, its concern only for the good of the beloved, was never disclosed by such " acts " and could not have been. Had such a disclosure been possible by such acts, acts whose form was impersonal, there is a sense in which the incarnation would have been a superfluity because it answered to no deep divine-human necessity. The standing objection, that an absolute *logos* incarnation is incompatible with the undeniable fact that *logos* continued throughout the incarnate experience to be immanently active in the creative processes, is not too easily met. How could the Word as the constitutive element of the divine nature which gave form and direction to the divine activities be at one and the same time " in the arms of his mother and on the wings of the wind " — to use the words of an early Christian thinker? To the extent that the question can be answered at all, it must be answered in terms of that very self-disclosure of God which the incarnation essentially is. God is not less under *logos* determination, nor is *logos* less immanent

and determinative in the work of God's hands, because *logos* is fully present and operative as the incarnate Son.

Our great need is to know with what kind of God we have to do. We can know this according as he discloses himself. His disclosure as Jesus Christ answers to our need, according to the measure of our faith that here indeed we are face to face with the Very God. The God we thus face in faith is Holy Love. He is a God who is Holy Love because he is a Fellowship. And as we reverently reflect on what else must be true because we accept this to be true, we are led into a realm which more and more helps to "make sense" of the complexities of existence. The God on whom our faith has laid hold is a God the alphabet of whose total Word is discernible in what he has said and done at this place and that, and at this time and that — " by divers portions and in divers manners." He is a God who does not cease to be active in one place to become active in another, nor cease to be active in one way to become active in another. He is a God therefore whose *logos* incarnation, so far from being an intrinsic impossibility and therefore an intrinsic incredibility, is provided for both by his own necessary and eternal constitution, and by the very methodology of his creative and provisional revealing activities. If there is a point where these provisional revealing activities reach their climax, it will be precisely that point where what is made most apparent is the fact of God's Holy Love. The incarnation of the Word is such a point. It declares, as nothing else can possibly be conceived as declaring, that God is Holy Love.

2. *The incarnation of the Word discloses God's concern for men.* The very process of revelation, as it has been described above, is a man-pointed process. If revelation takes place in terms of meaning — as it must — then it is self-evident that while its source is necessarily in God, and that while its conditions are provided from within the framework of creation, provision must be made for its reception. Revelation presupposes its own alpha — God; and its own omega — man. The indispensability of the human structure for the furtherance of the ways of God and the fulfillment of his purpose must be regarded as axiomatic. God's purpose with man determines the

way man is. " As the destiny, so the man," is just as true as
" As the man, so the destiny ": it may even be more true. No
one to whom the Biblical faith is profoundly significant because universally interpretive could possibly regard the human
structure as a creative accident, a creative blunder, or a creative incidental by-product. He will rather regard it as the
creative focus — the predestined " event " of that innumerable
series of " events " which creation is, the *microcosmos* of the
macrocosmos, the precipitate of the endless crisscrossings of
nature and history. The human structure provides the necessary correlative to the divine intent of self-disclosure. The existence of man in the image of God has ultimate reference to
the incarnation of God in the human.

And for whose sake? Primarily for the sake of man. The
cosmic climax is man in whom therefore the index is discerned.
Incarnation is conditioned on man's being constituted as he is.
Man thereupon becomes the beneficiary of his own constitution. The law of his being is such that it makes it possible for
God to accomplish on his behalf the mightiest Act of which
God is capable. To say that it makes no difference to a man
whether or not he believes that there was such an Act, that
it makes no difference to him whether or not he believes that
God is such a being as to be capable of the Act, that it makes
no difference to him whether or not he believes that the intent
of the Act was to accomplish a radical change in human life
at every point and a radical change in human destiny — to say
this is to say what simply is not true. " Faith — or no faith; this
faith — or another: it is all one." Who says that? Only he says
that who does not know this faith, and who has not gone to
the trouble of seeking to understand what it really is and what
it can accomplish. To be persuaded that the measure of God's
concern for men was in his sacrificial subjection of himself to
the operation of the law of the human, that so the human
might be lifted above " all bitterness, and wrath, and anger,
and clamor, and railing " to the level of kindness one to another, tenderheartedness, mutual forgivingness, reconciliation
with God, exemplification of the mind that was in Christ,
which is to say, to the level of the truly filial as respects the

relation to God and the truly fraternal as respects the relation to others — to be persuaded of this is also to be persuaded that human life, the most sunken equally with the most exalted, is surcharged with an inexhaustible significance.

3. *The incarnation discloses the effect on God of the human condition.* The process of revelation is the process of God's purpose to save men. What revelation might be if it were made to a sinless race we have no means of knowing, and in any event it is a question of only theoretical interest. The only race we know is this race, shot through with self-pride, rebellious, a house divided against itself, finding its satisfactions in impermanencies, beating in the void its broken wings in vain, nostalgic for the Father's home while groveling amid the husks — in a word, sinful, lost, and undone. This is the human race. This is man — ancient man, medieval man, Renaissance man, modern man, Eastern man, Western man, man individually, man collectively. Revelation is made to sinners, and its intent is to save sinners, and it is sinners who stand in the way of revelation to frustrate its divine intent. Sin makes men unbelievers. It blinds their eyes. It deadens their spiritual sensitivity. It creates a barrier to the very appeal of the God who would do it away. The parable of the unfaithful husbandmen who killed the representatives of their lord, and who, when their lord, as a last resource, sent to them his own son, killed the son also — this parable strangely illuminates both the ways of God in his approach to men and the all too common response of men to the divine approach (Matt. 21:33-46). " O Jerusalem, Jerusalem, that killeth the prophets, and stoneth them that are sent unto her! how often would I have gathered thy children together, even as a hen gathereth her chickens under her wings, and ye would not! " (Matt. 23:37).

That no approach of God to men through other men could ever be a complete approach and a successful approach may be regarded as implicit in the circumstances. It is equally to be regarded as implicit in the circumstances that an approach at once complete and successful would need to be *a personal one.* But a personal approach would be precisely the approach that would be most costly to God. For God to disclose by incarnation not only his love, and not only the self-giving quality of his love, but the cost that love must endure in order to save — this is where we come upon the Infinite Mystery. The Infinite Mystery is in the fact that when divine love goes to its redeeming uttermost, it does so by enduring a radical disruption of the internal relations in which is its perfect blessedness. *Logos* incarnation in the human, to constitute the means of redemption by first securing a Redeemer, is not merely a piece of divine routine. It is sacrificial action which, while not disrupting the divine fellowship, introduces into it a tragic note, indicated as to its ultimate poignancy by the cry of dereliction from the cross. By nothing less than this could sinful man be saved; by nothing less than this could the full measure of the holy love of God be disclosed. Sin when judged according to the divine intent is an abnormality in the human: the mark has been missed. It is met by an abnormality effected in the divine. But whereas the human abnormality is the fruit of self-will, the divine abnormality is the fruit of " amazing grace." So far is incarnation from being a mere dialecticism of the divine according to the impersonal Hegelian style that it is explicable only as a dramatic arrest of the habitual divine self-movement. The arrest is volitional, not mechanical. It is according to grace, not according to law. " By grace have ye been saved." The grace is of a sort that the warm and pictorial language of devotion can so much more effectively express than can the austere and restrained language of the precise analyst. Thus Charles Wesley:

> " He left His Father's throne above, —
>   So free, so infinite His grace —
> Emptied Himself of all but love,
>   And bled for Adam's helpless race;
> Amazing grace! how can it be
>   That thou, my Lord, shouldst die for me! "

In what God does to save sinful men he endures a hurt which leaves upon him a scar; that scar is there forever, for the throne of God is the throne of God *and of the Lamb*, " the Lamb that hath been slain "; but the scar is his glory; it is the print of the nail and the thrust of the sword; it is the wound that proclaims how hard went the battle, how dire was the foe, by how great a cost was obtained for us the heavenly citizenship. Never is it to be forgotten that what is crucial to the Biblical faith in its final reach is not what any man told us about God; not just one more of a series of " acts " whose God-meaning was discernible by some man under the leading of the Spirit — no; and not even anything that was told us about God by Jesus as we have this recorded in the Gospels. But what is crucial to the Biblical faith in its highest reach is *God's own self-declaration in and by Jesus Christ as the Incarnate Son.* Not Jesus revealing God to us: how could *any man* tell us the truth about God? Not that! But God revealing himself to us in the fact of Jesus, in the person himself, in the Living Word. *This Life is God in self-definition.* Here is the focal point of the Biblical faith. By this we are called to be judged. To this we are called to submit. In this we are called to rest. The self-containedness of the Creator is shattered, both to permit the entry of the creaturely into the realm of the Creator and to permit the entry of the Creator into the realm of the creaturely.

It does not follow that the Son of God in the flesh was fully aware of all his own significance. In fact, it was implicit in his " humiliation " that he should not be. He was aware of the supremacy of his Father's will; he was aware of the claim of that will upon him; he was aware that he must stop at nothing that was a manifest requirement of that will; he was aware that upon his own complete submission depended all that he included in the comprehensive term, " the Kingdom of God." Of all this he was aware. But the secret of his being, its profound mystery, was locked fast in the heart of God his Father. There were no incarnation but for this secret — a secret to be divulged in the Father's own good time. The Incarnate Son who knew that he was the Incarnate Son would not be the Incarnate Son, and could not be. Incarnation involves a certain process of obliteration. There is ontological continuity persisting through radical experiential change. The divine filial in entering the human filial did not cease to be the divine filial, but his knowledge of himself was as the human filial. That strange intuitions respecting himself may sometimes have flashed across his mind may be surmised. This is at least suggested in the words which the author of the Fourth Gospel puts on his lips: " Before Abraham was, I am." Such assertions as, " He emptied himself," and, " He humbled himself," and, " He took the form of a slave and the style and fashion of a man " (see Phil. 2:5–8), do but represent faith's justifiable effort to achieve philosophical justification. One may question them as assertions: one may not question them as the effort of a faith-engendered flame to maintain its connection with that divine source whose " consuming fire " the flame so ardently bespeaks.

Here, then, is the ultimate God of the Biblical faith. Here is the authoritative. Here is the all-determinative. Here is the redemptive. He to whom this faith is the very breath of his life needs nothing more. He is set free — free of verbalisms, free of legalisms, free of dogmatisms, free of ecclesiasticisms, free of sacramentalisms, free of ceremonialisms. What use he may make of any of these will be according to the requirements of his freedom, *and of what those requirements may be he only is the judge.*

This is not rank individualism. Rather, this is Christian personalism. Its ramifications are many, as we shall now see.

VIII

FREE FAITH AND THE OLD TESTAMENT

ALREADY it has been made clear that fruitful Bible study must steadily bear in mind the fact that the self-revelation of God to men to which the Bible bears witness was integrated with the processes of history. God deals with a man according to the man's time and place. The man's time and place are also factors conditioning his response to the divine dealing and his way of understanding and describing it. Nothing can happen to a man except in a historical situation, not even his experience of God. Many of the baffling aspects of the Old Testament are the inevitable results of God's recognition of the historical milieu in which even a " chosen " man and a " chosen " people must necessarily live and move. A certain relativism attaches to the divine self-disclosure just by reason of the fact that it is a self-disclosure made to men — and men are conditioned creatures. As Lotze has it, they can exist only in relations! No Word of God that ever came to a man was received and expressed in its utter original purity. Whatever is received by a man is modified by the fact that *a man* receives it and that it is received by *this* man. The fact is obvious, yet its relation to the movement of revelation is often entirely ignored, and the light it would throw on many a Biblical obscurity is therefore missed. Confusion is made worse confounded. The lawgiver was first a *man*. The priest, the prophet, was first a man. The scribe, the psalmist, the apocalyptist, was first a man. The fact that he was a man, and a man of a certain kind, and a man of a certain period, left its mark upon what he received from God and upon what he said about what he had received.

In an earlier chapter we dealt with some of the evidences

of the relativism that characterized the process of revelation. To read and interpret the Old Testament without any reference to this relativism is to misread and misinterpret. This indifference may easily lead to the claim, still not uncommonly made, that everything in the Old Testament, having come from God, is of equal value, equally binding upon us, equally to be taken over into the content of faith. One feels very helpless in the presence of a mentality than can lightly make such a claim. The necessary contingencies of history are waved aside. The best that was possible to men of faith at a given time is treated as binding upon men of faith for *all* time, in complete indifference to the fact that faith is characterized by lower and higher. The uncertainties of the human are thereupon attributed to the divine. God is judged by his least effective messenger!

If we are to be held to such an attitude to the Old Testament and all it contains, we are deprived of recognizing and applying the determinative significance of that Living Word of God who was Jesus Christ. We cannot allow him to make any difference either in the way in which we understand God or in our understanding of what God requires of us. On the one hand, because we are Christian men we declare our surrender to God as sacrificially, completely, and redeemingly self-revealed in the entry of the divine filial into the conditions of the human filial — our surrender, that is, to the Son of God become a son of man; and, on the other hand, we make our declared surrender a hollow thing because in actual fact, under a false view of the historical process by which the supreme revelation was anticipated and prepared for, we give the alleged surrender no practical significance. We refuse to allow the highest to make any difference! At times — when, for example, we are reading Judges or Leviticus or Nahum or Ezra or Ecclesiastes — we talk about God, what he is in himself, what he seeks for men and would do for men and would have men be, as though no such person as Jesus Christ had ever appeared in our history. We in effect judge him by what went before instead of, as we should, judging what went before by him. There is no declaration in the Old Testament respecting

God, his character, his purpose, his activity, no declaration respecting the requirement of this God as to the behavior of men, which can possibly be binding on the Christian man *if* the declaration in question cannot be reconciled with what God disclosed himself to be in the Incarnate Word, and with the requirement on human life and thought and action that is the proper issue and concomitant of this disclosure. The Old Testament declaration does, indeed, have its own proper significance, but its significance is in the evidence it affords to the historically conditioned variations attendant on the revealing process.

It does not follow from this that the Old Testament may now cease to be read. What rather follows is that we are to read it with Christian eyes, and when Christian eyes read the Old Testament, especially some of its more savage and unregenerate parts, they will necessarily read it as critical eyes. " The Christian criticism of the Old Testament " is, in the nature of the case, an inevitable criticism. Certainly the Old Testament throws much light on the character of God, and the purpose of God, and the ways of God, and on the rich possibilities that are open to men of faith. For this light we can only be grateful, and we shall use it as we may. But to read the Old Testament as men whose God is that God who was seen in the " face " — that is, in the whole personal life — of Jesus Christ is to read it differently from what it can be read from any other standpoint. It is not only to read it differently: it is also to read it truly, if " reading it truly " means reading it according to the original divine intent. One may read Ecclesiastes as one reads any ancient ethical treatise — the *Ethics* of Aristotle, the speeches and arguments and cogitations of Socrates in the *Dialogues* of Plato, the varied defenses of cynicism, and hedonism, and Epicureanism, and Stoicism, and the like: one may do this, and it is legitimate enough. But Ecclesiastes is in the Old Testament, and it is, in truth, an ethical medley. The writer has been called " the gentle cynic." Cynical he may be, but his gentleness is another matter. Let anyone read the section Eccl. 2:1–17, and then inquire what the Christian man is supposed to do with it. Pessimism, cynicism, hedonism, prudentialism, Stoicism, moralism — all these are set forth in this one book. Here and there the book expresses the insights of a truly " wise " man, and it is always a question whether the rest of the book is not simply a setting for these insights, climaxing as they do in the two closing verses respecting " the whole duty of man." If this is really the case, then Ecclesiastes strikingly exhibits — and justifies! — the contrast between the Word of God and the words of men. Even so, the Christian man will read Ecclesiastes, as he will any other book of the Old Testament, as one who will not necessarily be bound by its sentiments merely because the book is included in " the book of God." He will exercise his right of free judgment concerning it. His freedom in Christ is a freedom to reject whatever he deems alien to the meaning of his faith.

The Christian way of reading the Old Testament is therefore a creation of faith, and faith is quickened by the very difference it creates. The recognition and application of this difference is indispensable for the Old Testament interpreter. He has his own standard of interpretation: *God-in-Christ*. It may very well be that with this standard we shall find in the Old Testament very much more to undergird our faith than we should find in using a less exalted and a less exacting standard. It is simple and sober fact that the Old Testament as a witness to a divine self-revealing movement read in the light of the incarnation — " the Word come to be flesh " — takes on a meaning that it can never have when it is read in its own light alone. The Old Testament brings so much to the man of Christian faith just because the man of Christian faith brings so much to the Old Testament. Read in its own light alone, the most it can give us — and even this is set around with the questionable — is a God whom men were led to believe in because of certain " acts " which under the leading of the Spirit they were persuaded were his " acts," and therefore revealed to faith something about him, this " something " being plainly a variant. Were they right *in principle* about such " acts," about their significance? They were right *provided that Jesus Christ is what in the Christian faith he is held to be.*

If we describe Jesus Christ, as we have already done at some length, as an Act of God, it must be with the understanding that he is God's "mightiest Act." This Act differs, in part, from all God's other revealing acts in being unmediated. We see Jesus Christ as a direct divine disclosure, whereas elsewhere the divine self-disclosure is indirect — indirect because mediate. There was a point at which God laid aside the veil that pertains to his being, and God unveiled is Jesus Christ. Elsewhere God suffered himself to be discerned through the veil, but the veil was always there, and the eyes of faith, even at their clearest, were always blurred. It was the Hebrew belief that no man could look upon God, and live (Ex. 33:20–23; cf. ch. 3:6; Isa. 6:5). The only way men could really and truly "see" God was to see him as a man — yet when they saw him as a man they did not recognize what they saw: that is to say, they did not really "see." Jesus said, "He that hath seen me hath seen the Father," and the words conveyed no meaning. All they did was to evoke what was almost a command: "Show us the Father!" Having eyes, the disciples still saw not until Jesus was no longer there to be seen — and then they knew upon whom they *had* looked. "Was not our heart burning within us, while he spake to us in the way?" The words were susceptible of numerous applications. Of what greater Act could God be capable than an Act by which he unveiled himself by humanizing himself? The possibility of this self-humanizing, and the means of it, were intrinsic to his very nature from all eternity. Such an Act dispenses with the process of inference. When the act is one thing, and God another, there is necessarily a step to be taken from the act to the Actor. The step was one of faith, with always the shadow of uncertainty hovering near. It is true that many took the step: there had been no Old Testament otherwise. But what the step was held to uncover was at the best an approximation. An approximation was all it could be, because while God was given in the act, the act and God still stood in contrast the one to the other. There was no merging of the two into one. God was other than the act, and the act was other than God: wherefore by no such act could God be utterly self-disclosed.

The incarnation is an Act that dispenses with the distinction

between the Act and the Actor. The Act is verily a divine unveiling. That which conceals the divine from human eyes is
removed — for those who would have it so. The result is immediate revelation in contrast with mediate revelation. Faith
is still the condition of the apprehension, but *what is apprehended is already there,* depending on nothing besides itself to
make it what it is. Whatever men did with Jesus Christ did not
make him any other than what he actually was. They could
scourge him as a blasphemer, but they could not make him a
blasphemer. They could crucify him as a malefactor, but they
could not make him a malefactor. This " mightiest Act " of God
invests with credibility all those lesser alleged acts of God to
which faith had been a response and by the response had been
made revelatory, but these lesser acts add nothing to the credibility of this " mightiest Act." The many words do not substan-
tiate the One Word. It is rather the One that substantiates the
many.

Herein lies the relation between the Old Testament and the
New. There is a very real sense in which those various alleged
acts of God which provide the vehicle of the Old Testament
revelation may be said to constitute an expectation of that
supremely revealing Act of God which is the incarnation. We
must never forget that there were always a few who in even
the darkest hour waited for " the consolation of Israel." Her
King would yet come to Zion. The great deliverance would yet
be accomplished. Yet it is much more truly the case that the
New Testament confirms the Old Testament than that the Old
confirms the New. To the convinced Christian it is palpable
truth that the incarnation — the Word of God come alive — is
the one great Event which gives to the essential message of the
Old Testament, especially its message concerning God and his
purpose for men, a stability and an authenticity that in the
nature of the case it could not otherwise have. Undeniably
there is much in the New Testament, much in what Jesus said
and did, much in Romans, much in Galatians, much in Hebrews, much in the Apocalypse of John, that is illuminated by
being read in the light of the Old Testament. Where the issues
at stake are faith-issues, we may speak of " proof " in only a

very restricted sense. With this qualification, we may assert that it is much more truly so that the New Testament " proves " the Old than that the Old " proves " the New. He who has surrendered himself to the reality of the Incarnate Word, and for whom " God was in Christ reconciling the world unto himself," will not be under any compulsion to " believe " everything that is said or implied about God in the Old Testament, nor will he be under any compulsion to " approve " all that men did or required others to do in the name of this God, much less to suppose that he is to do the same. His very faith in the Living Word sets him free from bondage to the written word, even although he may find much in the written word that he accepts under the sanction of his freedom. But his fundamental freedom is in his fundamental surrender, and his fundamental surrender is to the Living Word. What is agreeable to this surrender will have his allegiance, but he must himself be persuaded of this agreeableness. This will often enough require of him a decision that will try his very soul to reach. Time and again he will have to risk himself on his own judgment. Speaking generally, the collective judgment of men of a like faith to his own will carry him, but not always. On occasion he will be, like Athanasius, *contra mundum* — against the world, even, perchance, against the Church.

For the God of the Old Testament is a complex figure enough. Clouds and darkness are round about him. In Micah 6:6–8, called by George Adam Smith " the high-water mark of Hebrew prophecy," and in Isa., ch. 40, called by Robert W. Rogers " one of the most magnificent expressions of theistic faith in all literature," we are confronted with a God who commands our complete allegiance. But what shall we do with Judg. 11:29–40 (Jephthah's vow and its acceptance); with I Sam., ch. 15 (the command to exterminate Amalek); with I Chron. 21:1–17 (the three penalties offered to David for " numbering " Israel); with Zeph., chs. 1; 2 (the dreadful destruction attending Yahweh's coming); with Jer. 49:7–22 (Yahweh's threat to ravage the Edomites in revenge upon Esau); with Ezek., ch. 35 (closely resembling Jer. 49:7–22; see also Obadiah, where the theme and the spirit are similar); with

Ezra, chs. 9; 10 (the banishing of the foreign wives and their children); and with Ps. 83 (the ruthless destruction of Israel's "enemies"). Surely much that is said here about God expresses purely human presuppositions and desires. The writers transfer to God their own purposes and passions. "Israel hates the Edomites: therefore Yahweh does," is the way thought moves. The psalmist spoke truly who put in God's mouth the words: "Thou thoughtest that I was altogether such a one as thyself" (Ps. 50:21). It is only natural that there should be much in the Old Testament that has been rendered insignificant by the mere passing of time, for example, some of the provisions of the various "Codes" (see Lev., chs. 13; 14). But there is also very much in the Old Testament that has been rendered irrelevant, even incredible, not merely by the passing of time, but by the coming of a more perfect understanding of God and of the ways of God. Such things we can readily enough *account for,* but having accounted for them we pass on. We give them no further attention, except it may be for their historical, social, or psychological interest. We certainly do not regard them as "authoritative," or as intrinsic and permanent elements of the rule of Christian faith and practice.

We can, for example, readily understand Abram's deception of the king of Egypt (Gen. 12:10–20), and his determination to sacrifice his son Isaac. We can understand the conquest of Canaan (did we not seek to possess the territories of "the Six Nations"?) — the ruthless dispossession of the inhabitants, the seizure by the invaders of cities that they did not build, and of houses that they did not furnish, and of wells that they did not dig, and of vineyards that they did not plant (see Deut. 6:10, 11). We can understand Gideon's mingled loyalty to Yahweh and to "the baals" (see Judg. 6:22–32; 8:22–28). We can understand Samuel's command to Saul to exterminate Amalek, every man, woman, child, and beast. We can understand Elijah's exultant assassination of the alien priests and prophets following the dramatic demonstration on Mount Carmel. We can understand the vehement protests of Amaziah, the priest of the shrine at Beth-el, against the intrusion of Amos (Amos 7:10–13). We can understand David's foul plot to get rid of

Uriah: many a man has learned how easily one sin leads to another! We can understand the attitude of the leaders of Jerusalem to Jeremiah: doubtless a vigilant Committee on Un-Judean Activities was deemed an essential to the national safety (see Jer. 11:8–23; cf. ch. 32: 1 f.). We can understand the growth of the Code of Holiness among the exiled priests anticipating "restoration," and the later attempt on the part of Ezra and Nehemiah to reorganize the life of Jerusalem on the basis of this Code, creating a "regimentation" in the interests of priestism, such as later became known as "clericalism" (Neh. 8:1–12; 10:28–39; cf. the ideal of "the Holy City" in Ezek., chs. 40 to 48). We can understand Isaiah's oracle on the nations (Isa., ch. 24); and Jeremiah's bitter prayer against his enemies: "Deliver up their children to the famine, and give them over to the power of the sword; and let their wives become childless, and widows; and let their men be slain of death, and their young men smitten of the sword in battle. . . . For they have digged a pit to take me, and hid snares for my feet" (Jer. 18:21, 22); and his equally bitter anticipation of the fate of Babylon (ch. 51), comparable to Nahum's song of hate concerning Nineveh (Nahum, ch. 3) and to Obadiah's "vision" concerning Edom and its fate.

We can understand, too, Job's petulant cursing of the day in which he was born (Job, ch. 3); just as we can understand the psalmist's praying, Jeremiah-like, that God will take away the sight of his enemies, and destroy their families, and blot their very name out of the book of life, leaving them without a posterity (Ps. 69:23–28); just as we can understand Deborah's exultant cry, "Blessed above women shall Jael be, the wife of Heber the Kenite!" — blessed for her cold-blooded murder of the sleeping Sisera, a guest in her tent at her own urgent invitation (Judg. 5:24–27; cf. ch. 4:12–22); and, let it be added, just as we can understand the crude barbaric humor of the Hebrew tradition — doubtless repeated with many a coarse jest around campfires of shepherds and soldiers — concerning the origin of the hated Moabites and Ammonites (Gen. 19:30–38; cf. Jer., ch. 48; and note the contrast in Ps. 60:7, 8: "Judah is my sceptre. Moab is my washpot"). All this, and much more like it, we can understand. How human it all is! " Human," be it said, not " humane "! And how human are we! — " all too human." Children of starry heaven, we trust; but no less children of the primeval slime — and the slime begrimes the star dust!

Understanding, however, is one thing; approval or acceptance is another. If we approve and accept, why do we? If we disapprove and reject, again why do we? These incidents and sentiments belong properly enough in the record, since the record is concerned with God's effort to domicile himself within the life of a people, and with all the barriers that stood in the way of his entry. But to make out of them so many "words of God," save, indeed, in a purely negative sense, is to undercut the Bible in respect of its ultimate meaning. They are certainly no " rule " for the Christian man's own faith, and no " guide " for his own practice, save again, negatively. Such thoughts, such feelings, such deeds are not for him, parts though they are of the Biblical record. So far as he has a " rule " for himself, it is provided by the character, the purpose, and the will of that God who disclosed himself sacrificially and redemptively in an Act — the incarnation — of which the form was Jesus Christ. He will assent to much that he finds in the Old Testament about God and his purpose and about human life and experience; he will make use of it for his own great enrichment respecting the things of the spirit, and for the deepening of his relation to God, and for the Christianizing of his social behavior and attitudes; but the final basis of this assent and the final basis of this use will not be in the mere fact that he finds what he assents to and what he makes use of in the Old Testament — for that would be documentary authoritarianism: not there; but it will be in the fact that he sees them as falling properly under the self-revelation of God in Jesus Christ. Let your Christian conscience be your guide, but let that conscience be exposed to more and more light, lest the light that is in you become darkness in the comparison!

Then let it be said once again: Just because God, in an Act whereby the divine filial entered the conditions of the human filial, sacrificially disclosed himself to men in his ultimate ac-

tuality of holy and self-giving love, thus creating, for those
who will have it so, "the sole and sufficient rule of Christian
faith and practice," he who in faith commits himself to the
Act both as real and as having this significance comes under a
law of freedom concerning that to which he stands committed.
It is a dangerous freedom, as all freedom is dangerous, but it
is a freedom by which he both tests and expresses the reality of
his faith. He takes that whose reality is necessarily an inward
apprehension, and which remains vital only as long as the inwardness continues, and he uses that as his "measure." He will
believe that nothing is important for his relation to God, and
that nothing is important for his relation to men, which does
not come under his understanding of what is required by loyalty to this "measure." On the other hand, what he is persuaded
does come under this requirement, wherever it may be found,
in the Old Testament or in the New, and whatever it may be,
takes on for him the quality of an absolute. "*Whatever it may
be.*" It may be the defiance of corrupting influences, as Gideon
in Judg. 6:25–32; it may be protest against oppression, as Nathan's parable and its application in II Sam. 12:1–15; it may
be rebuke of pretense, as in Amos 7:10–13; it may be the demand for renunciation, as Jeremiah's celibacy (Jer. 16:1) and
Hosea's continence (Hos. 3:1–3); it may be the championship
of the dispossessed, as Micah in Micah 2:1–5; it may be uncompromising adherence to a principle, as the Rechabites in
Jer. 35:1 f.; it may be the refusal to conform, as Daniel and his
three friends at the court of Nebuchadrezzar; it may be the
challenge of convention, as Jesus eating with sinners (see Luke
15:1, 2); it may be championing the unpopular, as Paul preaching to Gentiles (Acts, ch. 14; see also Peter and Cornelius in
Acts, ch. 10); it may be submission to obloquy, or surrendering
comforts, as in the case of Paul (I Cor. 4:9 f.; II Cor. 6:4 f.);
it may be making concessions for the sake of the weak (Rom.
14:13 f.); and it may be "forsaking all" when the occasion demands (Mark 10:17–31). There is one "must" under which
the Christian man incessantly stands: that "must" has to do
with what he sees goes properly with his belief that God is
such a One as through great tribulation entered the kingdom

of the human as the Incarnate Son in order that the kingdom of the human might be transformed into the Kingdom of God.

What has now been said is not intended to deny that the entire Old Testament is of value in its own right. It does have that value. It has value for the archaeologist, for the anthropologist, for the historian, for the sociologist, for the student of literary styles. The Book of Job deals with a problem. A man who is not the least interested in the problem as such, or who rejects the solution the book seems to suggest, may still find endless fascination in the book itself. The Song of Songs could hardly be called a profoundly religious composition. The custom of early Christian writers of regarding the " Song " as an allegory of Christ and his Church, carried over into the headings of the English Authorized Version — headings rightly omitted from the various modern revisions — was evidence of the difficulty they felt at the very presence of the book in the Word of God. The rejection of the fantastic allegory view, and the frank acceptance of the book for what it actually is, a series of love lyrics given some unity by being used to describe the experiences of a given pair of lovers, certainly does not rob the book of all significance. What it does is to give the song sequence the significance it was intended to have, suggested in the memorable words, " Many waters cannot quench love." As such, the book possesses an endless charm, but it keeps this charm only as it is allowed to keep its real character. The charm is lost when the book is forced into a frame of reference to which it is wholly alien. Its place in the Old Testament is justified by the fact that it reflects an aspect of that historical and social situation in Israel within which the continuing self-revelation of God was taking place. As to the revelation itself, however, it says little enough, and we lose nothing by saying so.

IX

AN OLD TESTAMENT INTERPRETATION

IN THE preceding chapter it was said that the Old Testament may be read in its own light, and that it may be read in the light of the New Testament. The conception of the Bible and its significance being set forth in this book does not preclude the first, nor does it deny the rich significance the Old Testament is known to yield for those who thus read it. After all, we can never forget what the Old Testament means to the faithful Jew. But the second way of reading it is necessarily the Christian way. It is the Christian way because the faith that Jesus Christ is God's ultimate self-disclosure puts upon the Old Testament the stamp of incompleteness. All that God seeks to say is not yet said because the Word has not yet become a Living Person. The New Testament is centered in that Living Person as God's final self-revealing Act. The Old Testament, therefore, in so far as it is " a book of God," finds its completion and fulfillment in the New.

The result is both repudiation and confirmation, as was shown in the preceding chapter. The Christian reads the Old Testament as a free man. His freedom is of his faith. His faith does not mean that he is set free of respect for historical fact, or for any other kind of actual happening that the Old Testament records. If what is said to have happened under Elijah on Mount Carmel and afterward at the Brook Kishon (I Kings 18:16–40) actually did happen, then there is nothing more to be said as to the fact itself. The freedom that comes of faith is not a freedom to deny events. But it may be a freedom to *deny* what is said about the relation of the events to God and about the kind of God the events are alleged to show that God is.

Equally it may be a freedom to *confirm* what is said about God in these respects.

There is much in the Old Testament that is confirmed by the self-disclosure of God in Jesus Christ. It is even so that there are Old Testament truths that the self-disclosure renders even " truer," so to speak, than was suspected either by the man who first stated them or by the men who later assented to them. There are two contrasting conceptions in the Old Testament of Yahweh's attitude to Nineveh. One is expressed in The Book of Nahum, and it nowhere suggests any divine mercy. The other is expressed in The Book of Jonah, and here wrath is tempered with compassion, justice with mercy. The man who has seen God in the face of Jesus Christ cannot doubt that God's attitude is more completely expressed in Jonah than it is in Nahum. God is " a devouring fire " (so Deut. 4:24); God is " a tremendous Lover " (so Francis Thompson). Can he be both? He can. But how can he be? The Old Testament sets the question by asserting both truths. The New Testament evidences the solution of the apparent paradox.

The paradox comes to light in the juxtaposition of the first two great " writing prophets " of Israel. These are respectively Amos and Hosea. It is no exaggeration to say that between them they provide the " text " of which all later Hebrew prophecy is the varied commentary. Amos is the earlier of the two, but not by very much. The difference in time, however, is sufficient to justify us in saying that but for Amos there might have been no Hosea — at least, no Hosea as we know him. All Hebrew prophecy is under obligation to Amos and Hosea, but to Amos chiefly, because Amos was largely the creator of Hosea. Amos is, in fact, the great prophetic enigma. " Yahweh took me from following the flock, and Yahweh said unto me, Go, prophesy unto my people Israel " (Amos 7:15). Yahweh had said and done something like that many a time before, but never with such dramatic consequences. He had, indeed, disclosed himself to Moses as Yahweh, but there was much in the content of that name that was withholden even from Moses. Moses is the chief point of reference alike for the prophetic understanding of Yahweh and for the prophetic interpretation of

Israel's history. Amos took over Moses' Yahweh, but greatly deepened the content of the august "Name," because in addition to what tradition had preserved respecting Moses, Amos had a vastly wider range of history to "interpret" than Moses ever had. For some five centuries the history of Israel since Moses had been weaving its complicated pattern. The anarchy of the period of the Judges; the growing stability of the monarchy; the division of the kingdom; the struggle between Yahwehism and Baalism, more severe in the North than in the South, but present even in the South under the very shadow of the Temple; the echoes of valiant prophetic voices — Samuel, Nathan, Elijah, Elisha, Micaiah — all this was in the heritage of the shepherd and orchardist of Tekoa in the wilderness of Judea.

And more besides. There was the spectacle of great prosperity in the Northern Kingdom under the leadership of Jeroboam II, existing side by side with incredible and indescribable depravity. Conditions were bad enough in Amos' own Southern Kingdom of Judah, but in the North they were infinitely worse. As Amos, following his lonely occupation, pondered all this — for the call to be a prophet never comes to a man who has not been *thinking* — there began to take shape in his mind under a sharper form and with a new urgency *the problem of the moral order*. In the tradition as Amos knew it, the concern of Yahweh had been a concern for his chosen people. He was the God of Israel. Israel would stand or fall by Yahweh; Yahweh would stand or fall by Israel. It was this limitation that Amos began to doubt. He saw that Israel was not a self-contained people. What happened in Israel and to Israel could not be independent of what happened elsewhere. The lines of history crossed each other, and Yahweh must be implicated in the fact. Amos looked at Syria; he looked at Philistia; he looked at Phoenicia; he looked at Edom and at Moab and at Ammon. What did he see? In every case he saw calamity. Why this calamity? Because of wrongdoing. The wrongdoing of these peoples was done in the name of their gods. It could not therefore be from their own gods that the calamities came. Whence then came they? Could it be that there was a moral order independent in its workings of the gods of the nations?

But Israel too had known calamity. The story was plain to be read. From Jeroboam I to the accession of Jeroboam II in the North — the story was not much different from that of other peoples; and from Rehoboam to Uzziah in the South, while the story may not have been quite so bad, it was still ominous. In the North were the alien shrines, ostensibly erected to Yahweh and for the worship of his name; actually centers of Baalism. All over the North, especially in the dark days of Ahab and Jezebel, the Baals were in command. What mattered it that the people cried, " O Yahweh, hear us! " when what they *meant* was, " O Baal! " Not whom they worshiped with their lips, but whom they worshiped in their hearts and deeds, was their real God. It was no less so in Judah. North and South alike " played the harlot," but the harlotry of the North was open and unashamed. Were the calamities that had befallen the North inflicted by the Baals? That would not make sense, any more than it would make sense that the calamities of other peoples came from their gods.

But the Northern Kingdom had flouted Yahweh. Could it be that the calamities of the North *had come from him?* And could it be that like calamities of other peoples had also come from him? And if they had, were these calamities *judgments?* Were these judgments the evidences of a universal moral order, and did this universal moral order, which embraced in its sweep the peoples who did not know him — Syria, Philistia, Phoenicia, Edom, Moab, Ammon — equally with the people of Israel, North and South alike, who did know him but had ignored him — were these judgments the expressions of the will and purpose of Yahweh?

This was Amos' epochal question, and to the question he gave an epochal answer. *The moral order is the will of Yahweh; the moral order is universal; therefore Yahweh is the universal God.* But the Northern Kingdom is now enjoying prosperity, such prosperity as it has never known before. Many have both winter houses and summer houses. They lie upon beds of ivory. They eat the choicest lambs and calves. Musicians add to the splendor of their banquets. Servants hold golden wine bowls to their masters' lips. Beauticians are present with their fragrant oils and cosmetics. Equally lavish is the worship at the shrines. There is no limit to the profusion of the sacrifices. Yet the prosperity of some is answered by the poverty of others, and religiosity by appalling degradation. The poor man who must borrow a little money to buy a pair of shoes is sold as a slave because he cannot pay it back. And when he grovels in the dust to beg mercy, throwing the dust on his head in his distress, his arrogant creditor threatens to charge him for the dust! The creditor, taking the money he has received for the slave, calls to his son, and together they go to the house of prostitution, and to the same prostitute. To ease their conscience, they then go to the altar — for " confession " and " absolution " — and the very robes they kneel on they have taken in pawn, and the wine they ostentatiously share with their indulgent god is the wine taken in excess from the sharecropper. When the oppressor is threatened with a lawsuit, he escapes by bribing the judge; and if the judge prove incorruptible, the oppressor combines with like-minded persons to secure the judge's dismissal.

This is what confronts Amos — and much more like it. Then what has become of the moral order? Where is the Yahweh who is allegedly in control? But Amos does not surrender. By whatever means he may have come to his profound insight — and it is here being suggested that it came to him by his reading of the history of Israel in the light of the " name " of Yahweh and under the guidance of the Spirit — his insight is clear in itself and uncompromising in his expression of it. The prosperity of the idolatrous North does not mean that Yahweh is helpless before the Baals. The moral order still stands; what a nation sows it shall reap; the moral order is universal; it represents the will of Yahweh; Yahweh is therefore not simply the god of one people — Israel; he is the universal God; he judges evil wherever it exists; the prosperity of the Northern Kingdom is no disproof of this; the Day of the Lord, which Israel professes to desire, approaches, and it is darkness and not light; Israel has known disaster before, and it is coming again; Yahweh has threatened before and then relented, but this time he will surely pass through the land; therefore, " prepare to meet thy God, O Israel." And what a God! " For, lo, he that formeth the mountains, and createth the wind, and declareth unto man what is his thought; that maketh the morning darkness, and treadeth upon the high places of the earth — Yahweh, the God of hosts, is his name " (Amos 4:12, 13).

In a word, Amos took the Yahweh of Moses and made him the God of the universe. He took the law of the Yahweh of Moses, and expanded it into the moral order under whose operation the universal God had set all mankind. *Here is the first announcement of a universalized, moralized, personalized theism in the Old Testament.* Amos applies it at the shrine at Beth-el with relentless logic. One has but to read what he said there to realize the burning moral passion that possessed his soul. His words cut like swords. They fall like the blows of a hammer. He uses one metaphor that is nothing less than devastating — the plumb line (ch. 7:7–9). What is more unerring, more revealing, more merciless, than a plumb line? God will hold a plumb line up against Israel — for that matter, against every nation, every man. Who can escape the plumb line? To measure by a plumb line is to measure, not by human relativities, but by the laws of the universe — God's laws. Truly, " God geometrizes." Wherefore the psalmist's question: " If thou, O Lord, shouldest mark iniquities, O Lord, who could stand? " (Ps. 130:3). We must answer, " No one."

Then is the plumb line of Amos absolute, final, without appeal? Are we doomed because we are not perfect — because even we are *not able* to be perfect? Then were we in sad case. Amos universalized his theism. Because he did that, he also moralized it. Because he universalized and moralized it, he should — shall we say? — have humanized it, if only by a hair, men being as they are. It is true that he represents God as saying, " Seek ye me, and ye shall live," but this involves no modification of the moral absolutism.

What Amos did not do, we find done by Hosea. Hosea magnetizes the plumb line of Amos, and it varies in favor of the human. But Hosea did that at great cost — a cost such as was paid by no other prophet. The story haunts us. Amos belonged to the South, but he delivered his message at Beth-el in the North. Hosea at the time was a young man, a citizen of the Northern Kingdom, apparently recently married. Life was good to him. He shared his country's prosperity, and saw nothing wrong with its religion. News seems to have reached him of the strange preacher at Beth-el, and he went to hear him. This is surmise, but safe surmise. For Hosea came to think much as Amos did. Imagination likes to play with the thought that Hosea was the one lone "convert" of Amos' Northern mission! Conditions that had not disturbed him before began to disturb him now. Yahweh took on a quite new character. The altars where he was supposed to be honored were seen now as places where he was defamed! The "nature" worship symbolized in the pole, the pillar, and the green tree was license, not religion. Hosea saw his people as an apostate people, and himself as apostate with them. He had learned from Amos the primacy of moral demand, and this as the proper corollary of the character of Yahweh and of his universal sway. In a word, Hosea became as severe a prophet of judgment as Amos himself.

The evidence to this is in the names he gave to his children in the next few years. The names were symbolic, as later in the case of Isaiah. His first child, a son, he called Jezreel, to indicate that the bloody revolution which had put Jehu on the throne of Israel, and to whose dynasty the reigning Jeroboam II belonged, would yet have to be paid for. The second child, a daughter, he named Lo-ruhamah, the Hebrew for "There is no mercy." The third child, a son, he named Lo-ammi, the Hebrew for "Not my people." All this is in the spirit of Amos. Hosea begins his ministry as a disciple of the prophet of Tekoa.

But a new note crept into the preaching of Hosea. It is anticipated in Hos. 2:1. The children's names do not properly represent Yahweh. The negatives must be dropped off. Why? Because there *is* mercy, and because Israel *is* Yahweh's people.

What had happened? A shattering experience had befallen Hosea. His wife Gomer had proved unfaithful. She had gone from bad to worse, and at last had left him for a life of open shame. Her lovers grew tired of her, and offered her for public sale. Hosea himself purchased her, and brought her back to his home.

It is necessary to distinguish Hosea before the purchase from Hosea after the purchase, a distinction too often overlooked. When Gomer first left him, Hosea saw it as a confirmation of his message of judgment. Gomer had played fast and loose with her vows. Gomer had known no law but her own wishes. Gomer had laughed in the face of decency. Gomer had sown the wind, and she must now reap the whirlwind. It was all plain.

But Hosea sat by his lonely hearth in his desolated home. He must still go about his daily tasks. He must keep the home together for the children's sake. Doubtless he had the sympathy of the community. Kindly women stopped at the door with little gifts of food; perchance came in at times to help the little ones to "straighten up the house." But all the time the forsaken husband is thinking, thinking, thinking. He has told the people that Yahweh is a God of judgment, one who is of purer eyes than to behold evil, and who cannot look upon iniquity. Yahweh must feel about Gomer as Hosea feels, and he must feel about Israel as he feels about Gomer. But at the heart of Hosea there is a hurt, a deep hurt, a hurt that never eases. Hosea has been forsaken by one he used to love. He cannot forget her. Everything around him speaks of her. It speaks of old and happy far-off things, and pleasures long ago. It is not that he loves her still: no man could do that. But the hurt is there, and his days are sad, and the nights are long. A question haunts him. If Gomer is like Israel, if Israel has treated Yahweh as Gomer has treated Hosea, then in spite of the fact that Israel and Gomer alike deserve their punishment and that the punishment bespeaks Yahweh's moral integrity, does Yahweh feel his forsakenness as Hosea feels his? Is there a hurt even at the heart of Yahweh?

This is Hosea's searching question. It leads him to reconsider Israel's history and the truth is burned into him. He sees that while again and again Yahweh has judged Israel for infidelity, he has never forsaken Israel entirely. He has never been content just to judge. He would recover as well. He is not content to be a forsaken God. He has made a covenant with Israel, and he would still see it kept and fulfilled. Of this Hosea becomes convinced. God's dealings with his people not only reveal his moral integrity: they reveal the fact that he is not satisfied just to punish. Punish he must, but the punishment is not an end, but a means. In his people's suffering he too suffers. His very righteousness makes him a lonely God. Israel is a faithless bride. The wounds and bruises and putrefying sores of her dalliance with strange lovers are upon her, but she is still not forgotten.

So, Hosea gets a new message. Jezreel is not irretrievable. *Lo-ruhamah* may yet be *Ruhamah. Lo-ammi* may yet be *Ammi.* This is what Hosea begins to preach. The God of judgment is a long-suffering God. Ephraim is joined to his idols, but God will not let him alone. "How shall I give thee up, Ephraim? how shall I cast thee off, Israel?" (Hos. 11:8). Yahweh, is God, not a man. A forsaken husband will not *forget* his faithless wife: the hurt will be there; but he will not seek her return. How can he? The bond has been shattered, and such a shattered bond is beyond repair. But Yahweh, being God, will do what no man would do: he will restore his faithless bride to her old position, *because he is God and not man.* He speaks the incredible words: "I will heal their backsliding, I will love them freely; for mine anger is turned away." It is thus that Hosea preaches, and few there be that listen.

This indifference is what leads Hosea to consider an audacious step, and at last to take it. How long he wrestled with his thought, we do not know. There were a thousand opposing reasons — his own reputation, his own comfort, his children, his peace of mind. But had he not been brought into his present situation just so that Yahweh might use the situation on behalf of his purpose with his people? This voice that keeps ringing in Hosea's ears — is it not the voice of Yahweh? Preaching leaves the people unmoved. Hosea can see that; certainly Yahweh can. Still the people play the harlot at every altar, and under every green tree. Still they do not "return." *Preaching is not enough.*

Thereupon Hosea takes his fateful step. He will do the impossible. News has come that Gomer can be bought by anyone who is willing to pay the brothel keeper his price. The price will not be high for a woman whom few any more desire. With a word to no one, the grim-faced man sets out on his journey, and when later in the day he returns, Gomer, pocked under her paint, reeking with the perfumes of her trade, slouches along by his side.

What an evening was that in the little village! Unbelieving eyes stared out of open windows and doors. Raucous laughter followed the pair down the village street. Even the scavenger dogs snarled as they passed. As Hosea opened the door of his house, his children stared in shocked silence. " Children, this is your mother." Jezreel mutters something under his breath, and walks out. Ruhamah becomes Lo-ruhamah. White of face, she utters the word: " Father, if that woman stays here, I go." Hosea's jaw tightens, but he whispers, " She stays." Slowly — very slowly, one prefers to think — the girl moves toward the still open door, stops, turns, looks at little Ammi, holds out her hand, speaks one word, " Come, Lo-ammi! " and the two walk out together. It is then that Hosea turns to Gomer, to disabuse her mind of any false ideas as to why she is home again: " Thou shalt not play the harlot, and thou shalt not be any man's wife — *not even mine* " (see ch. 3:3).

The common practice is to sentimentalize this action of Hosea. We are told that this is the evidence that Hosea still loved Gomer, and that on the basis of his love he was able to realize that in the same way Yahweh still loved Israel. Although it was Hosea's own words that Yahweh was God, and not a man, we are told that Hosea argued from himself to Yahweh. This quite misses the obvious fact that already Hosea had been led to grasp the boundless compassion of Yahweh for Israel as revealed in his past dealings with his people, and that *the reason why he went for Gomer was just because of this*.

Then did not Hosea still love Gomer after all? No! Those who have asked us to believe that he did can never have attempted to imagine the situation. No man with the fine delicacy of a Hosea could ever receive back *as his wife* an abandoned woman like Gomer. Hosea himself declared that he was not doing so. In the face of that declaration, why the insistence that he did? This that Hosea had done is what no high-minded man could ever do in the sense it seemed to carry. He could not have *wanted* to do it. He did it under a sense of divine command: "Yahweh said unto me, Go and purchase Gomer, and bring her home." Would any man *want* to do that? Would any man *want* to make himself a laughingstock? Would any man *want* to wreck the peace of his home? Would any man *want* to live in the same little house with a woman who was still his legal wife, yet withal take — *and keep* — the vow of celibacy? No! Hosea did not "still love Gomer." The love of a man for a woman could never have survived the Gomer self-degradation.

What, then, are we to say? We are to say that Hosea endured self-crucifixion as he did in order, by his action, to give dramatic force to his message concerning Yahweh's will for faithless Israel, and the love it expressed. Hosea undertook to *act out* what he had been preaching. Perchance what did not move the people when he *said* it would move them when he threw it into a living parable. This that Hosea did was truth declared by symbolic action. It was a *word-made-flesh*. Hosea was the first Hebrew prophet to preach by giving his children symbolic names, and he was the first Hebrew prophet to preach by using a symbolic deed. Many of his successors followed his example. Isaiah did (Isa. 20:1 f.), and Micah (Micah 1:8), and Jeremiah (Jer. 13:1 f.; 18:1 f.; 27:2–11; cf. chs. 28:10; 32:6 f.), and Ezekiel (Ezek. 4:1–13; 5:1 f.). We must remember that Hebrew prophets were unusual men, who said and did unusual things. Hosea did the unusual, even the dramatic, in order to arrest the attention of the people, and because he believed it was what God wished him to do. He was not saying thereby, "This is how much I love Gomer." He was saying rather: "Gomer stands for Israel. Look upon Gomer, and you see yourselves. I seek to save Gomer that you may see how Yahweh seeks to save you. But there are differences. I brought Gomer back by main force, but Yahweh cannot do that with you. He seeks to allure you [Hos. 2:14]. Gomer can never again be my *wife,* but you can again be as Yahweh's chosen people. And this he desires, because his compassions die not. 'The love of God is broader than the measure of man's mind; and the heart of the Eternal is most wonderfully kind.' "

What Hosea is portraying, then, is the agony of divine love. Hosea knows agony too. He could do what he was doing only because of what he had endured. The agony of Hosea is the agony of having been forsaken. It is the agony of having had his love destroyed. It is the agony of having his name and the name of his children besmirched. It is the agony of the public bearing of a shameful cross that so he might set forth the love of God. And if anyone insists that Hosea could never have done what he did for the sake of the love of God alone and to declare God's love for the sinful, but that the old love for Gomer was still there as a driving motive, the plea may be allowed on the one condition that it be understood that what love Hosea still had for Gomer was not *romantic* love, but, so to speak, *evangelical* love.

Romantic love is destructible; evangelical love " endureth all things, and faileth not." It was not his *wife* that Hosea would save, but a *human soul.* In romantic love there is always a touch of self: it is *eros* rather than *agape.* But evangelical love is other-centered. It is as near selfless as love can be. We miss the mark utterly when we add a romantic coloring to our thought of the love of God. God's love is *agapaic,* and what love was in Hosea's heart for Gomer was likewise *agapaic.* When Gomer went away, perhaps even before she went away, *eros* went too. If when Gomer came back, love also came, it was not *eros* but *agape.* So far forth, the drama of Hosea's living parable was a love drama, but it was not a love drama cast in the terms of The Song of Songs: rather, it was a love drama cast in the *agapaic* terms of Gethsemane and Golgotha. And whatever may be the appeal of The Song of Songs, and whatever may be the reason for its inclusion in the Word of God, both the appeal and the reason sink, in comparison with the appeal and the deep underlying reason of Gethsemane and Golgotha, into insignificance. Hosea could preach the suffering and self-giving love of Yahweh because he had paid the price for proclaiming it. He died daily. He was obedient even unto the death of a cross. If one may dare put it that way, he bore in his body the dying of the Lord Jesus, that the life also of Jesus might be made manifest in his mortal flesh.

Amos and his terrifying plumb line; Hosea and his vicarious cross. The one — incorruptible rectitude; the other — helplessness surrendering to pursuing love. The word of Sinai; the word of the cross: which is it? Or is it both? And if it is both, how can it be?

What we know is that the Amos emphasis and the Hosea emphasis entered into the Hebrew prophetic tradition. In varying degree, it meets us everywhere. Yahweh-God is righteous; Yahweh-God is compassionate. Circumstances, however, made it easier to believe in the first than in the second. Jeremiah had a place for the compassion, but not until the righteousness had had its way. In the horror of the destruction of Jerusalem, and as the dark days of the Exile settled down upon a disillusioned people, Amos' plumb line must have haunted many an exiled soul, so that " to sing the Lord's song " any more seemed as impossible as it was hopeless. Amos must have seemed the authentic voice for days such as these: " Therefore thus will I do unto thee, O Israel; and because I will do this unto thee, prepare to meet thy God, O Israel! " (Amos 4:12). And how little they had been prepared, and how devastating the visitation!

Nevertheless, there had been a Hosea as well as an Amos. And if among the exiles the voice of Amos seemed chiefly to prevail, reinforced as it was by memories of Jeremiah's solemn pronouncements, there was at least one among them who had not forgotten that there was once a Hosea, and that Jeremiah himself had foretold that " a new covenant " would arise from the ashes of the old. We do not know who the exile was. He is called variously the Second Isaiah, the Prophet of the Return, the Evangelist of the Old Testament. His mind became dominated by the conception of " the Suffering Servant of Yahweh," whom he described in four so-called " songs " (Isa. 42:1–4; 49:1–6; 50:4–9; chs. 52:13 to 53:12). The " servant " is the theme of them all, but the treatment varies. The longest, and much the most impressive of them, is the last. The "servant" is Israel, but the conception of Israel is certainly not the same throughout. The conception is individualized: Israel though the "servant" may be thought to be, the pronoun used is always "he." In the fourth "song," however, the individualizing is startling in its dramatic sharpness. In the first and second "songs," it is not difficult to believe that the writer is thinking of Israel under the form of one individual. It is not difficult to believe that in the third "song" he is thinking of the smaller group of "the pious," perhaps of "the faithful remnant," within the nation. In the fourth "song," however, one feels constrained to believe that he has forgotten both the nation as a whole and the smaller faithful group, be it "the pious" or "the remnant," and is thinking definitely of some one individual in whom he discerns the characteristics that that "Suffering Servant" must have whose vocation is the vocation of Israel, but who will fulfill it as Israel — the nation or the special devoted group — could never do.

Is there someone in the prophetic tradition in whom these characteristics are found? It has been suggested that Jeremiah may have supplied some of them, and the likelihood of this is strong. But may it not be that there had lingered in the tradition, in a form that has not come down to us, some of the experiences of Hosea which were admittedly surmises in what was said about him above. Surely they were not unreasonable surmises. Surely anyone who understands human nature will have no difficulty in believing that Hosea was ostracized in the village where he lived! Surely it is safe to suppose that the old friendly knocks on Hosea's door were heard no longer; that the women of the village no longer stopped in to give a helping hand; that Jezreel and Lo-ruhamah and Lo-ammi came to see their mother no more; that the message which Hosea was enduring his cross to make more authentic and appealing was listened to by very few and received by fewer still — if any; safe to suppose, *mutatis mutandis,* that they stripped him, and put on him a scarlet robe, and platted a crown of thorns and put it upon his head, and put a reed in his right hand; and kneeled down before him, and mocked him, saying, Hail, King of the Jews! Hail, man who would be God! and spat upon him, and took the reed and smote him on the head, and gave him wine to drink, mingled with gall. It is not difficult to believe that the Second Isaiah knew things about Hosea, things such as these, over and above anything written in the book. Did he sense the contrast between this and Amos, and did he little by little come to see in Hosea a hope that was not present in Amos — *a Messianic anticipation expressed in the terms of a God of suffering love?*

The last thing one would wish to be here is dogmatic. Where one does not know, one may at least ponder. What we do know, however, is that the last of the " servant songs " is redolent of Hosea. Despised; rejected of men; man of sorrows; knowing grief; burdened with woe; smitten of God — *and for others.* Afflicted — but silent; bruised and broken; innocent — but tormented; forsaken and alone — *and for others.* Bearing iniquities; pouring out his soul; cut off from life; storming the mercy seat; interceding with strong crying and tears — *and for others.* One trembles at the analogy!

Centuries later an Ethiopian visitor to Jerusalem was on his way home, and was passing the time by reading aloud the last of the " servant songs." A stranger overheard the reading and accosted the traveler: " Do you understand the words? " The stranger confessed that he was puzzled. He was but recently in Jerusalem, he said, and heard strange things about a man having been crucified for blasphemy, whom his followers were declaring was the God-sent Saviour of the world, and these words he was reading brought the rumors back to his mind. And the stranger sat down by the perplexed traveler, " and beginning from this scripture, preached unto him Jesus." Jesus! The name is loaded with significance. It has strange antecedents — Joshua; Jeshua; Hosea. All mean the same. It was the battle cry of the Maccabees in their epochal struggle. It stands for " Yahweh saves."

And the angel said, " Thou shalt call his name Hosea; for it is he that shall save his people from their sins " (Matt. 1:21). When the Hebrew Hosea is Hellenized it becomes *Iēsous,* which is Anglicized as Jesus, described by Charles Wesley as " the Name high over all, in hell, or earth, or sky."

We have held that the New Testament sheds a great illumination over the Old. At no point is this more true than it is with the respective Amos and Hosea emphases. It is not being implied that the emphases are found in Amos and Hosea alone. They are present in the Biblical story before these prophets appear, and they provide the prevailing notes in the story that follows. But it was given to Amos to realize the universality of the moral order and to identify this with the nature and will of Israel's Yahweh, who then is set forth as the God of all creation and the God of all mankind, and who is therefore a God of absolute righteousness. It was given to Hosea, on the other hand, to realize that this same God was a God of long-suffering love. Amos himself had called upon Israel to repent and to return to God, and by that much had lightened his moral absolutism. Hosea had insisted that sowing must be followed by reaping, and had therefore not lost the moral quality out of the absoluteness of love. Yet the characteristic metaphor of Amos is still that of the plumb line, as the characteristic metaphor of Hosea is that of the forsaken lover seeking the recovery and restoration of the faithless beloved. An insistence on the equal truth of the two metaphors creates a paradox. This is only to say that the divine self-disclosure in the form in which it was apprehended by Amos and Hosea was incomplete. They were confronted by no one Act of God that would constitute the solution of the paradox. In the fourth of his " songs " of the Suffering Servant, the Second Isaiah shows that he had apprehended the *principle* of the solution — a suffering that expresses and satisfies equally, at one and the same time, and by one and the same activity, the imperative of absolute righteousness and the imperative of absolute love, but a mere principle is not sufficient.

Central in the Christian faith, and making the Christian faith what it is, is the belief that in the incarnation of God in Jesus Christ both imperatives are equally met. Here Law and Love are seen to be one, and the Law and the Love are seen as the Law and the Love of the same creative and universal

God. It is not possible to ponder the New Testament in its totality without realizing that it is undergirded and pervaded and motivated by the faith that God was in Christ; that for God to be in Christ in the way he was constituted his most self-costly and most self-revealing Act; and that the Act was of such a nature that while it perfectly met the imperative of Law it as perfectly met the imperative of Love. God in Christ paid the price of human redemption according to the requirements of his own eternal nature as Holy Love — holy in his intolerance of sin, love in his concern for the sinner. In the fact of God in Christ, every least flicker of Old Testament belief in a forgiving God — "a God merciful and gracious, slow to anger, and abundant in lovingkindness and truth; keeping lovingkindness for thousands, forgiving iniquity and transgression and sin" (Ex. 34:6, 7) — is confirmed; in the fact of God in Christ is equal confirmation not only of the entire Old Testament system of expiation, but also of what is sometimes held to be in complete opposition to it, namely, the prophetic insistence that God forgives only on the condition that the sinner does something about his sinfulness and sins. Repentance, confession, reformation, restitution, and the like, stressed as they were by the prophets, are so many recognitions of a moral absolute, no less than are expiatory sacrifices — perhaps, indeed, more so.

For the New Testament not only treats the self-disclosure in Jesus Christ as God's "mightiest Act," attesting his reality, his nature, and his purpose, but it also treats the cross as the climactic point in the Act. It is toward the cross that all that went before is directed; it is from the cross that all that followed after — including the "rending of the veil," the resurrection, the creation of faith, the gift of the Holy Spirit, the Fellowship of believers — necessarily proceeded. The absolute of righteousness and the absolute of mercy co-exist at the cross conceived as the disclosure of the absolute of Holy Love. Where personal relations are in question, righteousness without mercy is something less than perfect righteousness, and mercy without righteousness is something less than perfect mercy. It belongs to God alone to be perfect in both respects, and the In-

carnate Son enduring the tragedy of the cross is judgment —
judgment pronounced by holiness and endured by holiness.
But the cross is judgment that there might be deliverance —
deliverance of the judged from the evil which had been exposed, and robbed of its finality by the judgment. By the cross,
Love stoops to conquer. The cross is the tragic divine descent
to man to create the redeeming human ascent to God. The cross
represents the totality of human sinfulness taken upon itself
by the totality of divine Love, whereby divine Love reveals
and establishes forever its right to forgive the sinner, and the
right of the sinner, if he will, to be forgiven and reconciled.

In a word, the cross, as the climactic point in the self-disclosure of God by the incarnation of the eternal Son, and as
the point where sin and holiness are at the death grapple,
means that God is such a God as that his ultimate deed of
judgment is at the same time his ultimate deed of love. By
what God judges sin, by that he redeems sinners. By what God
redeems sinners, by that he judges sin. In a way neither could
ever have anticipated, the partial and apparently irreconcil-
able insights into the nature of God granted to Amos and Hosea
(we say nothing here of their successors) are confirmed by being brought to completion, and in the very completeness of
the revelation consists at the same time their reconciliation. In
God, Love is Law and Law is Love. Sinai and Calvary are not
contradictions, since Calvary is seen at last to be the summit
that is Sinai's crown.

Doubtless there will be those who will feel that in this suggested interpretation of the final significance for divine revelation of the two great Hebrew prophets dealt with, too much
rein has been given to imagination. The use of imagination will
not be denied, but neither will it be apologized for. The coherence of a process that was integrated with a continually
changing historical situation, and conditioned by all those contingencies which are the necessary attendants on human freedom and human differences — this coherence is ascertainable
only as one surveys the process as a whole, and from the point
of view yielded by the accepted climax of the process. The
Hebrew prophets played an important part — in fact, the most

important part — in the process. In the attempt to understand this part we must seek to reconstruct the prophet's situation. We must " sit where he sat." We must enter into his limitations — limitations of time and place and circumstance and capacity and outlook. Much of this is supplied by ascertainable facts, but much of it is not. We have nothing like a complete biography of any prophet. Jeremiah comes the nearest to it, but even in his case the chronology is confused, and there are many gaps. Interpretation must pay respect to known fact. Beyond that, some use of the imagination is imperative. It is a justifiable expectation that imagination shall be restrained by intrinsic credibility and probability, but within that limitation we cannot dispense with it. What can reverent imagination not add to the interpretation of Abraham's sad journey to the mountain in Moriah, the dedicated Isaac by his side? What can it not add to the interpretation of Jeremiah's purchase of the field in Anathoth? And what can it not add of meaning by being brought to bear, as has been done above, first, on the interpretation of Hosea's domestic tragedy; second, on Hosea's own interpretation of the tragedy; and third, on the interpretation of the tragedy itself and of Hosea's interpretation of it, according as both are read in the light of the cross, understood as God's own tragedy arising from the requirements of his innermost nature as Holy Love confronting the contrasting tragedy of human sin. This last interpretation, however, allows for the plumb line of Amos, as it must, since no interpretation of any fact or event or experience involving men in the moral order is deeply Christian in which broken law and redeeming love are not alike recognized and alike satisfied.

CHAPTER X

THE SYNOPTIC GOSPELS

THE attempt has become common in recent times to distinguish between the Jesus of the Gospels and the Christ of faith. The view underlying the attempt is that the Jesus of the Gospels is a historical reality, whereas the Christ of faith is largely an imaginary figure superimposed upon the historical. It is further claimed that the Christ of faith — represented chiefly by the Epistles and the Fourth Gospel — has colored even the accounts of the historical Jesus. This coloring is apparent in the birth and infancy narratives; in the descriptions of Jesus' "mighty works," especially in the more dramatic of these; and in the stories of the resurrection appearances. The task of criticism is that of removing this coloring, so that we may get a more realistic view of the actual Jesus. It is declared that even after this has been accomplished, considerable confusion and uncertainty still remain, due to the way in which the Gospel records were affected by the situation obtaining in the Church, especially by the fact that "oral testimony" played so large a part in the early spreading of "the good news." We have in the Synoptics, however — so goes the claim — enough dependable knowledge of the life, teaching, and activity of Jesus to serve the purpose of a "standard" for our determining the nature of original Christianity. Much patient scholarship, and an amazing ingenuity, have been brought to the support of this conception.

The conception, of course, rests — often admittedly so — on certain presuppositions. One of these is that such a figure as the Christ of faith is held to be is an essential incredibility. One who *could not* have existed obviously *did not* exist, and no records, however reverently regarded, could validate the impossible.

The stubborn fact remains, however, that what is left when

the process of "reducing" the Christ of faith to "a credible figure" is complete is not original Christianity at all, nor does it account for original Christianity. That original Christianity consisted in the following by a few men and women of the "simple teaching" of Jesus is an assumption pure and simple. Something other than these teachings is necessary to account for the "first Christians." Lacking this "something other," human knowledge of Jesus, including the knowledge of his teaching, his example, and his experience, would have passed into oblivion. For a little while, the threat of this oblivion was a genuine one. Only one thing averted that threat. It was averted by the birth of a faith whereby Jesus was lifted out of the realm of the merely historical and the merely human and integrated with the eternal and the divine. The immediate cause of this change and of the related faith was the evidence that he who had "suffered under Pontius Pilate" and "was crucified, dead, and buried" was still alive and that he had manifested this fact to a few disheartened friends in a fashion that effected their complete transformation. Precisely in this transformation and all its far-reaching implications lies the reason for what knowledge we possess of the Jesus of history. The Jesus of history was not destroyed by the Christ of faith. *The two are one and the same.* The first led to the second, but the second was the crown and consummation of the first. The attempt to separate the Jesus of history and the Christ of faith is therefore an attempt to divide the indivisible. What God has made one, let not man regard as two.

Christianity, then, originated in a faith, or, better still, *as* a faith. It was a great faith, an audacious faith. It was a faith to which an alternative was always possible, as it is still. Without this alternative possibility it had not been a faith. There is no faith except as there is venture. The leap from an "appearance" of one known to have been dead to a suffering God, an incarnate Son, an atoning Sacrifice — this was "a leap of faith" indeed, and it can never be anything other. The one thing that "original Christianity" was *not* was an irresistible compulsion, exerted either by a message or by a person. If ever a band of men made a crucial choice, it was those men who were confronted by an "appearance." The first Christians had to *choose*

to be Christians and from their time to our own there has been
no other way of becoming a Christian — that is to say a conscious and open-eyed and convinced Christian — except by
choice. Circumstances may make the choice easier for some
than for others but no circumstances can make a choice un-
necessary. The first Christians had to choose how to construe
the death of Jesus on the cross. They had to choose how to construe what he had said about the Kingdom of God and about
his own relation to that Kingdom. They had to choose how to
construe the empty tomb. They had to choose how to construe
his " appearances." They had to choose how to construe the
profound emotion that swept over them with increasing power
according as their other constructions began to focus at a single
point. And they had to choose how to construe the Man himself, the stark fact of his presence in the world, in whom all this
centered and from whom it was inseparable; because it would
be according to that construction that all the rest of the construction would be given its final form.

For these men saw everything looking increasingly in one
direction and coming increasingly to have one meaning. This
Man — so they were led to affirm — came from God; he brought
God with him; God was in all his life and work; God was in his
shameful death. This Man was still with God, for death had
not been able to hold him, and it could not hold him because
he was who he was. The coming of such a Man into the world
and his enduring all he endured was no small matter, either
for the God by whom he was sent or for the world into which
he came. In his coming, the love of God was sacrificially revealed, and what was sacrificially revealed was sacrificial in
itself. The love was revealed for the salvation of men, since
no man can be " lost," no man can fail of the destined end of
life, who takes to himself this God as the one great reality. This
was what the handful of men who ran away from Gethsemane
found themselves being led to see. This is what became in
them an irrepressible conviction. This is what took on for them
the ever-expanding dimensions of an imperishable, determinative, dominating, and redeeming faith.

This is what formed the substance of what they at once began to proclaim, to Jew and Gentile alike, as " the Gospel," as

" the Way," as " the new covenant," as " the power of God unto salvation to every one that believeth."

And all this was so before there was any such body of writings as that which comprises the New Testament; or any such closely articulated organization as that which ecclesiastical minds insist on *identifying* with the Christian faith; or any such elaborate rites, ceremonials, sacraments, and pageantries without which, so it has often been declared, there is no salvation. In respect of all such things as these, " original Christianity " was a *free faith*. It was a faith centered in Christ as the divinely given Saviour and Lord, who was *able* to save because he was the Son of God with power; who created an actual salvation by his death and resurrection; and who through the ministry of the Holy Spirit made his redeeming work increasingly effective in human hearts. Under the force of practical considerations, this free faith devised various instrumentalities — officials, writings, ceremonies, procedures, rules of faith, and the like — but always the instrumentalities presupposed the faith; always their proper function was to be servants of the faith; always it was possible for the faith to change them, to dispense with them, to devise new ones, and always it was a fact — as it still is — in the very nature of the case that the primacy belongs to the free faith, and that all the instrumentalities, *of whatever sort they be,* are secondary, subservient, adaptable. The absolute is the free faith whose focus is the living Christ to whom the whole being of the believer is held in the willing subjection of love; all else — *all else* — traditions, documents, organization, rites, sacraments, confessional statements, ecclesiastical orders, is relative.

Faith that " God was in Christ reconciling the world unto himself," and that God himself paid the cost of this and that the cost took the form of such a sacrifice on the part of God the Father as corresponded to the sacrifice made on the part of God the Son — this is the faith that was declared to an astonished audience of devout Jews as Peter preached in Jerusalem on the Day of Pentecost. It is when this is clearly comprehended, and not until then, that the existence of the Church and of the New Testament alike is by way of being accounted for. The Synoptic Gospels are inevitably implicated in what is thus accounted for.

They are implicated not as the bases of the faith, since the faith existed before they did, but as so many means of tying the faith into actual history on the one hand and of its elucidation on the other hand. Let every reasonably defensive view of the composition of the Synoptics be fully recognized. Let the differences in the final records be frankly faced. Let whatever appears to be uncertain be left uncertain. Let chronological inconsistencies be admitted for what they are. When all this is done — recklessly as it may be by a Schweitzer or a Loisy, or with a proper restraint as it is by a Vincent Taylor or a Manson — it remains that these are still the records, and the only records we have. They cannot be exscinded from the life and activity of the early Christian Community, from which they emerged substantially as they now stand. The contingencies that necessarily attended their composition are apparent in many ways, so much so that any claim respecting their "plenary inspiration" and their "verbal infallibility" is so utterly incredible that one wonders whether it is ever sincerely made. What is clear is that what they signify and what they represent is reflected in all the other writings of the New Testament, many of which — perhaps most of which — antedate the Synoptics in the forms the Synoptics finally took.

Because, however, the Synoptic Gospels may not be in all respects perfect and complete does not mean that they are not sufficient for the purpose for which they were first composed and are therefore to be thrown aside as utterly unreliable; or that they are so mutilated as to leave unaccounted for the Community from which they emerged. Synoptic criticism is legitimate enough so long as it is reasonably objective. The one thing it cannot do is to invalidate the faith to which the very existence of the Gospels bears constant witness. It is perfectly certain that "the Sermon on the Mount" was never delivered as a single discourse. Because "Matthew," or someone else, threw into this form the various "sayings" of Jesus can hardly require that we strike out Matt., chs. 5 to 7, as historically worthless and of no Christian bearing. Matthew, in fact, follows a fairly definite scheme in his presentation of all his material: the scheme is imposed upon the material, but the material is not thereby rendered suspect and useless. It is highly improbable that the numerous parables brought together in Matt., ch. 13, were all spoken at one time: their significance is not in the least affected thereby. The so-called "Little Apocalypse" in Mark, ch. 13, more fully elaborated in Matt., ch. 24, has been the subject of endless critical consideration. It may at least be said to be strategically placed, even if what Mark did, as Matthew later, was to gather around the remark of "one of the disciples" (Mark 13:1) about the imposing character of the Temple many words concerning an impending judgment that in actual fact had been spoken by Jesus on numerous earlier occasions. If this were the Mark-Matthew procedure, it is as justifiable as it is understandable. The Synoptists were biographers, and a "biographer" is not a mere "reporter." The critical view concerning the last chapter of Mark is that "the original ending" of this Gospel was lost from ch. 16:8 on, and that later two other endings were prepared, one known as "the longer ending," the other as "the shorter ending." The English versions give the longer ending; the shorter has been included in the translation of Moffatt. Tradition attributes the longer ending to a Christian of the early years of the second century. The one certain fact is that we do not have a part of Mark's original Gospel, but a substitute for it, and we do not know definitely to whom we owe the substitute. It is difficult to see that the matter is one about which to get excited. The gospel of Christ as the power of God unto salvation is not going to stand or fall by any theory of "the Marcan ending"! As a matter of fact, the first eight verses of Mark, ch. 16, report the resurrection, and the resurrection per se is much more important than any detailed descriptions of its attendant circumstances. The loss of what originally followed v. 8 is therefore not serious: it cannot be construed as indicating the possibility that our oldest Gospel did not attest the resurrection. Moreover, the "ending" that follows v. 8 supplies details about the resurrection manifestly gathered from recognized sources already in use in the Church. And in any event, we are still in possession of what was not lost, namely, an account of the life of Jesus, ending with the empty tomb, which everywhere bears the signs of having originated with a close intimate, in all probability Peter himself.

That "mighty works" characterized the ministry of Jesus is not only the testimony of the records: it is also entirely congruous with his mission in the world and with faith's conviction respecting who he was. In saying this, however, we are not precluded from a critical examination of the records. The presence of miracle in the records, both by direct description and by indirect reference (the latter being much more abundant than is generally realized: cf. Mark 1:34; Matt. 4:23, 24; Luke 6:17–19; etc.), is to be taken as the evidence of at least a "charismatic" quality in the activity of Jesus. *The actuality of this quality is the important consideration,* not the verbal accuracy of the detailed descriptions of its exercise. It does not follow that every alleged "mighty work" was in fact a "miracle." The very fact of "mighty works" inexplicable to the onlookers created a disposition to see them where they did not exist. The question we need to ask is, What did Jesus do that led to the widespread belief that "miracles" attended his ministry? It is not at all a matter of this particular miracle or that particular miracle having occurred exactly as described. Years ago, J. M. Thompson, an Anglican scholar at Oxford, tried to eliminate miracle from the Gospels by a critical examination of the several recorded miracles. He claimed either that the evidence was insufficient or that the event could be accounted for on quite natural grounds. He did not seem to realize that getting rid of specific "miracles" was not also necessarily getting rid of "miracle." The category may remain even although the examples may be imperfect. *The belief that Jesus did mighty works* is the fundamental fact, and it still stands even when detailed criticism has done its worst. The connotation of this belief is so entirely of a piece with what faith affirms respecting Christ himself that the question ceases to be one of documentary evidence alone. It becomes in addition a question of *natural concomitance with a divine self-revealing activity.* If this position be allowed, then one may be quite convinced that Jesus wrought "mighty works," and still have grave doubts concerning the authenticity of a given miracle, for example, the restoration to life of the little daughter of Jairus — if she were actually dead! — and of the son of the widow of Nain. James Denney had not the least doubt about the reality of the resurrection, but commenting once upon the "appearance" recorded in Luke 24:36–43, he said, "I confess I cannot go the piece of broiled fish!" There are those who will sympathize with his admission, while still firm in their faith in "the risen Christ."

In a word, verbal exactitude is not to be expected of the records of the activity of Jesus. Neither is it to be expected of the records of his teachings. As a matter of fact, we know that we do not have this exactitude, as may be seen by even a casual examination of the Synoptic Gospels. From the total account we have of the activity of Jesus we can generalize the impression it makes upon us, and we may do the same in respect of his teaching. What we may think about the account of a specific activity on his part, or about the account of a specific piece of teaching, is quite apt to be influenced by this generalized impression. It would be true enough to reply that the generalized impression is derived from the total account. But this does not necessarily preclude *the possibility of the generalized impression rendering some detail of the account suspect.* The skeptic may reject this or that part of the record on purely naturalistic a priori grounds. The man of firm faith — the man to whom Jesus Christ is verily the Son of God in the flesh — may reject some part of the record on the ground that "I do not believe that Jesus would have done that" (for example, "cursing" the barren fig tree, an incident against which Adolf Deissmann so passionately protests in *The Religion of Jesus and the Faith of Paul*), or "I do not believe that Jesus would have said that" (for example, the words with which he seemed to disparage his mother and brothers — Matt. 12:46 f.). Doubtless this suggestion of the right of independent judgment on the part of the believer will shock many; but how many of the "shocked" exercise a much more subtle form of independence in ignoring *in practical life* great areas of the teaching of Jesus which they profess to accept *in toto*!

Doubtless this recognition of verbal inexactitude in respect of the records of Jesus' teaching can be deeply disturbing. We might wish that what he said had been phonographically recorded at the time, but the fact remains that it was not. He entrusted his cause to the care of fallible men, and he entrusted his message to the exigencies of fallible human speech. Yet the fallible men did not betray his cause, and the fallible speech did not fail to preserve and to spread abroad the essential meaning of his message. We know exactly what Abraham Lincoln said at Gettysburg; we do not know whether any words attributed to Jesus are exactly as he spoke them. To make the value of the records depend entirely upon this kind of exactitude is both to put the stress of faith in the wrong place and to misapprehend the very nature of the gospel. The gospel is not in any " saying " of Jesus or in any one of his deeds. The gospel is in who he was and what he did and what he represented and what he accomplished, *totally considered.*

For any man ultimate authority is in what he takes to be ultimate reality, and this reality he must formulate for himself. He will recognize many lesser and subsidiary authorities, according to what is required by his immediate purpose. Often enough, these lesser authorities will savor of the arbitrary: they will impose themselves upon him, leaving him no alternative. But the authority by which he elects to live and die, the authority to which he assigns absolute control of his existence here and of his destiny hereafter, the authority by which in the end he will determine his use of all other authorities, of whatsoever kind and of whatsoever range — this is the authority which for him is the ultimate. For the sake of this he will surrender all else. According to this he will decide all else. There is a Christian view of what constitutes this authority. This authority is in what the Christian takes that God to be who at unimaginable cost to himself broke into human history in the person of Jesus Christ, to show men what in himself he actually is, and through Jesus Christ as his Incarnate Son to create a new and redeemed humanity. The Christian sees all else with reference to this. He understands all else with reference to this. It is the rock upon which he builds his house of life. It is the rock to which he clings when all else is swept away. It is the rock whose endurance is relative to his own endurance, and because " the great swelling tides of death and destruction cannot prevail " against him, neither can they prevail against the rock. All else can be dispensed with, but not this.

FREE FAITH AND THE GOSPELS

T HE life of that Christ by whom God laid himself bare in
the way and for the purpose that has been described will
necessarily be a life that accords with its own significance. The
account of the life as we possess it agrees with the expectation.
We must add that it agrees with the expectation in the by and
large. The congruity of the *Gospels* with the *gospel* is simple
fact, but that does not release us from the necessity of examination and judgment respecting difficult points. That One
such as Jesus will have much to say to men about God, about
themselves, about their conduct, about the manifold relations
of their life — this too is implicit in the situation. And here, as
with his life, the things he said were precisely such things as
his racial backgrounds, his moral and religious heritage, his
deep intimacy with the Father, his sense of high vocation, even
the high vocation of being the Saviour of the world, and his
consequent awareness of involution with the whole creative
and re-creative purpose of God, would in the main lead us to
expect him to say.

This very expectation helps to set us free from bondage to
a crass literalism. There is nothing irreverent, nothing dogmatic, in the surmise already expressed that words may be
attributed to him in the record which he not only may not have
spoken but which do not properly represent him. Certainly he
said much — and did much — on which the records are silent
(see John 20:30, 31; 21:25). Paul quotes Jesus as having said,
"It is more blessed to give than to receive," but the words are
in none of the Gospels. Yet who would deny their perfect
agreement with "the mind of Christ"? In the record of his
words as we have it there are things that startle us, sometimes

in one direction, sometimes in another. This needs to be considered.

The subservience of the Gospels to the gospel is a fact of very great importance. The men who produced the Gospels were already committed to the gospel. It is because of this commitment that they produced the Gospels. So much has already been pointed out. This being the case, it follows that no literary or historical criticism of the *Gospels* can ever affect the underlying *gospel*. The man of faith can be quite undisturbed by all that is said about the so-called Synoptic problem.

But it further follows that the man of faith can do some criticism on his own account. And not only that he can, but that he must. If we are right in claiming that all Old Testament revelations and the associated interpretations and applications are to be examined and judged in the light of the supreme and final revelation which is Christ, then the same principle must be allowed to be valid in the case of the New Testament. In what follows, the use of this principle will be illustrated from the Synoptic Gospels. The principle is that anything in the Gospels that does not seem to the man of faith to be in harmony with the gospel or with Him who is himself the gospel may be treated as of no Christian significance.

1. Matthew, ch. 23, has caused a good deal of heart-searching among Christians. The "sayings" here collected express a severity at times approaching harshness. A whole class of men are described in terms that certainly were not applicable to every member. All the evidence indicates that there were many honorable Pharisees and many high-minded scribes. On the other hand, it is clear that there were those whom the descriptions properly fit. The descriptions appear the more devastating because they are brought together, according to Matthew's customary style, in one chapter or section. It is in the highest degree improbable that Matt., ch. 23, represents a single discourse. What Jesus said about the group on various occasions is here assembled, and the total impression created is dark indeed — and not only dark, but in some respects unjust. It is not being implied that Jesus was an easygoing sentimentalist, to whom severe language would be alien. We know

better than that. He was an uncompromising moral realist. Some of his most graphic parables are parables of judgment (see Matt., ch. 25), and the apocalypticisms of Matt., ch. 24, are those of a man who did not hesitate to warn of the dangers that waited on life. But, as elsewhere in the Gospels, what chiefly matters in Matt., ch. 23, is the total impression it creates on the mind. It is an impression of deep moral urgency. Great issues are at stake. Men charged with religious responsibilities have in their keeping the souls of others, and they endanger these souls when by superficiality, self-love, and pretense, they endanger their own. This, and not the details of the metaphors and the strong colors of the language, is what is chiefly to be apprehended. We do not need to question Jesus' use of such metaphors and of such scathing language; but neither do we need to imagine every word of Matt., ch. 23, as falling directly from Jesus' lips. What is likely is that much of the language he used in his references to the scribes and Pharisees was made more graphic and more severe as it passed through the mind of the Early Church. There was good reason for this. Some sections of the Church suffered severely at the hands of Jewish leaders, both scribes and Pharisees, and it is not unlikely that the tradition concerning what Jesus said about these leaders was greatly augmented by the victims of their harsh treatment. One would like to believe that the section ch. 23:33–36 is an extreme example of this probable procedure, and of what it led to, rather than an exact verbal transcript of an utterance that fell from the lips of Jesus.

2. The " saying " reported in Matt. 10:37 is " hard " even at the best: " He that loveth father or mother . . . son or daughter more than me is not worthy of me." But " hard " though it is, it strikes the authentic note. This agrees with the significance that Jesus Christ had for the world. It is congruous with his " Leave all, and follow me." It implies the absoluteness of the loyalty that it was his intrinsic right to command. To the question, " Does that sound like Jesus? " the man of Christian faith will answer, " It does — exactly." The words are of a piece with his whole attitude: they mean that by great tribulation one enters the Kingdom, even as he himself said and himself

exemplified. But turn to the form of the " saying " as given in Luke 14:26. " If any man cometh unto me, and hateth not his own father, and mother, and wife, and children, and brethren, and sisters, yea, and his own life also, he cannot be my disciple." Is that merely a " hard " saying or is it not in truth a " harsh " one? Admittedly the exegetes have tried to show that " hate " here does not really mean " hate." It only means a form of behavior such as, if exhibited under different circumstances or for a different reason, would be construed as expressing hate. This, however, is only an attempt to make the words mean what they do not say, the attempt being inspired by the conviction that what the words do say they do not mean. But what is the origin of this conviction? Is it not precisely what we are contending for? What we are not in ourselves convinced is of a piece with the " deposit " left in our mind by the combined reading of the *Gospels* and of the *gospel,* we are not willing to believe that Jesus ever did or said, or if he did do it or say it, then we are not willing to accept it as finally representing him. After all, Jesus could very well have said at one time what he would not have said at a later time. One commentator (A. J. Grieve) on Luke 14:26, referring to the Matthew form of the saying, writes, " It is better for us to think that Matthew has softened the saying than for us to do so here." But why is it better? Why is it not justifiable to believe that Matthew reports the saying in its original form, and that Luke reports it in the form of a later " hardening "? Why be afraid to say that we think that one of the forms is nearer the mind of Jesus than the other, and that the form that is nearer to his mind is the form that he himself used? A regard for the " words " of the Gospels that is so tender that it prevents us from pronouncing an adverse judgment where an adverse judgment is manifestly permissible and even, it may be, mandatory, is a regard that comes very close to indicating authoritarian verbalism. In view of the fact that we cannot be absolutely certain that we have the *ipsissima verba* of Jesus in a single instance, why do we act, and encourage others to act, as though we supposed that we had them in every instance? Certainly we have a right to *choose* when the Gospels present us with different forms of the same teaching and different accounts of the same incident, and, if the differences are anything more than purely verbal and therefore carry a difference of significance, to choose that significance which seems to us more nearly to agree with our faith-reading of Jesus Christ as God's Living Word, God's Incarnate Son.

3. Or what shall we say of the words, " Till heaven and earth pass away, one jot or one tittle shall in no wise pass away from the law, till all things be accomplished " (Matt. 5:18)? Luke's form of the saying is not only briefer, but much less emphatic (Luke 16:17). The saying is suspect in both of its forms. The reverence for the " jot " (the smallest letter in the Hebrew alphabet) and for the " tittle " (perhaps the little " tip " that distinguishes one Hebrew letter from another letter closely resembling it) was characteristic of the scribes " who sit on Moses' seat" (Matt. 23:2), and who " bind heavy burdens and grievous to be borne, and lay them on men's shoulders " (ch. 23:3). The terms were in common use to indicate those *minutiae* of requirement which had grown up around the law throughout many centuries. This sort of crippling demand is entirely alien to all we know or can surmise of the attitude of Jesus. So far from encouraging it, or approving those who were devoted to it as the central form of service to God, Jesus was exactly antithetical to it. This sort of externalism did not simply " leave him cold ": it aroused his ire. It was the very thing from which he would release men. He simply did not care as to the precise manner in which men washed their hands before eating; or as to whether some garden herb was tithed or not; or as to the precise width of the hem of the robe; or as to the bodily attitude in prayer, and the like. The Son of God did not come into the world to promote the dictatorship of trivialities. The concern that sent him to the cross was not a concern for any " jot " or for any " tittle." It was a concern for much weightier matters than these. Such concern would better be ours, even to the extent that we are led to say that Matt. 5:18 represents a " gloss " originating in some Pharisaical mind in the early Jerusalem church rather than the mind of him who could " touch " a leper, dine with " sinners," receive the minis-

trations of a woman of doubtful character (Luke 7:36–50), and heal the sick on the Sabbath day.

4. Among the most fateful words contained in the Gospels are those allegedy spoken by Jesus to Peter: " Upon this rock I will build my church; and the gates of Hades shall not prevail against it. I will give unto thee the keys of the kingdom of heaven," etc. (Matt. 16:18, 19). The words are admitted to be "well-attested" so far as manuscript authority is concerned. But there is one attestation they indubitably lack, at least so long as they are regarded in the usual way. *They lack the indispensable attestation of intrinsic credibility.* It is true that Matthew reports the words about "binding" and "loosing" as having been repeated a little later to all the Twelve (Matt. 18:18), which at least serves to modify the so-called "primacy" of Peter. The objection, however, is to the whole suggestion of ecclesiasticism contained in this section of Matthew. Not only is there nothing like it in the other Gospels (see especially the Marcan account of the Caesarea-Philippi period, ch. 8:27–38; cf. Luke 9:18–27), but even the word "church," used in ch. 16:18 and ch. 18:17, occurs nowhere else in the Synoptics. When we remember that the Gospel of Matthew has very definite associations with the church at Jerusalem, as B. H. Streeter has so clearly shown (in *The Four Gospels*), and that in this church Peter, James, and John were "pillars," the ecclesiastical coloring of Matthew becomes entirely intelligible. Indeed, "tell it unto the church" in Matt. 18:17 almost certainly means the church in Jerusalem, which greatly lessens the possibility that Jesus himself ever used any such words. The mere intelligibility of the "church" references in Matthew is, however, very far from authenticating them. The probability that ecclesiastical pretensions appeared quickly within the Christian community at Jerusalem, and were given support by the natural device of tracing them to words put on the lips of Jesus by those who needed the support, is not to be discounted. The device is human enough, and has been duplicated often enough in the history of the Church since, for example, the forged *Decretals of Isidore.*

The choice is between some such view and the supposition

that Jesus had the ecclesiastical mind as revealed in this Matthew section. But the last thing we can suspect Jesus of having is the ecclesiastical mind. He no more had it than he had a Pharisaical mind. Only a person who himself possessed the ecclesiastical mind would ever impute a like mind to Jesus. To say it bluntly, the Petrine " rock," and the Petrine " keys," and the Petrine " binding " and " loosing," *in the sense which came to be attributed to them,* and with the august claims they have been used to support, are entirely out of harmony with the nature of the gospel, with the impression created by the Gospels as a whole, with the original Christian faith, and with the whole conception of Jesus and of the Kingdom that so deeply concerned him, which our minds gather from the records. That there were good reasons for the organizational form which the Church eventually took, and for the associated procedures, is to be admitted; but the attempt to trace all this to a few words which it is doubtful that Jesus ever spoke, or if he did speak them at all, almost certainly did not mean what they have been so widely held to mean, is another matter. The hierarchists may have their hierarchy; the sacramentarians may have their seven sacraments (the medievalists tried to give them still more); the authoritarians may have their closely graded prescriptions — so much penance for so much defection, so much pay for so much service, and the like; and they may make a plausible case, *pragmatically,* for their devices and their activities. But one thing they may not do: they may not justifiably claim that all this is the inevitable explication of what lay implicit in something that Jesus said or did. The characteristics of essential Christianity, which are few, simple, but exacting, and the characteristics of historical Christianity are by no means to be identified. That the characteristics of essential Christianity have never been wholly absent from the vast pageantry that is historical Christianity is to be emphatically affirmed, and is something for which to give God thanks, but it is here as it is with the Bible — there are many more " words " than there is " Word," more that speaks of man and his frailties than of God and his will.

We shall return later to what was said above about the ecclesiasticism in Matthew's Gospel, its probable origin, its significance, its fruitage. It will suffice to say here that the possible retort that what has been said above represents simply so much a priori subjectivism is not so crushing as it may seem. The vital issue respecting the gospel is precisely that of faith-inspired subjectivism or external authoritarianism.

5. Most of the recorded parables of Jesus " sound like him." We know of no ancient teacher who used the parable so effectively as he did. Who but he could have constructed such self-interpretive parables as those of the Prodigal Son and the Good Samaritan? The one thing that amazes us is that they should have been preserved only by Luke! It might be added that we are also amazed by the fact that only Luke records the parable of the Dishonest Steward. The amazement in this case, however, is that Luke should have thought the parable worth preserving! It is safe to say that we should have been none the worse off in any respect if this parable had been omitted from the Gospel narrative. Countless interpreters have wrestled with it, and the interpretations have been almost as numerous as the interpreters. " I say unto you, Make to yourselves friends by means of the mammon of unrighteousness; that, when it shall fail, they may receive you into the eternal tabernacles " (Luke 16:9). It sounds like an endorsement of the dubious procedure of the dishonest steward. Similarly in v. 11, which seems plainly to imply that the steward had been " faithful in the unrighteous mammon," and v. 12 seems to repeat the implication. But at v. 13 the tone changes. This verse is reproduced by Luke from Matt. 6:24, and is therefore not to be taken as a part of the original parable. The verse reads: " No servant can serve two masters: for either he will hate the one, and love the other; or else he will hold to one, and despise the other. Ye cannot serve God and mammon." Is not this verse an adverse comment on the steward, who in v. 9 has apparently received Jesus' commendation? One suspects that Luke reports the parable because he found it in his sources, but that he was not happy over the possibility that Jesus would be charged with approving double-dealing. He therefore introduces a saying of Jesus, already in circulation, which clearly condemns the sort of double-dealing in which the steward had engaged. And

here at least we can make use of one of the central principles of "form criticism," and surmise that an original parable of Jesus which would have supported Luke 6:13 had become garbled in the process of oral repetition by various "teachers" expounding Jesus' teachings to varying groups, until it assumed a "form" which was a complete reversal of the original.

It is a maxim in Biblical criticism that "the more difficult of two readings is likely to be the true one." The assumption is that the "easier" reading grew up as an attempt to simplify a more difficult original. The maxim is reasonable enough, and has often proved very useful, but it is of no use here for the reason that the parable exists only in this form. There is no question of two different reports of a parable between which we may choose. We have to take it "as is."

Taking it "as is," we simply do not know what to make of it. The very ingenuity of commentators to make something out of it only indicates the complexity. When such ingenuity is required to find the meaning of a parable, it becomes a fair assumption that a corruption of the parable has somewhere taken place. The very purpose of a parable is to help to make plain a great truth. It is true that in Mark 4:10–12, Jesus seems to imply that he uses parables to conceal, but in the parallel reference in Matt. 13:10–16, Jesus tells his disciples that he speaks in parables, not for their sake, because they already understand "the mysteries of the kingdom," but for the sake of the people at large, to whom these "mysteries" are not clear. But what is made clear by the parable of the dishonest steward? Does not the confusion that the parable creates render the parable itself suspect? Only by the most violent forcing of the language may a respectable meaning be deduced from it. We say flatly that Jesus would not say this sort of thing having the sort of meaning it palpably bears. Jesus himself creates in us that very canon of judgment by which we are led to repudiate statements allegedly made by him. Herein we are not judging him. Instead we are making him the judge. We will not attribute to him anything that we cannot but feel is unworthy of him.

Some will regard all this as an attack upon the veracity of the Gospels. But it is not that at all. Rather, it expresses a determination to maintain *the veracity of the gospel.* Much in this book is directed to the danger of supposing that the Christian faith stands exclusively upon the Gospels; that it is determined exclusively by the Gospels; and that it is to be measured exclusively by the Gospels. No discounting of the Gospels is intended because attention is called to this danger. The Gospels are here clearly recognized as so many written records which testify to a great Act on the part of God, an Act by which he made manifest his love for men in the most costly way that could be devised. The cost was in the coming of his own Son, his "eternal Other," into the world to endure the human lot, and in that condition, and in the face of all that men could do to him, to maintain the life of perfect Sonship and of perfect Brotherhood, because of which he could be constituted the "mediator also between God and men, . . . who gave himself a ransom for all," and could be designated "the firstborn among many brethren."

The *gospel* is in the very fact that this is what God in Christ did for men. The *Gospels* tell us enough for us to know how this was done; what manner of person he was through whom it was done; what mighty words proceeded out of his mouth; what mighty works — works of healing, works that defied the powers of evil, works even that disclosed that nature was not a finality — attended his activity on men's behalf; how he was treated at the hands of men; in what way he was driven to his death; the meaning he himself believed his death to have, and in what way he continued after death to be a dominating reality to a few who had been his followers, and who would henceforth proclaim him as the God-sent Saviour of the world. The form his impact upon the world might have been expected to take was precisely the form it did take. Such a life as he lived, such words as he spoke, such deeds as he performed, are of a piece with faith's judgment concerning him and with faith's conviction concerning the reason for his presence in the world.

Faith that in Jesus Christ men are confronted with the self-disclosure of God, and that the self-disclosure is such that not only the reality of God but his nature, purpose, and will as Holy Love is put beyond all doubt for one who shares this faith — this is what is borne witness to by the very fact of the New Testament and by the very fact of the Christian Community to whom we owe the New Testament. But what is witnessed to is anterior to the witness. *What is witnessed to is this God self-disclosed in his way.* It is in the light of what is witnessed to that we are to read, use, and evaluate the witness. If in the witness we find that which does not ring true to what deep in ourselves we have come to understand and believe concerning that which is witnessed to, then our first loyalty must be to that understanding and belief. If in the witness it is asserted that Jesus Christ laid it down as a condition to giving him the supremacy that one must repudiate family relationships and obligations; that he applied to men opprobrious epithets; that he endorsed meticulous legalistic requirements as attendants on religious faith; that in calling and commissioning his first little group of disciples, he had it in mind to make them the nucleus of a vast ecclesiastical organization rightly exercising prerogatives of Deity, including the authority to close in the face of men the gate to heaven and to close behind their back the gate to hell; that he used a story of double-dealing for personal gain as an analogy to life in the Kingdom of God — if things such as these are asserted in the Synoptic witness, then the man who sees Jesus Christ as the personal self-disclosure of God, through whom and by whom new life is made possible to men, will construe his faith as justifying and even demanding his rejection of these features of the witness.

There is only one alternative to this. The alternative to this is the acceptance of the witness verbatim and *in toto.* And who does that? *Nobody does that.* The most passionate advocate of the " verbal inerrancy," " inspired infallibility," and " objective authority" of the Synoptic witness does not do it *except in theory.* He does not do it actually, because no man could. Whatever he may *say* about his attitude, in reality he picks and chooses. The reason for his picking and choosing may be a debatable question, but that he indulges in it is not. We all do it, and we must. What has been written above constitutes a frank recognition of the universal Christian practice, and deals with the principle that would lift the practice out of the realm of pure arbitrariness and personal prejudice and would ground it instead in the very nature of that freedom for which Christ " set us free " (Gal. 5:1).

XII

THE EPISTLES AND CRITICISM

IT HARDLY needs to be said that there are numerous critical questions connected with the New Testament Epistles as there are with the Synoptic Gospels and with The Acts of the Apostles. These questions have their own importance, and for a scientific study of the New Testament a careful consideration of them is indispensable. The conclusions arrived at by those who have devoted themselves to such matters have often been disturbing to persons of weak faith. The suggestion that a letter ascribed to Paul may have been written by somebody else seems to carry devastating implications. It is difficult to see why. If, for example, Paul did not himself write Ephesians, it still remains that we have Ephesians, that it is a deeply Christian book, that it comes out of the Early Church, and that it could not possibly have been written by anyone for whom Christ was not, as the epistle itself says, " far above all rule, and authority, and power, and dominion, and every name that is named, not only in this world, but also in that which is to come " (ch. 1:21). If it is actually true, as is now generally supposed from the tenor of the letter, that II Peter was not written by Peter at all — at least not by the apostle Peter — and that its probable date was about A.D. 150, which makes it the latest writing of the New Testament, we are not thereby required to treat the letter as of no significance because of no proper " authority." The little letter is, in fact, of very great contemporary relevance. It makes plain the fact that a large number of people had been received into various churches who had had no adequate preparation for understanding the Christian faith and its requirements, and who by their cheap views and loose living were putting Christ to an open shame, being as "springs without water, and mists driven by a storm" (ch. 2:17). If anyone thinks that a writing dealing with such a situation has no bearing on the modern Church, he has not looked about him very carefully. What is chiefly significant about II Peter is not who wrote it or when it was written, but what it dealt with and how it dealt with it. The fact that the Christian faith carries great ethical imperatives, and that he who does not recognize them, and in himself carry them out, is thereby self-accused as deficient in both his understanding of the faith and his commitment to it — this is the clear meaning of the letter; this is what makes it deeply Christian; and this is what justifies not only its ascription to Peter, even although the ascription was a literary device to add weight to the letter, but also its inclusion in the New Testament as constituting the body of early written testimony to the revelation in Christ.

These remarks may serve to indicate a point of view with reference to the New Testament writings outside of the Synoptic Gospels. These writings are for the most part expositions of a common faith, or of some aspect of it. The faith is that of the Christian Community. The faith centers in Jesus Christ; in his relation to God, usually expressed in terms of a Sonship that was his alone; in what he did for men; in what he suffered on behalf of men and an account of sin, particularly in his submission to "the death of a cross"; in his resurrection and present activity; in his presence in the life and experience of the believer as a transforming, redeeming, and sanctifying influence; and in his power to bring a like influence to bear, the appropriate conditions being met, upon all the life of all men everywhere, "to the end that the Kingdom of God may come upon the earth."

This is the faith in which consists that gospel to which the Gospels bear witness. The various New Testament expositions of it are not in all respects identical. It is not to be expected that they would be, nor would identity be desirable. The Synoptic Gospels bear a common witness through a varying witnessing, and the same is to be said of the other writings of the New Testament. These writings are by six or seven different authors and the circumstances of the author, his purpose in writing, his cultural backgrounds, the cast of his mind, and his own personal experience were all factors in helping to determine what he wrote. The New Testament offers perfect evidence that men whose faith had an identical point of reference yet variously expressed and expounded it. There was even an element of progress in the clarification of the faith. The immediate effect on Saul of Tarsus of his Damascus experience was a conviction that the Jesus he had been persecuting through his followers was indeed the promised Messiah (" the Christ " — see Acts 9:22). What he learned from Ananias and the other disciples in Damascus with whom he tarried a few days after he recovered his sight we can only surmise, but the main theme of his immediate disputations in the synagogues of Damascus was quite clearly that of the Messiahship of Jesus. The term, " the Son of God," in Acts 9:20 is as certainly a purely Messianic title as it is in Peter's so-called " confession " in Matt. 16:16. Jesus became " Saviour and Lord " for Saul of Tarsus at Damascus, but Saul — " who is also called Paul " (Acts 13:9) — could hardly have written as early as that in his Christian life the Epistle to the Colossians or the Epistle to the Romans of his later life. Even Paul was " a babe in Christ," needing " milk" before he became a mature man in Christ equal to " strong meat " (see I Cor. 3:1, 2). It took time for him, as it does any man, to " grow up in all things into him, who is the head, even Christ " (Eph. 4:15). Paul had the " rudiments " — what the author of Hebrews calls " the first principles of Christ " (ch. 6:1) — from the beginning, else he could never have begun to " press toward the mark "; but while a knowledge and an experience of the " rudiments " qualified him to be a witness, it did not in itself qualify him as an authentic expounder of the Christian faith in all its immense ramifications. The authenticity of the New Testament expositions of the common Christian faith is an authenticity that comes of long tarrying in the school of Christ.

What has now been said is preliminary to a statement of a few — a very few — of the critical questions that arise in connection with the New Testament writings other than the Gospels.

1. An interesting example has to do with the teaching on the final resurrection and its association with the so-called "Second Coming of Christ" — a phrase, incidentally, nowhere occurring in the New Testament — found in I and II Thessalonians. I Thessalonians is Paul's earliest extant letter. It seems to have been written from Corinth early in A.D. 51, although some would place it in A.D. 49, during Paul's second missionary journey. He had therefore been preaching for perhaps as many as ten years, and we must assume that this letter fairly represents him on the questions dealt with. One of these questions is that of the circumstances attending the promised return of Christ. The relevant section is chs. 4:13 to 5:11. The description of the return, of the associated resurrection of "the dead in Christ," of the upsweep into the air of the faithful who are still living, of the uncertainty of the time of the event, and of the consequent necessity of unceasing watchfulness, makes use of traditional apocalyptic language. That is to say, it is highly pictorial, even dramatic. It is language of the sort attributed to Jesus in the reports of his parables and discourses dealing with judgment (see Matt., chs. 24; 25). It is such language as abounded in certain Jewish writings of the second and first centuries B.C. Undoubtedly the language was common in the speech of early Christians as they talked with great fervor, and even with deep desire, about their Lord's promise to return "at the end of the age." Paul could hardly have escaped being influenced by this element of the Christian hope as it was first explained to him by his instructors in the faith. It should be said that the autobiographical section in Gal. 1:11–24 is a problem in itself: it is utterly impossible to harmonize it with the story in The Acts of the Apostles; it contains statements that are not clear as to their meaning; and its declaration that he did not owe to any man his knowledge of the gospel is incredible on the face of it, if it really means what it seems to say. Certainly it is difficult to believe that the words, "Neither did I receive it from any man" (Gal. 1:12), apply to all that Paul writes in I Thess. 4:13 to 5:11.

There has been a disposition on the part of some to question Paul's authorship of II Thessalonians, or to make it a late writing, but the case is very far from having been established. It reads very much like a sequel following closely on the first letter, and this is the traditional view. Our immediate interest is in the section ch. 2:1–12, and its comparison with chs. 4:13 to 5:11 of the first letter. The theme of both sections is " the coming of our Lord Jesus Christ, and our gathering together unto him " (II Thess. 2:1), but it would be difficult to maintain that the treatment is identical. One gathers that what Paul had written on the theme in his first letter had caused a good deal of confusion among the Thessalonian Christians, and naturally so, considering that they were such recent converts, mere " babes in Christ." They evidently thought that " the end of all things " could be expected at any moment. In the second letter Paul seems to set himself to subdue the confusion and to lessen the tension of immediate expectancy by introducing an idea not found in the first letter, namely, that of " the lawless one," the cause of " the mystery of lawlessness," who is already being brought under control, but who must be still further controlled before his devastations can be ended by the coming of Christ. In a word, the " coming " or the " manifestation " will be " according to the working of Satan " (ch. 2:9), meaning that evil delays the outworking of the purposes of God. This would seem to suggest that Paul had thought out " a philosophy of the delayed Parousia," precisely as was done much later, and probably for much the same reason, by the author of II Peter (see ch. 3:8–13). It also seems likely, in view of his conception of the function of " the lawless one," that Paul no longer entertained or encouraged the hope of Christ's speedy return, which, he said, will be according to the appropriate time (cf. I Tim. 6:14, 15). Meanwhile, although he has a " desire to depart and be with Christ " (Phil. 1:23), a plain indication that he does not expect Christ's return during his lifetime, he must continue to serve the cause of Christ as best he may.

2. A question that has interested certain scholars in recent years is that of the location of the churches to which the Epistle to the Galatians was addressed. There was in northeastern Asia Minor an ethnic kingdom known as Galatia. The Romans extended the name " Galatia " to include a considerable area reaching south and west of this kingdom. Such cities as Perga,

Lystra, Derbe, Iconium, and Antioch (Pisidian) were certainly visited by Paul on his missionary journeys (Acts, chs. 13; 14; 15:36 to 16:6), and they were all located in this southwest territory. If it was to these churches that Paul sent the letter, then " Galatians " means " the churches of South Galatia." If the letter was sent to the ethnic Galatia, then it is implied that Paul carried on in that territory a considerable missionary activity of which we nowhere have any account. The question cannot be regarded as one of any vital importance for the interpretation of the mind of Paul as it is revealed in the epistle. If, however, " Galatia " means the ethnic kingdom of that name, then we must conclude that the account of Paul's missionary labors contained in The Acts is by no means complete, a conclusion further strengthened by what Paul writes about himself in Gal. 1:11–24.

3. A much more complicated and important question has to do with the structure of the Epistles to the Corinthians. There are good reasons for believing that the two letters as we now have them were made up out of an original four, and possibly even five. The first of these is alluded to in I Cor. 5:9: " I wrote unto you in my epistle." The tone of II Corinthians 6:14 to 7:1 has led many to feel that this passage is a part of that first letter. The second letter is what we know as I Corinthians, in which Paul deals with factions in the church at Corinth (cf. I Cor. 1:11), and answers a series of specific questions submitted to him from Corinth, apparently in reply to the first letter referred to above. A bitter controversy led to Paul's making a brief visit to Corinth (see I Cor. 2:3; cf. II Cor. 12:14; 13:1). The controversy had to do in part with the validity of Paul's apostleship, which had been called in question by the Judaizing party in the Church, and news of which had reached the Corinthian Christians, themselves largely Gentile, recent converts from paganism. From this visit Paul returned to Ephesus, writing thence a third letter. It is a fair surmise that this letter consisted of II Cor., chs. 10 to 13, or that it at least included these four chapters. The letter is firm, and even sharp (cf. ch. 13:5–10), and Paul seems to have been disturbed as to its possible effect at Corinth. In due time, however, he received a

report from Titus, specifically referred to in II Cor. 7:5–16. The report warmed Paul's heart, and he wrote another letter — the fourth. This fourth letter makes up most of our present II Cor., chs. 1 to 9.

It will be seen that the analysis does not cover the entire contents of the two epistles in the form in which we have them, which leaves open the possibility that Paul may have written to Corinth more often than four times. The analysis is, however, well-substantiated by the internal evidence. The main value of it is, of course, in its complete incompatibility with any literalistic theory concerning the " inspiration " and " authority " of the New Testament.

4. Four of the letters traditionally ascribed to Paul are known as the " Imprisonment Epistles." They are Ephesians, Colossians, Philemon, and Philippians. A question here is whether they were written during the Roman imprisonment, the older view and still widely held, or whether they were written during the Caesarean imprisonment (see Acts 23:12–35; 24:22–27), a more recent view, with able advocates. The probable dates of the Roman imprisonment are A.D. 58–60, assuming that Paul was released after " two whole years " (Acts 28:30), and exercised a ministry (unrecorded, but reaching, one would like to believe, into Spain), between the time of his release and his death in, probably, A.D. 64 (cf. Rom. 15:22–29).

There is also a question on the part of some concerning the authorship of these epistles, although the question is rarely extended to Philippians, which is so manifestly Pauline, bearing throughout the stamp of his personality and of his distinctive thought, and everywhere implying that the author is in prison in Rome. To question that Paul wrote Philippians, or that he wrote it from Rome, is one of those over-refinements of criticism which reflect on the critic. As to Ephesians, Colossians, and Philemon, it is practically certain that whoever wrote either one wrote the other two. The little Philemon letter almost settles the question. Everything would suggest that the runaway slave Onesimus was in Rome rather than in Caesarea, and that it was there that he was recognized by no other person than Paul. If the letter to Philemon, who lived at Colossae, was written by Paul in Rome, and sent from that city, then it is difficult not to suppose that Paul also sent from Rome, having written it there, the Epistle to the Colossians. In the case of Colossians, however, the place of origin cannot be held to have any least bearing on the significance of the letter or on its interpretation nor is the significance affected even if, as seems apparent, the letter was intended not merely for the Christians in Colossae, but for the group of churches in the Lycus Valley, running through the Roman province of Asia, the church in Colossae being one of the group.

Nor is the question of the place of origin of Ephesians particularly important. It *could* have been written during the Caesarean imprisonment without any change being thereby effected in its significance. The really important question, with Ephesians as with Colossians, is that of authorship. The arguments against the Pauline authorship have to do chiefly with style, vocabulary, certain of the problems dealt with, in particular the type of Gnosticism appearing in Colossians and the general theological point of view. One may familiarize oneself with these arguments, especially those having to do with the theology and the "world view," and still feel that one is in the presence of the same mind that is operative in the writings that are undeniably Paul's. That the Christology and Soteriology of Ephesians and Colossians show a "development" beyond that found in Paul's earlier life is to be admitted; but it is difficult to see any cogency in the assumption that what Paul says about the faith and its "frame of reference" in, say, I Thessalonians, must be taken as the absolute standard by which the later and more mature Paul is to be judged.

And if the Pauline authorship of the two epistles still be denied, those who make the denial have not thereby gotten rid of the testimony of the epistles. "Ephesians and Colossians, there they stand!" There was *somebody* in the Early Church, if not Paul, who herein gave powerful expression to his faith respecting the centrality of Jesus Christ and his universal supremacy; who assumed that it was the faith of the Church itself; who was concerned about the signs that the faith was being departed from; and whose writings were so highly regarded in the Church that they were esteemed worthy of preservation, and certainly in due time of being assigned to Paul.

The witness of the two epistles to the Christian faith is independent of the questions of authorship, of date, of place of origin, of destination. Surely it cannot be deemed a small matter that a mind equal to writing Ephesians and Colossians was a mind in thrall to Jesus Christ — like Paul himself, " a bondservant of Jesus Christ." It is a curious illusion, which we shall do well to abandon, that if any of the books of the Bible were not written by the persons whose names they bear, or to whom tradition, often for very poor reasons, assigns them, they lose their significance for the history and elucidation of revelation.

5. Romans is chiefly important for what it has to say. The critical questions are not numerous, but there is one concerning the closing chapters that should be mentioned. The body of the epistle consists of a carefully worked out presentation of the gospel of Christ, with continual references to objections that might conceivably be offered by a devout Jew. The scope of the gospel, however, is held to include Jew and Gentile alike, and Paul so presents it. The epistle is least like a personal letter of all Paul's known writings, and most like a general treatise. Indeed, although twice in ch. 1 as we have it the letter appears to be addressed to the church " in Rome " (vs. 7, 15), there is some evidence of early forms of the epistle that contained neither " in Rome " nor yet the closing section from ch. 15:14 to ch. 16:27. The usual critical view is that Paul wrote the letter from Corinth late in his career, but not later than A.D. 57 or early A.D. 58, as an exposition of the gospel suitable for general circulation. Then in anticipation of a visit to Rome he inserted the words " in Rome," and also added ch. 15:14–33, sending the emended treatise to the church in Rome by messenger. Chapter 16 as far as verse 23 was no part of the original treatise at all. Instead, it was a separate short letter addressed by Paul to the church at Ephesus, commending to that church a devout Christian woman, Phoebe, whom Paul held in high regard. The little letter included greetings to Paul's numerous friends in Ephesus (cf. Acts, ch. 19). It also contained a warning against unfaithfulness (Rom. 16:17–20). At an early period — so runs the critical view — this letter became attached to the larger and much more important Romans, perhaps to ensure against so small a letter being lost. Whether

or not the view is correct cannot be deemed to affect the message of Romans as a whole.

6. The three so-called "Pastoral Epistles," I and II Timothy and Titus, are traditionally assigned to Paul. Two questions connected with them have been discussed at great length, namely, the authorship, and the ecclesiastical organization implied in the letters. Both questions have their own interest, the second one especially, and this we shall need to consider later. Whether Paul actually wrote them all or whether letters that he did write have been expanded by other hands or whether they were the work of an unknown person who adopted a common literary device of the ancient world and used Paul's name to add weight to what he wrote, we may not be able to determine. All three views have their own advocates. What is perfectly clear is that the epistles express the Christian faith in terms closely agreeing — sometimes completely identical — with those that were used by Paul. What the letters emphasize is the necessity of keeping uncontaminated the faith that "Christ Jesus came into the world to save sinners" (I Tim. 1:15), he having given himself "a ransom for all" (ch. 2:6; cf. Titus 2:13, 14; 3:4–7; Matt. 20:28). This is represented as having been God's purpose from the beginning (II Tim. 1:9, 10), who raised him from the dead (ch. 2:8), and will judge by him the living and the dead alike (ch. 4:1).

Whoever the writer was, he was deeply concerned that there should be no departure from this "doctrine" (I Tim. 1:3, 10, 11; 4:6; 6:3–5; II Tim. 1:13, 14; 4:1–5). That the Pastorals testify to a faith; that the center of this faith is Jesus Christ; that Jesus Christ is the gift to men of the grace of God, whereby is fulfilled God's eternal purpose of salvation — that this is the testimony of the Pastorals is an undeniable fact; and the most elaborate and plausible arguments designed to show that they were not written by Paul leave this testimony entirely undisturbed.

7. For the purpose that this book is designed to serve, it is not necessary to dwell at any length on critical questions connected with epistles other than those assigned to Paul, since the principle being followed — that of the subservience of the witnessing to that which is witnessed to — applies just as

properly to James, I and II Peter, Jude, I, II, and III John, and Hebrews. It should, of course, be noted that the variety of authors represented by these epistles greatly increases the *spread* of the New Testament witnessing. The fewer writings by Paul, then the more writers; and the more writers, the more witnesses!

James emphasizes the ethical rather than the doctrinal, but it is quite evident that he does this, not because he does not agree with the doctrine — in particular the doctrine that forgiveness is the gift of the grace of God through Jesus Christ, who will come again to complete his saving work — but because he is concerned lest the doctrine be made an excuse for evading "the perfect law," which he clearly takes to be the law of love (chs. 1:25; 2:8, 12). In this respect, James is in complete agreement with "the Sermon on the Mount" (Matt., chs. 5 to 7), and with such great ethical passages in Paul as Rom., ch. 12; I Cor., ch. 13; Gal. 5:13–26; Eph., ch. 4; Col. 3:1–17.

III John has to do almost entirely with the pride of place of a church leader named Diotrephes, with whom John contrasts the humility and love shown by a certain Demetrius; but I John and II John have as their theme the reality of the manifestation of the Son of God in the flesh. In this manifestation is revealed the holy love of God, to the end that "the works of the devil" might be destroyed and propitiation be made for sins. Thus the great declaration: "Herein was the love of God manifested in us [or, in our case], that God hath sent his only begotten Son into the world that we might live through him. Herein is love, not that we loved God, but that he loved us, and sent his Son to be the propitiation for our sins" (I John 4:9, 10). The passage is reminiscent of John 3:16, and may truly be described as a statement of the central theme of the New Testament. The similarity between much of the language of the three epistles and that of the Fourth Gospel makes it plausible that the same "John" wrote the epistles and the Fourth Gospel, but here again the question of authorship is quite subsidiary. The faith of the epistles is, as implied above, identical with the faith the entire New Testament presupposes and to which it everywhere bears witness, namely, that in Jesus

Christ, God personally and sacrificially manifested himself for the salvation of the world. The witness expressed in the three epistles in no least degree depends upon our knowing precisely who the John was to whom the witnessing is ascribed. If the witness here offered to Jesus Christ is not witness to *truth,* then all the impressive concomitants of the witness, chiefly that of the centrality and supremacy of love as the final requirement made on men by a God of love, cease to be anything more than so many devices upon which men may agree for easing the pathway of life.

The problems of The Epistle of Jude are much the same as those of II Peter, briefly considered at the beginning of this chapter, and concern chiefly date and authorship. The name Jude (or Judas) is fairly common in the New Testament. The writer of the little letter identifies himself as "the brother of James" (v. 1), but what we do not know is *which* James. It is not impossible that the "brother of James" is a later insertion, added to give weight to the letter by associating the author with a recognized leader of the Early Church, either with that James who was the brother of the Lord (Matt. 13:55; Gal. 1:19) or with that James, brother of John, who was one of the original Twelve, and later a leader in the church in Jerusalem (Acts 12:1, 2). If the "James" referred to was either of these, the letter could hardly have been written later than A.D. 70. If the "James" referred to was "the Lord's brother," then Jude would be the Judas mentioned as one of the four brothers of Jesus in Matt. 13:55. But if that were the case, then he would more likely have begun his letter, not by identifying himself as "a servant of Jesus Christ" and as the "brother of James," but by identifying himself rather as "the brother of Jesus Christ."

The matter is mentioned here at all chiefly for its critical interest. Actually, the letter must have been written much too late for the author to have been the "brother" of any church leader of the first century. The purpose of the letter is obvious: it was to warn against a dangerous type of moral perversion that was creeping into the Church. The perversion was that of "antinomianism," the claim that faith in Christ released the believer from the requirements of the moral law. It was not until well along in the second century, when Gentile influence was becoming predominant, that this was a serious problem. The problem is that dealt with in II Peter, which, as already explained, was the latest writing in the New Testament, the probable date being about A.D. 150. The burden of both Jude and II Peter is therefore "ethical" rather than "doctrinal," which adds to the significance of the implied doctrine, especially in II Peter. The latter epistle emphatically grounds salvation in Jesus Christ — "the Master that bought them" (ch. 2:1) — through whom there may come to believers such a renewal and transformation as in effect makes them "partakers of the divine nature" (ch. 1:3, 4). Note also in Jude 3 the exceedingly suggestive phrase, "our common salvation."

There is little critical objection to assigning the authorship of I Peter to Peter the apostle. What objection there is is based chiefly on the language. The Greek is easy, fluent, and correct, and we have no reason for supposing that Peter, the fisherman of Capernaum, whose rough speech once gave him away (Matt. 26:73), was a good Grecian. But we owe the *form* of the letter to Silvanus (ch. 5:12), whose name is Greek, and who apparently, like a good amanuensis, expressed in his own stylistic way the thoughts he received from Peter. And even if Peter be in no sense the author, nothing is thereby taken from the significance of the faith that the letter so powerfully expresses. Instead, we have in the author one more convinced and dynamic witness, unknown though he may be. In fact, in the entire New Testament there is nowhere a sustained description of "the word of good tidings" (ch. 1:25) that excels in power, grasp, and comprehensiveness the first chapter of this epistle. It could truthfully be described as "the quintessence of evangelical Christianity." The eternal Christ, the incarnate Christ, the sinless Christ, the suffering Christ, the crucified Christ, the risen Christ, the glorified Christ, the redeeming Christ — all these are held together as one great, overpowering Reality in the mind of the writer. And if the writer really is Peter, and if the tradition be sound that Peter was martyred during the Neronic persecution, and if the purpose of the letter is in part to encourage the persecuted Christians scattered throughout the Empire to stand fast in their faith, then we are compelled to an inevitable inference — this: *that within thirty years after the death of Christ the faith for which great numbers of Christians are prepared to suffer and to die is such a faith as is described in this first chapter.* In the comparison with this fact, the question whether Peter could have written such Greek becomes something less than a bagatelle!

8. The Epistle to the Hebrews will be considered in the next chapter. It is one of the greatest writings of the New Testament. Both its authorship and its destination are matters of conjecture. Few now suppose that it was written by Paul. The conviction that it was not written by Paul — nor, for that matter, any other apostle — was one chief reason for its wide rejection in the Early Church. In general, the Church of the East, attracted by its Hellenistic flavor and its markedly philosophical tone, had no difficulty in accepting it as an authentic and authoritative presentation of the faith. The Church of the West, on the contrary, strongly committed to the principle of " apostolicity," and being ignorant as to its authorship, came only slowly to the recognition of the epistle as worthy of a place in the " canon " — the body of authoritative writings. The famous dictum of Origen, that " only God knows " who wrote The Epistle to the Hebrews still stands, and is likely to do so. Barnabas, Apollos, Philip, all have been suggested as the author, and many others, including even Priscilla, the wife of Aquila, friends of Paul. These two evidently played a large part in the life of the Early Church, and in the New Testament references to them Priscilla is frequently named first (Acts 18:2, 18, 26; Rom. 16:3; I Cor. 16:19; II Tim. 4:19), but that she wrote Hebrews is pure conjecture. In many ways, the epistle has the marks of being a general treatise intended mainly for the group of Hebrew Christians, but the last chapter is somewhat particularized, and suggests that the author is addressing a definite community. As good a suggestion as any is that he is writing to those Jewish members of the church in Rome in whom Jewish sympathies are still strong, and who need to be strengthened in their faith in the face of persecution (cf. Heb. 10:26–39) — probably the persecution then being waged by the emperor Domitian.

As to this, one says again that it has its own proper interest. But it still remains that we have no certain knowledge of the writer of the epistle, of the date or place of the writing, or of the intended recipients. The epistle is therefore to be considered in its own right and as it stands. It stands or falls by itself. No adventitious supports of any kind can be adduced in its support. We know that it was in use by A.D. 95, for Clement of Rome refers to it at that time. We know therefore that it emerged from the Early Church. Consequently we can assert that it reflects the faith of that Church. It belongs in the body of witnessing. The character of the witnessing and the nature of that to which the witness is borne — these are the matters of primary importance. These are what we need to know. These are what can be transmuted into the actualities of living experience here and now. Where there is not this transmutation as a result of Biblical study — whether it be of The Epistle to the Hebrews or of any other book — the study may still be academically defensible, but it has not brought to light the Word of God.

9. The book of The Revelation of John is not one of the New Testament epistles, although in the early chapters it uses epistolary forms, and its purpose was much the same as that of, say, Hebrews and I Peter — the strengthening of faith in a time of persecution. A brief mention is made of it here, however, because of its bearing on the main point of the chapter.

The controversy that has centered, and that still centers, in this book is nothing less than a tragedy. One of the most impressive statements we possess of the centrality and universality of Jesus Christ as respects divine-human relations on the one hand, and the overthrow of evil through the self-disclosing sacrifice of God on the other hand, has been mangled beyond recognition by the transposition of the central to the peripheral and of the peripheral to the central. Symbols have been mistaken for realities; poetic outbursts for sober statements of fact; imaginative flights for changeless truth; word pictures for mathematical exactitudes; literary borrowings from Jewish and even pagan sources for immediate and infallible dictation by the Holy Spirit; climactic moments in the unfolding of a dramatic form with an exact chronology of events reaching into the far-distant future. If there is one book in the New Testament that profits in its interpretation by the critical approach,

it is this Revelation of John. Without this approach, the interpretation is likely to be unrestrainedly dogmatic, and of no
book is dogmatic interpretation less defensible or less likely to
represent the writer's real thought. The immediate concern
of the writer — about whom the only thing we know is that his
name was John and that he was in prison for his faith, a first
century anticipation, shall we say, of John Bunyan! — was with
the contemporary situation, the Domitian persecution of the
closing years of the first century, and with how the Church
could meet and survive it. What he set out to do was not to
construct a crossword puzzle. It is true that he makes use of
devices whose meaning may not be clear at first sight. But his
steady and undeviating aim throughout the entire course of
his bold and even audacious construction is *to keep faith alive,
vibrant, and resolute, there and then.* The object of faith was
Jesus Christ, described as the Lamb who shared the very
throne of God. The faith was in dire danger from the machina-
tions of the Beast, described as the ruthless enemy of the
Lamb. The Lamb was concretely represented by the Church
(Zion; Jerusalem). The Beast was concretely represented by
Rome (Babylon). The struggle between the two was attended
by great upheavals, not only among men but even in nature.
The struggle would continue into the future, but the confidence of the Church *at any time* is always in the Lamb, both
slain and enthroned. The weakest is the strongest. The slain
Lamb is ontologically and sacrificially — that is, in himself and
in his suffering — inseparable from God, and therefore represents, as the Beast does not, the ultimate power of existence.

John may have supposed that there would be other crises
resembling that of his own time, and he implies that what is
adequate and dependable *then* will continue to be so, even to
the point of final and complete victory. But that he had in
mind as the specific initiators of future crises Mohammed, the
papacy, Napoleon, Hitler, Stalin — this is pure fantasy. There
are in Revelation fundamental truths and principles that we
never dare surrender. They constitute the very heart and essence of the Christian faith. It suffices that we understand
these, make them our own, cling to them whatever befalls,
meanwhile sitting lightly to the pictorial concomitants within

which John sets them, since it is by the centralities, not by the concomitants, that the faith must continue to stand.

The critical questions so briefly indicated in this chapter are very far from being exhaustive. The rapid review has only one purpose, namely, to illustrate the main thesis of the book, which is the propriety and the necessity of distinguishing between the contingent nature of the Biblical witnessing and the continuity, self-expansion, permanence, authority, and absoluteness of what is witnessed to.

A quite different group of critical questions have to do with the meaning of certain words and phrases found throughout the New Testament, and for that matter in the Old. Their number is endless. They include " Yahweh," " Spirit," " Messiah," " chosen," " sin," " atonement," " grace," " salvation," " propitiation," " reconciliation," " ransom," " justification," " holiness," " faith," " good tidings," " Son of Man," " Son of God," " Kingdom of God," " law," " flesh," " eternal life," " body of Christ," " church," and so on. The meaning of such words and phrases is a question falling within the broad area of interpretation. One principle at least must be laid down and rigidly adhered to in this regard, namely, that no interpretation of crucial words and phrases can be accepted as valid that involves a radical modification of that faith respecting Jesus Christ and his relation to God on the one hand, and to mankind on the other hand, to which it is the manifest intent of the Bible, *totally considered,* to bear witness. What does a man set out to say? This is a fundamental question. Nobody has the right so to manipulate a man's language as to make him say what he did not mean to say, or to make him mean what he did not mean. We may refuse assent to his palpable meaning: that is our right. But it is not our right to dictate to any man what he shall mean, the more so when in dictating to him his meaning we are also dictating to him his faith. For example, we may not like the palpable meaning of John 3:16, or of Phil. 2:5–7; or of Heb. 1:1–5; or of Col. 2:13–15; but our dislike does not endow us with some mysterious authority to transform the palpable meaning into a meaning so innocuous that what the statements are now held to declare is neither arresting, humbling, nor profound. Paul's words, "Him who knew no sin he made to be sin in our behalf; that we might become the righteousness of God in him" (II Cor. 5:21), may be so "interpreted," and have been, as to make Paul contradict much that he says elsewhere. The words as they stand have a palpable meaning. Embodied in the statement are the great principles of substitution and mutuality, and they can be redeemingly operative because Jesus Christ is himself so constituted as to be able to act representatively at one and the same time for both God and man. To interpret the statement in such wise as to make it mean something other than this is to confess to having presuppositions which make the palpable meaning of the statement impossible from the outset.

The immediate concern of this chapter, however, has been with the question of how far critical theories respecting the date, authorship, occasion, destination, purpose, editorial rearrangement, additions and polishing by other hands, and the like, affect the manifest testimony of the writings themselves. The answer is that they do not affect them in any essential regard. They are still expressions and witnesses of a common faith. The object of the faith is God self-revealed in Jesus Christ, conceived as the Son of the Father, who came sacrificially into the world, there to experience the human lot in obedience to the Father's will, even unto the death of a cross, and having been raised from the dead by the same will to which he had so completely submitted, remains forever the mediator between God and men — man's way to God as he is also God's way to man. The way was created by divine suffering. How effective the way shall be depends on faith, faith that God is such a God as all this requires, consequently is a God of love, whose purposes are love, whose activities are motivated by love, who is the enemy of whatever may be the enemy of love, who pays the price of his hostility to love's enemy, and who would bring love to prevail in all the affairs of men. In this faith, the anticipatory faith of Israel witnessed to in the Old Testament is brought to fulfillment. The God of the Bible is one and the same God, but it was not until he "spoke in a Son" that he was fully and finally self-revealed.

XIII

NEW TESTAMENT EXPOSITIONS OF THE FAITH

RECENT examinations of early Christianity have made much use of the word "kerygma." Underlying the word is the Greek *kēruks*. A *kēruks* was a herald, and the *kērugma* was his proclamation — that which he heralded. The kerygma was the message that lay at the heart of early Christian preaching and teaching. The sources of our knowledge of this message are the New Testament and the nature of the Community to which it gave rise and by which it was represented. The message itself had become possible because of some great Act of God: the message, indeed, included the affirmation of the reality of the Act. The form taken by the Act was Jesus Christ, to whom and to all that he did and endured belongs therefore a solitary significance. He is the most meaningful of all the acts of God. The intent of the Act was the securing of a Community of men and women in which would be realized the original purpose of God in creation as this began to be disclosed in his "calling" of Israel. Through the sacrificial sufferings and resurrection triumph of one Son — one because primal, originative, and archetypal — God would win for himself many sons, who because they were his sons would be also brothers — a family, a household, a body united in Christ its Head.

The intent of God's Act was conditioned as to its realization in any given man on faith. Faith was self-commitment to God as his Act of Jesus Christ revealed him to be. Such a self-commitment involved a new relation to God. Love, submission, service, were the fruitage of this faith. The committed life was a "life hidden with Christ in God," and finding in this experience such a present sense of the Holy Spirit that the life became itself a channel of redeeming and transforming power.

What lies at the heart of the primitive Christian kerygma therefore is the declaration that Jesus Christ is the means, provided from within the very life of God himself and forever inseparable from him, to overcoming the evil and the sinfulness of the world, the means becoming effective according as there is the response of faith and the proper fruitage of faith. The declaration formed the substance of the discourses preserved in The Acts of the Apostles, beginning with Peter's discourse on the Day of Pentecost — "the first Christian sermon." C. H. Dodd, in *Apostolic Preaching and Its Developments*, has made this clear once and for always, although in such earlier works as James Denney, *The Death of Christ* and *Jesus and the Gospel*, and Vincent Taylor, *Jesus and His Sacrifice*, the same insistence was present. This declaration gives the ultimate reason for the Church, and the ultimate reason for the New Testament — in fact, for the Bible itself, according to the view set forth above. According as this declaration does or does not prevail in the hearts and minds of men, to dominate all their thought, all their affection, all their activity, the hope of a redeemed and transformed world, whose promise and power are here, does or does not approach fulfillment.

The presentation, exposition, and application of this fundamental declaration is the reason for every letter, treatise, and similar writing found in the New Testament. There is a contingent and variable element in the presentation, exposition, and application as there is not in what is declared. Authority pertains to that with which the declaration is concerned, not to the presentation, exposition, and application. The writers of the New Testament are not only messengers — men charged with the kerygma — but they are interpreters as well. More commanding than their interpretations, however, is that which they are seeking to interpret. *The most prolific cause of confusion in the Christian Church has been the supposition that what Paul and others wrote in the New Testament about the gospel is to be identified with the gospel about which they wrote it.* It was Paul himself who wrote: "We have this treasure in earthen vessels" (II Cor. 4:7). He could only have meant, referring to his own ministry of the gospel, that the treasure was one thing and the vessel another. " For when one saith, I am of Paul; and another, I am of Apollos; are ye not men? What then is Apollos? and what is Paul? Ministers through whom ye believed " (I Cor. 3:4, 5). As *ministers,* they deal with the same faith; as *men,* possessed of different characteristics, they deal with it in their own distinctive way. The necessity of the vessel, of the intelligible presentation, is self-evident, and it has its own proper function. The treasure is the gospel, and the gospel is constituted of the self-disclosure of God in Jesus Christ and of the intent of that self-disclosure. Our jealous concern must be for this gospel. This will not prevent our appreciation of the vessel; our determination to preserve it for our own use and for its significance as witness; our recognition of its pedagogic necessity; our realization that again and again there is achieved such a perfect mutuality of treasure and vessel, of gospel and epistolary exposition, that their separation would be, if not destructive, at least impoverishing. Always, however, our first loyalty must be to that which the vessel exists to serve — and to preserve! The loyalty must be to that which lies at the core of any presentation, exposition, and application, even as we find these in the New Testament. To quote Paul again, " Though we, or an angel from heaven, should preach unto you any gospel other than that which we preached unto you, let him be anathema " (Gal. 1:8).

These are observations preliminary to calling attention to the similarities and the differences that characterize what may be regarded as the outstanding examples of New Testament exposition. These will be the Epistle to the Romans, the Epistle to the Colossians, The Epistle to the Hebrews, and the Fourth Gospel. They represent at least three different writers, and possibly four. There is no question that Paul wrote Romans. He probably wrote Colossians, but we cannot be certain. If Paul did not write it, then we do not know who did. We do not know who wrote Hebrews. And we do not know, beyond any reasonable doubt, who wrote the Fourth Gospel. We have therefore in these four writings not only an amazing body of Christian witness arising from several different persons, but a body of witness that is largely anonymous. We can infer a good deal about the character, temperament, and intellectual tendencies of the unknown writers, but that does not tell us who they are. Our response to the witnessing in its markedly varied form is not based on our knowledge of the witnesses, nor *merely* on the fact that it is contained in the New Testament, but on *our recognition of its central reference*. It is a faith-reference. The reference is to Jesus Christ and to his Godward and manward meaning, and to all the other meanings that go with this meaning. Our very assent in faith to the central reference of the varied witnessing of the known and unknown witnesses creates our appreciation of the witnessing at the same time that it sets us free from bondage to its varied forms.

As already said, Romans approaches a formal treatise. This is one reason why it has been seized upon with such avidity by the commentators and the theologians. Romans is essentially an argument. Paul *reasons* his case. He is unashamedly an advocate. His method is frequently that of the dialectician. What he proposes to expound and defend he states explicitly in ch. 1:16, 17: "The gospel . . . is the power of God unto salvation to every one that believeth; to the Jew first, and also to the Greek. For therein is revealed a righteousness of God from faith unto faith: as it is written, But the righteous shall live by faith." Paul, however, in the opening verses of this first chapter, indicates the central place the argument will assign to Jesus Christ, whom he describes as born of the seed of David according to the flesh, but according to the spirit of holiness declared to be the Son of God with power, by the resurrection from the dead. As he conducts his argument, Paul keeps in mind a possible opponent, whose objections he states and answers. This opponent is a devout Jew, to whom the faith of his fathers is sufficient. Paul can state his case so effectively because the opponent is in effect Paul himself before his epochal Damascus experience, when he was zealously persecuting the Christians. He had emerged from his Judaism, but he had not forgotten it. He knew it from within, and he knew how he had escaped from it, and he knew what he had escaped into; but he also knew that what he had escaped from and what he had escaped into, profoundly different though they were at the crucial points, were yet related as preparation and fulfillment in the redeeming purpose of one and the same God. God, he said, promised the gospel, and therefore "his Son," through his prophets "in the holy scriptures" (ch. 1:2).

Although Paul slants his argument toward the non-Christian Jew, he is not thinking of him alone. The gospel is for Jew and Gentile alike, but there is already a Church comprising both Christian Jews and Christian Gentiles, and both need all the help they can get. But they do not need it simply according as they were former Jews or Gentiles: they need it according to what they are now, no longer Israelites after the flesh and no longer Gentiles after the flesh, but sons of God through Jesus Christ who dwells in them through his Spirit (ch. 9:11). "For as many as are led by the Spirit of God, these are sons of God. For ye received not the spirit of bondage again unto fear; but ye received the spirit of adoption, whereby we cry, . . . Father. The Spirit himself beareth witness with our spirit, that we are children of God: and if children, then heirs; heirs of God, and joint-heirs with Christ" (ch. 8:14–17). In a word, Paul in Romans develops an argument for the gospel designed to convince the unbeliever and to strengthen and clarify the faith of the believer.

The formal features of the argument in Romans owe much to the concept of *substitution*. Paul makes large use of the possibility of one thing being treated as though it were another thing. The meaning of "this" is exchanged for the meaning of "that." What is not actually so is regarded as though it were actually so. Adam, the first man, disobeyed the law of God, and he was punished by moral disorganization and death. Every other human being is treated as though he were Adam, as though Adam's disobedience were his own disobedience, and he is therefore punished with Adam's punishment. He is a sinner because Adam was. Moral disorganization and death are not a form of punishment for his own free and deliberate sins: that punishment rests upon him because of his sinfulness, and his sinfulness is of his nature first, and is only of his will afterward. He is sinful before he sins because Adam sinned for him and because Adam's punishment is made his. We are lost by a substitution that was not of our own will; and our sins, the free equally with the inevitable, do but express and accentuate our original state.

The universality of sin is therefore accounted for. God provided for a righteousness of obedience in two ways: by a law written on the heart, and by a constituted law. The law written on the heart is " natural." Adam had this law, and he disobeyed it. Every other man has it, but he too disobeys it because he is what he is through Adam. The constituted law is that which was given to the chosen people of Israel through Moses. Herein was the possibility of a righteousness other than a " natural " righteousness. But the inability in respect of natural law reached over into the area of constituted law. The Jew's very advantage in having the law of Moses did but serve to render him " without excuse " (ch. 2:1). All alike, the Gentile with his conscience and the Jew with his law, " have sinned " (ch. 3:23), and all alike are " under the judgment of God " (ch. 3:19). The result is the certainty of all men being lost on account of unrighteousness. The only hope left is in the grace of God. " For God hath shut up all unto disobedience, that he might have mercy upon all " (ch. 11:32).

The grace and mercy of God are revealed through another form of substitution. Over against Adam is set Jesus Christ. Over against Adam's disobedience, which renders all men subject to sin and death, is set the perfect obedience of Jesus Christ, which, being " reckoned " to men, brings about their reconciliation to God. The substitution is not because of any obligation God is under. He makes it of his own free will, and because he is gracious. The failure of the son he created, Adam, with all its tragic consequences, is compensated by the triumph of the Son whom he did not create, but " sent " to be " a propitiatory," to set forth God's own perfect righteousness by showing that it is a righteousness that must always be satisfied if sin is to be forgiven. The God who attaches results to sin receives those results into himself, as the evidence not only of his righteousness, but of his grace as well — " that, as sin reigned in death, even so might grace reign through righteousness unto eternal life through Jesus Christ our Lord" (ch. 5:21).

This substitution, however, becomes effective only through faith. There is no perfect " natural " righteousness, and there is no perfect " law " righteousness, but there is a perfect " faith " righteousness. The perfection of faith-righteousness is in the fact that it is Christ's own righteousness " reckoned " to the believer. My sins were " reckoned " to Christ through his perfect obedience; his perfect obedience is " reckoned " to me through my faith. God takes him for me, and me for him. Christ the sinless is made to be sin, and I, the sinful, am made to be the righteousness of God in him (ch. 5:17–19; cf. II Cor. 5:21). This, however, is not a mere bookkeeping transaction, a paper transfer without a substantial basis. Faith is not antinomian. Christ's righteousness is " reckoned " to the believer in order that it might be actually reproduced in him. The servant of sin is made " the servant of righteousness unto sanctification " (see Rom. 6:17–23). The life of faith is a life by and in the Spirit, whereby God's eternal purpose to secure " many brethren " who should be " conformed to the image of his Son " is by way of being fulfilled (ch. 8:2 f., 28–30). What is involved in this " conformity " which is the fruit of a true faith is set forth in Rom., ch. 12.

This is in no sense a complete presentation of the argument of the epistle. But it does suggest what Paul undertakes to do. He undertakes to show in what sense the gospel " is the power of God unto salvation to every one that believeth " by relating the gospel to the universal human moral predicament under the dominant concept of substitution. We may not agree with every aspect of his argument. For the modern man, with his quite different idea of human origins, and of the development of the moral consciousness, from anything that was possible to Paul, some of the things that Paul says may be entirely unacceptable. That is not the point. Even the author of II Peter was frank to say that he found in the epistles of Paul " some things hard to be understood " (ch. 3:16), and he has had many successors. All that is being contended for is that the

Epistle to the Romans is an early witness to the Christian faith, made in the form of a carefully constructed argument centering around the concept of substitution, but that what is chiefly important is not the cogency of the argument, which may be questioned, but the fact that its purpose is to show how the gospel " is the power of God unto salvation to every one that believeth."

In Colossians, the movement of thought is radically different. Paul — assuming him to be the author — is writing to a specific situation in a group of churches which have been infected by what he believes is a false philosophy (ch. 2:8). The proof that the philosophy is false is in the fact that it takes Christ from the place of centrality in divine-human relations. The philosophy appears to have been a mixture of Gnostic dualism, Judaistic symbolism, and Mystery Religion rites and ceremonies. It made much of secret knowledge, hidden mysteries, and esoteric procedures. It assumed a gradation of celestial powers in contrast to a gradation of demonic powers. Man through his body was related to the demonic; through his spirit to the celestial. His problem was to subdue the body — " the flesh " — and to release the spirit. To do this required initiation into closely guarded secrets, illumination of the understanding with true wisdom, participation in symbolic rites, the putting on of robes appropriately designed and marked. By faithful engagement in these privileges and obligations, the initiate was assured of freedom from the control of the lower and of progressive appropriation of the celestial with its resources of wisdom and power. In this was redemption, which was therefore largely a matter of what a man did on his own behalf.

In his letter Paul attacks and seeks to undermine this philosophy by showing that what it seeks is already provided for in Jesus Christ. He makes free use of the terms common in the philosophy; alludes continually to the allied practices; and shows that what these terms and practices connote is already more amply provided for in a proper comprehension of Jesus Christ, who is not simply one more in a gradation of celestial powers, but is himself that all-comprehending divine Reality in which all such powers have their own existence. Being dependent upon him, they are therefore subject to his will. The two crucial passages are chs. 1:12–20 and 2:8–15. Throughout the epistle occur such terms as the following: " wisdom "; " understanding "; " knowledge "; " darkness "; " light "; " redemption "; " things visible "; " things invisible "; " the fulness "; " reconciliation "; " the blood "; " without blemish "; " hidden mystery "; " mystery of God "; " the treasures "; " putting off "; " putting on "; " buried in baptism "; " raised "; " the bond "; " the rudiments "; " the old man "; " the new man "; " the girdle of perfection." Such terms were in common use in the type of thought Paul is combating. Colossians is therefore very largely what is known as an *argumentum ad hominem.* That is to say, Paul is speaking to the premises of his opponents. A world view which they put forward as depriving Jesus Christ of his supremacy he makes use of for the exactly opposite purpose. Whatever achieves the end sought by the Colossian philosophy, but manifestly not achieved thereby, will involve a truer philosophy. Faith in Christ as " pre-eminent," as " the image of the invisible God," as that " firstborn " (the *logos* of John 1:1–3) through whom and for whom all things were created, led to the end promised but not reached by the Colossian philosophy. Therefore the truth is in Christ and all that he means.

One says of this what one says of Romans: the significance of the epistle is in what it sets out to do and in the motive of the undertaking, not in the success of the thought structure and its philosophical plausibility. Many would disagree violently with the picture of the universe that Paul makes use of: perhaps Paul himself did not really approve it. But it still remains that what chiefly counts is *why Paul uses it.* He uses it to set forth his faith that in Christ is redemption; that through him is reconciliation to God; and that the mystery of the ages is disclosed according as he reigns in the life of the world.

The philosophical framework in which the Christian faith is set in The Epistle to the Hebrews is apparent on even a casual reading. Although it makes much use of the Jewish sacrificial system, and although it uses that system for the elucidation of Christianity, it goes to Plato for its fundamental principle. That principle may be simply enough stated: *The temporal is the passing shadow or reflection of the abiding eternal.* The Jewish sacrificial system is such a passing shadow, whose substance is in eternal and heavenly realities. Christ and his self-offering, however, is not simply one more shadow. Instead, it is the eternal reality itself. This could be true only as Christ was as he was. What he was is stated in the opening verses of the epistle. He is that Son who images the very substance of God and who is the means whereby God could create and sustain all things. This inseparability of the Son from the very being of the Godhead is central to the Christian faith. It sets its tone, because such inseparability is the presupposition of the incarnation — " the Word come to be flesh " — and consequently of redemption. In the epistle this relation of the Son to God is treated as the philosophical requirement to making intelligible the claim that Christ and his self-offering are not one more example of a common fact that reflects the eternal, but that this is the eternal reality that is everywhere reflected every time a priest offers a sacrifice for sin, and not only reflected but also anticipated as to its final appearance and enactment in time.

It is obvious that what we have here is an expression of the mind of an early Hellenistic Jewish Christian, writing for other Jewish Christians who needed to be held steady in their faith (see Heb. 10:19–39). The Greek of this epistle is the best Greek in the New Testament. The quotations from the Old Testament are always made from the Greek translation — the so-called Septuagint. The writer was a man of culture. He discloses a well-disciplined mind. There is every reason to believe that he moved in intellectual circles — perhaps the Jewish-Hellenistic philosophical colony in Alexandria, whose brightest luminary was Philo Judaeus. He has himself become a " partaker of a heavenly calling " (see ch. 3:1), and he was concerned to help others, also partakers, against the neglect of " so great a salvation " (ch. 2:3) and against resting easily in " first principles " instead of pressing on " unto perfection " (ch. 6:1). The epistle is a piece of finely conceived exposition and edification.

As already said, the ultimate frame of reference used by the writer is "the heavenly realities" understood after the fashion of Plato. These realities are the uncreated and unchangeable "ideas" in which lies the possibility of whatever is created in time or of whatever can happen in time. Applied to Old Testament institutions and ceremonies, this can only mean that they are themselves temporal in their nature, but that they point to a reality that is not temporal. More specifically, the Old Testament priest reflected an eternal Priest, but the earthly priest, being subject to death, continued only for a time. The Old Testament sacrifices reflected an eternal Sacrifice, but they availed only for a little while, and needed to be often repeated. The Old Testament tabernacle — the place of offering — reflected an eternal Tabernacle, but since it was "made with hands" it was only "an example of the true." Therefore upon the Old Testament priesthood, the Old Testament sacrifices, the Old Testament tabernacle and altar, lay the necessary stamp of the imperfection of mortality. The most solemn of all Old Testament ceremonies, the annual Day of Atonement itself, charged as it was with a symbolic significance unimaginably rich, was but a shadow of the real. Even that original covenant with Abram upon which all Old Testament religion was predicated, did but reflect an eternal Covenant, and was therefore imperfect and the prediction of a "better" (chs. 8:6; 9:15).

This "better" Covenant — (the word "better" occurs frequently in the epistle) — involves that there shall be a "better" Priest, a "better" Sacrifice, a "better" Altar. Only He can be that who himself belongs of native right in the very center of the divine, eternal, heavenly realities. Such a One is "a Son" (chs. 1:1–4; 3:5, 6), who is "better" than all else — better than angels, better than Moses, better than any high priest. But to make his intrinsic superiority effective, he must make himself one with men, because only so could he be their Priest, representing not only God to men but also men to God. Such a Priest would be not after the Aaronic order, of which there were many, but after the order of Melchizedek, that strange, mysterious figure of an ancient day, who came none knew

whence and returned none knew whither, one "without genealogy" (ch. 7:3), whose function in the providence of God
was to foreshadow the uniquely solitary priest of the Melchizedek order. This was Jesus Christ, the Son of God, "made . . .
after the power of an indissoluble life" (ch. 7:16), who, "because he abideth for ever, hath his priesthood unchangeable"
(v. 24), as no Aaronic priest could ever have.

What did Jesus Christ, being such a priest, offer? He offered,
not the scapegoat offered by the high priest on the annual Day
of Atonement, but himself. Where did he make his offering?
He made it, not on an altar built by hands, but in that heavenly Holy of Holies toward which all sacrifices offered by men
are directed, but which they can never actually reach. What
did the perfect Self-offering of the perfect Priest in the perfect
heavenly Tabernacle accomplish? It accomplished for men "an
eternal redemption" (ch. 9:12), and at the same time, in keeping with the unchangeable law that "apart from the shedding
of blood there is no remission" (v. 22), created and sealed
"a new covenant." What follows from such a self-offering of
such a Priest at the very heart of the eternal world and securing such a redemption? It follows that the offering needs not
to be repeated and cannot be repeated (ch. 9:25–28). It is
an offering made once and for always and for one and for
all. The Priest is eternal; the Offering is eternal; the Tabernacle is eternal; the propitiation is eternal; the redemption is
eternal; the Covenant is eternal. "He, when he had offered
one sacrifice for sins for ever, sat down on the right hand of
God. . . . By one offering he hath perfected for ever them
that are sanctified" (ch. 10:12, 14). Here is "a new and living
way" to the fellowship of man and God. It is a sacrificial way
created by God through his eternal Son consenting "in all
things to be made like unto his brethren" (ch. 2:17), and
"though he was a Son, yet learned obedience by the things
which he suffered" (ch. 5:8). Such a "way" was foreshad-
owed and anticipated by all the imperfect "ways" that had
gone before, and in this new, living, and perfect "way" the
foreshadowings and anticipations are fulfilled.

We cannot but be impressed with the magnificent sweep of

the mind of this early unknown Christian witness. What he writes represents an intellectual effort to throw his faith into a clarifying, impressive, and convincing form. The result is a truly arresting philosophy of the Christian faith — perhaps the first such philosophy. The characteristic features of the Jewish religion, and the fundamental principle of the philosophy of Plato, are laid under tribute for the formation of a thought structure that will support that finality and supremacy of Jesus Christ which faith makes central to the gospel. It is a thought structure that relates Jesus Christ to God by the necessities of the divine nature; which relates him to man by virtue of the fact that these same necessities provide for his voluntary entering upon the human lot; which finds in this twofold relationship both the universality and the permanence of his sacrificial self-offering. The thought structure shows the eternal acting in time in and through the Incarnate Son, so that such action of the eternal in time was also, and of necessity, an acting of the eternal upon itself. In one and the same self-revealing and world-redeeming Act, Creator and created, eternal and temporal, the eternal Son and the Son in the flesh learning by experience the " tears of things " (see ch. 5:7), are equally involved, but the Act is initiated by the Creator and constitutes his own personal presence within his creation to redeem, transform, and perfect it.

Romans, Colossians, Hebrews: these are three different expositions of one and the same basic faith. The faith is that in Jesus Christ the one God sacrificially disclosed himself to accomplish the redemption of men, in changing them from rebellious and self-willed creatures into loving and obedient sons. These three writings expound the same gospel. They passed into the life of the Early Church, where they were reverently regarded and carefully preserved. Yet they are anything but identical in their procedures. The only constraint the writers were under was that of the faith to which they were bearing witness. Outside of that, they implicitly claimed a wide range of freedom. The reader may claim a similar range of freedom in his attitude to the forms in which these writers gave expression to their witnessing. There is a familiar saying that every man is born either a Platonist or an Aristotelian. The born Platonist will revel in Hebrews; the born Aristotelian may have some grave doubts, but his doubts will respect, not the writer's faith, but the formal way in which he sets it forth. Indeed, it might be a matter of regret that there was not included in the New Testament an epistle that set forth the gospel by the help of the Aristotelian philosophy. Thinking of Thomas Aquinas, one could hardly say that such an epistle *could not* have been written!

For the Biblical literalist, the use of various "frames of reference" by the New Testament writers creates a serious problem. If he wants to insist on the "inspiration" and consequently upon the "authority" of Paul's theory of "Adam" and of "law" in Romans, he can hardly do less for the "Gnostic dualism" of Colossians and for the "Platonism" of Hebrews. This might lead into awkward complications, complications readily avoided by recognizing the "freedom" of the New Testament writers in their choice of a *methodology* of their witnessing. Paul was "all things to all men," and the principle was operative in his presentation of the kerygma, whether he was confronting the pagans of Lycaonia (Acts 14:5–18), or the Athenians in the Areopagus (ch. 17:15–31), or the Ephesians in the school of Tyrannus (ch. 19:8–10), or the angry mob of Jews before the Tower of Antonia ("the castle" of ch. 21:34), or the curious and inquiring Agrippa (ch. 26:1–29). As "the bondservant of Jesus Christ," he had no other desire than to "preach him," in season and out — to preach him as the Son of God crucified and risen on behalf of sinners, to live "in Christ" and "for Christ," and to know Christ as living in him "by his Spirit." But "the preaching," whether spoken or written, was according to the situation and according to the immediate purpose, and Paul had no doubt about his right to determine what that required. Herein was his "liberty of prophesying." He would have been the last man to deny a similar "liberty" to others. So long as there was "the same Spirit," a wide-ranging "diversity" of "ministration," of "workings," of "manifestation," was not only proper; it was inevitable in a "body" which, although itself "one," had

" many members," each the complement of the others (I Cor. 12:1 ff.).

We can but repeat, on the basis of the variety present in the New Testament itself, that the gospel, understood as God's self-revealing and redeeming action in Jesus Christ, made effective only by faith since it is only to faith that it is apprehensible — that this gospel is one thing, and its varied presentation, exposition, and application, even in this same New Testament, is another. If what has been brought out above concerning Romans, Colossians, and Hebrews does not mean this, then it is difficult to see what it does mean. The different forms of the different expositions have their own proper function, but the function is not that of so many rigid molds in which all future expositions must be run. In the New Testament one finds utter loyalty to the gospel combined with freedom and variety of interpretation. The modern interpreter, provided he displays the same utter loyalty, may rightly claim and exercise the same freedom. For example, a recent writer has made a notable attempt to use the contemporary " philosophy of organicism " as a framework within which to set the Christian faith. In view of New Testament procedures, does anyone dare to challenge his right to make this attempt? " What matters, so Christ be preached? " (cf. Phil. 1:15–18).

The most perfect illustration of this combined loyalty and freedom is provided by the Fourth Gospel. It is difficult to see how anyone with the Fourth Gospel before him could be a Biblical literalist, to whom " form " and " substance " were indistinguishable, either in themselves or in their absolute authority. The author of the Fourth Gospel follows his own course in his own way. He treats the gospel with an originality with which it is nowhere else treated in the New Testament. We owe to him the most profoundly Christian book ever written. In language unbelievably simple he brings to the surface the truths that lie in the deep places of thought and of existence. The little child can read them understandingly; the keenest mind admits that the apparent horizons of meaning recede as he approaches them. " Leagues beyond those leagues, there is more sea." The Christian faith was never more attractively and persuasively presented than here. The timeless is made timely in a fashion that must forever remain the despair of the less richly endowed. Nobody will ever write another Gospel fit to stand side by side with the Fourth. We could be deprived of the New Testament, but if the Fourth Gospel were left to us the substance of the New Testament would still be ours. We should still know the truth that makes men free.

Yet we do not know definitely who wrote this book, or when, or where. His name appears to have been John — but which John? Discussion on that point is endless. The determination of many to identify John the son of Zebedee, "the beloved disciple," and the author of the Fourth Gospel, betrays a fear that unless the author were a personal disciple of Jesus, his Gospel lacks authenticity. But why? Luke was not a personal disciple of Jesus; Mark is at best an echo of Peter; and there are no very good reasons for identifying Matthew the tax collector (the "Levi" of Luke 5:27; cf. Matt. 9:9) with the "Matthew" of the Gospel bearing that name. To assume that to write such a book as the Fourth Gospel the author must have known Jesus intimately "after the flesh" is to question the interpretive value of practically every epistle in the New Testament. Paul may have "seen" Jesus, and may even have "heard" him, but he was certainly not a disciple until his Damascus experience. The probability that the Fourth Gospel was written in the last decade of the first century would make the writer a very old man if he were John the son of Zebedee. It is true that here and there the writer seems to possess a knowledge that only a disciple could have had, but there is nothing of that kind in his book which he could not have learned from others. The writer was quite clearly a member of the Christian Community; long before he wrote, the Gospels of Mark, Matthew, and Luke were in circulation in the Church; the events of the life of Jesus were common knowledge among Christians; and for the purpose of this writer — be he "John" or another — this common knowledge was all that he needed.

For he did not set out to write one more account of the life of Jesus after the manner of the Synoptists. If he did, then he signally failed. With all their differences, the Synoptics permit of being arranged as a " Harmony." The extent to which this can be done may be seen in Huck's *Synopsis* (still the most useful). But it would be utterly impossible to incorporate the Fourth Gospel into such an arrangement. The bulk of what is found in the Fourth Gospel is not found in the Synoptics at all, or if it is, it is found (usually) in a different form. It may well be that the account of the Capernaum nobleman's son in John 4:46 ff. deals with the incident of the centurion's servant in Luke 7:1 ff., but who can miss the differences? The long discourses in the Fourth Gospel have nothing comparable to them in the Synoptics. We have no least reason to suppose that the long high-priestly prayer of John, ch. 17 is a verbatim report of a continuous prayer uttered by Jesus. On the other hand, there is in the Fourth Gospel nothing like the so-called " Sermon on the Mount " (Matt., chs. 5 to 7). The Fourth Gospel omits practically all the miracles found in the Synoptics. The exceptions are two: the walking on the sea (ch. 6:15 ff., and found in Matthew and Mark), and the feeding of the five thousand (ch. 6:1–14, and found in all the Synoptics). But found only in the Fourth Gospel are four, possibly five: the water made wine (ch. 2:1 ff.); the impotent man at Bethesda (ch. 5:1 ff.); the man born blind (ch. 9:1 ff.); the raising of Lazarus (ch. 11:38 ff.); the fifth is the nobleman's son (ch. 4:46 ff.) if this be not the same as the centurion's servant of Luke 7:1 ff. It is significant that these four miracles peculiar to the Fourth Gospel are all susceptible of symbolic interpretation. In respect of parables, it is a striking fact that the Fourth Gospel records none, although it has the three extended metaphors of the living bread (ch. 6:32 ff.), the shepherd, fold, and door (ch. 10:1 ff.), and the vine and branches (ch. 15:1 ff.), besides numerous brief similes. Moreover, the Fourth Gospel shows no particular interest in chronology or in proportion. It is the only one of the Gospels that indicates that the public ministry might have continued for almost three years as against the barely more than one year of the Synoptics, yet the writer devotes only eleven of his chapters to this long period. From ch. 12:1 to ch. 20:31 he is concerned with the events of the closing week, and with the resurrection. The closing chapter (ch. 21)has the appearance of being a supplement: it deals with the late "manifestation" at the Sea of Tiberias.

All this suggests that the author was very far from supposing that he was writing one more Gospel in the style of Matthew, Mark, or Luke. He does, in fact, frankly say that he selected his material, and that he dealt with it in his own way and for a particular purpose (ch. 20:30, 31). "These are written, that ye may believe that Jesus is the Christ, the Son of God; and that believing ye may have life in his name." He is admittedly an interpreter rather than a narrator. He has seen the gospel at work in the world for some half a century. He knows the Church from within. He is himself aware of the Spirit's presence. He has the advantage of looking at what Jesus said and did from the standpoint of the experience of these many years.

In addition, he has the philosophic mind. He sees things in their relations. He has patiently pondered the gospel and its fruits. Under his prolonged meditations these have gradually fitted into a pattern. It is undoubtedly true that the pattern reveals a Platonic cast, but this can be exaggerated. The author of the Fourth Gospel is not simply "a Christian Platonist of Alexandria." He writes much that Alexandrianism would never tolerate. He has a world view, but it is a world view much more determined by the Christian faith than by even a modified Platonism. His interest is centered in man and in what Jesus Christ can admittedly do for him, and in what Jesus Christ must be in himself to be able to do it. He has a *logos* doctrine, but he does not interpret Jesus Christ according to a prior understanding of the *logos:* rather, his understanding of the *logos* is reached through what he knows that God has accomplished in Jesus Christ. He wants men to see not only that Jesus Christ was "the Word [*logos*] come to be flesh," but what must be the nature of the *logos,* and consequently of God himself in his totality, that it belonged to him to "become flesh," and what was the effect upon God of this *logos* experience, and what was the reason for his enduring it.

His interest in man is what chiefly leads him to fasten on

the concept of *eternal life*. He sets in contrast two kinds of life: life that is " of the flesh," life that is " of the Spirit." The one is perishing life; the other is eternal life. The conceptions are qualitative primarily, durational only secondarily. Perishing life is life lived according to the flesh; eternal life is life lived according to the Spirit. Christ came to give to men eternal life. To pass from one quality of life to the other quality of life is " salvation." Where the Synoptists speak of Christ as the bearer of the Kingdom of God, the author of the Fourth Gospel speaks of him as the bearer of eternal life. Christ could bring eternal life to men because he was in himself Eternal Life. He came from God in order that men might find God through him. All the "mighty works" and many of the "mighty words" of the Fourth Gospel are analogous to this transition. The water and wine of the Cana marriage; the birth of the flesh and the birth of the Spirit of the Nicodemus interview; the water from the well and the living water of the conversation at Sychar; the impotent man and the whole man of the Bethesda pool; the barley loaves and the living bread of the miracle of the feeding; the blind eyes and the opened eyes of the pool of Siloam; the incident of Lazarus dead and Lazarus raised to life — all such words and works illustrate or emphasize the contrast between life from which Christ is absent and life in which he is present. Repeatedly throughout the Fourth Gospel we meet some form of the statement that Christ came into the world to bring to men eternal life. Eternal life is the realization of that life for which men were intended from the beginning, but to which they could not come of themselves. God provided the *possibility* of this life by the gift of his Son, the Incarnate Word. The possibility passed over into *actuality* according as there were faith and love on the part of men — faith that this is indeed who and what Christ was, and love for him who thus gave himself on man's behalf. " He that believeth on the Son hath eternal life " (ch. 3:36). " He that heareth my word, and believeth him that sent me, hath eternal life, and cometh not into judgment, but hath passed out of death into life " (ch. 5:24).

Words of this meaning are put many times and at varying

lengths upon the lips of Jesus by the author of the Fourth Gospel. Considering the differences of vocabulary between this Gospel and the Synoptics, it is not likely that Jesus used these actual words at all. The author is not *quoting* Jesus: he is expressing in his own language his understanding of the *meaning* of what Jesus said, of the *meaning* of what Jesus did, and of the *meaning* of Jesus' being who he was. The long speeches that Plato puts in the mouth of Socrates in the *Dialogues* are not intended to be verbatim reports. They are Plato's *words,* but they represent Socrates' *mind.* It is not unfair to say that in the Fourth Gospel the author is giving us Jesus as he saw him through years of experience and under the guidance of the Spirit, precisely as he wrote in ch. 14:25, 26, and ch. 15:26, 27. He *knows* that through faith in Jesus Christ men pass from death unto life. He sets himself to present such an interpretation of Jesus Christ as makes intelligible the fact that he accomplishes this and the process by which it is accomplished.

The greatest book in the New Testament is therefore the greatest illustration of the freedom of Christian faith. The Fourth Gospel is a man of faith presenting and interpreting Christ in his own way. We may not ourselves follow his way. We may not care about his analogies. We may not care about the way he makes Jesus talk. But what we cannot escape is the fact that he is a convinced witness of the Christian faith; that this is the form of his witnessing; that it is a form that keeps central things central; and that no suspicion that one might feel about the form of the presentation can ever of itself dispense with, undermine, or destroy what is being presented. " I am the way, and the truth, and the life." Did Jesus actually say this about himself? We have little reason to believe that he did. But is he still the Way, still the Truth, still the Life, even although he may not have *said* that he was? This is the real issue. *What men of faith discovered for themselves about Jesus Christ must always be more important for the purpose of witnessing than a mere report of some statement he may have made about himself.*

To witness to his faith is a constraint laid upon any man who sees in Jesus Christ the ultimate truth of God and the ultimate truth of himself. The form which his witnessing takes will be determined by a variety of circumstances, but the circumstances will never bind him to the extent of robbing him of his right to witness in his own way. This is clearly seen in the most outstanding writings of the New Testament. A corollary of this is our own freedom both in the estimation and use of these writings and in the form and method that we follow in our own witnessing. I can appreciate Paul's theory of the relation between Adam and human sinfulness without feeling any compulsion to approve or to use the theory; and I may give a quite different answer, couched in quite different terms, to the question, How and why do men sin? I can appreciate the way the author of Hebrews makes use of a distinctly Platonic concept as he seeks to relate Christ to the divine-human situation and to show how a reconciliation may be effected. But I may myself not be friendly to the concept, and I may elect to use a different concept altogether in my own presentation of the faith. This is nothing novel, nor is it anything blamable. It is but following the example of the New Testament. For the New Testament is not a mechanical device for shackling the Christian mind: rather, it is a permanent example of the fact that a vital Christian faith has freedom for its offspring.

XIV

FREE FAITH AND THE CHURCH

THE doctrine of the Church is a live issue today. It goes with the interest in what is known as ecumenicity, that is, the question of the unity and universality of the Church. The question is vastly complicated by sharply antagonistic theories of the Church itself. Nothing would more quickly ease the tension that the question always evokes than a recovery of the original Christian faith, with its utter directness, simplicity, and freedom, and a consequent recognition of the fact that *all* organization, *all* procedure, *all* ceremony is, in relation to the Christian faith itself, instrumental and therefore fluid, rather than essential and therefore fixed.

There are two main theories of the Church of the New Testament. Considering the divisions, the controversies, the bitternesses which have arisen in connection with them, so that the place where Christ is chiefly crucified is in the house of his friends, one can only think of the tragedy of Romeo and Juliet, and exclaim, " A plague on both your theories! " Gallant Romeo and gentle Juliet had to die to disclose the folly of their respective houses and to destroy the barrier that kept the families apart. Is this an ominous parable for the Church to consider — ominous, yet hopeful? Is it still so that " apart from shedding of blood there is " — *nothing!* Is it of the purpose of that God who is the God of history as well as the God of the faith that the churches must die that the Church may live?

The two theories of the Church may be stated briefly as follows: (1) The organizational form of the Church as we meet it in the New Testament is of the *esse* (" the being ") of the Church, and this has remained and always will remain unchanged and unchangeable. (2) This organizational form is of the *bene esse* ("the well-being") of the Church, its function being to serve the purposes of the Church as the situation required, with the implication that the organization is not unchangeable, and that, in fact, changes have taken place to the good of the Church.

(1) More fully, the first theory traces the organizational form to the will and purpose of Christ. He founded the Church when he "appointed" the twelve apostles, in due time "breathing" upon them the Holy Spirit to fit them for leadership in the Church, and authorizing them to appoint their own successors and to transmit to them the qualifications he had bestowed upon them. The first ordained appointees of the Twelve were deacons and elders (presbyters). It was from among the elders that the Twelve, as occasion arose, appointed and "ordained" those who were to be "bishops." The bishops were the direct and proper successors of the twelve apostles. The succession has never been broken, and in that unbroken succession — "apostolic succession" — is established the unity, the apostolicity, the catholicity, and the sanctity of the Church. The validity of the sacraments depends upon the validity of the ministry, and only that ministry is valid which is threefold in order and episcopally ordained, thereby reaching back to Christ himself. The priest is a channel of the grace of God. In baptism, the grace operates through him to regenerate, and to incorporate the baptized person with the Church as the body of Christ. Thus baptism is the fundamental Christian rite. The Eucharist, as the sacrament of the body and blood of Christ, whereby the communicant "receives Christ" and is absolved from all his sins, is valid only when administered by a properly qualified priest to a person who has already been baptized. The theory underwent numerous refinements, until it eventuated in the imposing hierarchical, sacramental, and penitential system of the medieval Church.

(2) The second theory does not dispute that the Church early assumed some organization, but holds that the forms adopted were such as seemed to be required for the more effective discharge of its mission on the part of the Church. It

disputes the entire theory of apostolic succession and sacramental validity. It denies that there is any clear evidence that Christ consciously and deliberately created a definite form of organization to be self-perpetuated unchanged for ever, or a sacramental procedure contingent upon it. It denies that the Early Church was organized under only one form. It finds ample evidence for the view that there were churches congregationally governed, churches presbyterially governed, and churches episcopally governed. It claims, however, that there was no difference between the elder (*presbyter*) and the bishop (*episcopus*) except in the range of the supervising function. Local churches were ruled by "elders," men chosen to do this by reason of their maturity, stability, and Christian character. As the need arose for cultivating fellowship between local groups of believers in the same general neighborhood, one or more of the "elders" was charged with the responsibility of encouraging this fellowship by being made an "overseer" of the group. He was called *episkopos,* a Greek word which "overseer" exactly translates. This same simplicity is held to have characterized church procedures. Neither Baptism nor the Lord's Supper was the awesome thing it is made to be under the other view. Baptism was a simple dedicatory rite, certainly not in itself regenerative; and the Lord's Supper was a Christian communal meal, the gathering of the Church for "the breaking of bread." In a word, the primitive Christian Community was essentially a believing brotherhood whose faith, relations, and procedures were characterized by a marked simplicity. For many years, Christians who were Jews — as most early Christians were — continued their synagogue and Temple connections. It was the spread of Christianity among the Gentiles, combined with unceasing tension between Jewish Christians and Jewish non-Christian authorities, and the natural necessities of a spreading Community increasing in numbers and influence, and becoming increasingly self-aware — it was this, more than anything else, that led to the Church's creating its own organizational separateness, its own formal characteristics, its own distinctive procedures.

An original complexity in which faith and form are in effect identical; an original simplicity constituted in faith alone, but devising its own forms as occasion arose — which is it?

What troubles us is the fact that both theories claim to be the reading of the same limited *data.* In attempting to decide between them — if we can! — we are hampered by one of Bacon's *idola* — this time *the illusion of language.* It is impossible — or so it seems — for either a Roman Catholic or a Protestant to read the New Testament with complete objectivity. We look at the New Testament down the corridor of history, and long before our eyes reach the distant object, they have been " conditioned " by what they have seen on the way. One has simply to consider the connotation for most people of the word " church." It at once suggests one of the greatest institutions the world has ever known. It suggests splendid buildings, elaborate rituals, stately processions, sonorous liturgies, transporting music, and all the thousand and one concomitants of the church as it has come to be. At last the eye reaches, say, The Acts of the Apostles, with its frequent references to "the church " (if twenty references can be called "frequent"). But what was this church of The Acts? It had no buildings; it received no generous public recognition; it had no distinctive hymnody; it had no processionals; it had no " paid ministry " in any sense approaching what appeared later; it had no liturgical services; it had no theory of sacramental grace. It certainly had no images, no stained glass windows, no organ, no carillon, no high pulpit, no marble altar decorated with gold. It had nothing of what " the church " means to most people today — except one thing. And the one thing it did have — *a faith* — is the one thing that all too often is not present in the modern connotation of " the church."

The church of The Acts was in sober fact a simple Community of believing men and women, or a given group of such communities, or the totality of such communities. The Community existed by virtue of a common faith in Jesus Christ as Saviour and Lord. Membership in the Community was conditioned on the profession of such faith, and the acceptance of its obligations. The natural leaders of the Community were the apostles, but, apart from the general reference in Acts 1:13, only three of them are ever again mentioned in Acts by name, Peter, James, and John. Matthias vanishes after his election (ch. 1:26). By any calculation the most effective and far-ranging leader of the Early Church was Paul, who was an "ecclesiastical irregular," not having been one of the original Twelve, and not having been "episcopally ordained." What "laying on of hands" Paul knew was by "prophets and teachers" (ch. 13:1–3). A theory of "the apostolate" that cannot find a place for Paul — to say nothing of Barnabas and Silas — might very well re-examine its premises. The early expansion of the Christian faith was due much less to the apostles who *stayed in Jerusalem* (ch. 8:1–4) than it was to the rank and file who, scattered by persecution, "went about preaching the word." Early Christianity began as essentially *a lay movement*. We see that it could not but have been so the moment we realize that what Jesus chiefly talked about was "the Kingdom of God," never "the church," and that what he was concerned to do was not to create any organization, but to let loose upon the world a new faith, a new life, a new power, a new relation of God to men and of men to men, of which would come a new Brotherhood. "Wait for the Spirit," he said, in answer to a question which was, in the thought of the questioners, equivalent to asking, "Dost thou at this time establish the church and assign us our positions?" (cf. Matt. 20:20–28): "Wait for the Spirit," he said, and he told them why. They would then become his "witnesses" in all the world (Acts 1:4–8). This was all he was concerned about: anything more would take care of itself — *as it did*. But all that, the offices, the organization, the procedures, the varied ministrations, was *consequential*, not *originative and constitutive*. It is this that we have overlooked, to our great confusion.

A similar linguistic illusion attends the word "bishop." We tend to identify the "bishops" of the New Testament with the bishops of the later Church. The attempt to transform the "appointing" and "commissioning" of the Twelve into a solemn "ordination" ceremony, such as characterizes "episcopal" bodies, is a clear case of "reading back" into a perfectly natural procedure a meaning that there is no least reason to suppose it had at the time. One has only to consider the first reported " gathering " of " the brethren " after Jesus' final departure to realize how lacking it was in any so-called " apostolic authority." It was necessary to choose someone to take the place of Judas Iscariot. The requirement was that he should have been one of the companions of Jesus from the beginning. Two names were presented, neither of which is mentioned anywhere in the Gospels, namely, Joseph Justus and Matthias. The choice was made " by lot," and went to Matthias. It is not clear whether the use of the lot was limited to the Eleven, or whether it was extended to the entire one hundred and twenty " brethren," but the latter seems to be the implication. In that case, the first reported official appointment in the history of the Church was by democratic congregational procedure! Curiously enough, the " unsuccessful candidate " is the only one of the two whose name is ever again mentioned in the New Testament! (See Acts 15:22, 27, 32.) Throughout the story in The Acts, it is quite evident that there was a recognition of the *leadership* of at least Peter, James, and John of the original Twelve, but this leadership rarely assumed what might be called an *ecclesiastical* quality. The visit of Peter and John to the Samaritan converts of Philip the evangelist is an exception (ch. 8:14–17). The Jerusalem decision concerning Gentile Christians was " written " by James, but in consultation with " the apostles and the elders, with the whole church " (see ch. 15:1 ff.). There was certainly nothing there to suggest that any " primacy " attached to Peter, nor is this suggested anywhere else in the New Testament. On the contrary, the " Judaizers " sharply criticized him (ch. 11:1 ff.); he made one of the " pleas " at the Jerusalem council (ch. 15:7 ff.); and for his wavering on the Gentile issue he was " talked to " by Paul at Antioch in a way hardly indicating any recognized " primacy."

Nevertheless, the word " bishop " confronts us in the New Testament, in both The Acts and the Epistles. There are modern churches that have a modified episcopal system, but, curiously enough, few people seem to think of the leaders of this modified system when they meet the word " bishop " in the New Testament. They think rather of the leaders of the highly organized liturgical and hierarchical churches, and the word is heavily loaded by this fact. They think of men adorned with rich robes, who carry an official staff, who wear a miter, who live in palaces, who have the control of huge funds and often of landed property, who can by a word affect the policies of nations, whose authority approaches the absolute, who have a retinue of followers, who may be recognized by others groveling before them in abject humility. Men such as this appear, or may appear, before a countless number of minds, at the mere sight or mention of the word "bishop." That there have been an abundance of such figures in Church history is simple fact; that the bishops of the New Testament resemble them is simple fantasy. Turn to the account in Acts, ch. 20, of Paul's farewell address to a group called "the elders of the church at Ephesus." The word rendered "elders" is the Greek *presbuteroi* (presbyters). During the address, Paul says: "Take heed unto yourselves, and to all the flock, in which the Holy Spirit hath made you bishops to feed the church of the Lord which he purchased with his own blood" (v. 28). The word rendered "bishops" is the Greek *episkopoi*. The two words are manifestly used as synonyms, a fact which has always troubled the hierarchists. Paul addresses his Epistle to the Philippians to "the saints in Christ Jesus that are at Philippi, with the bishops and deacons" (ch. 1:1). Does this mean that the Philippian church had no elders, but several bishops and deacons? Or does it not rather mean that the same men are called "elders" and "bishops" indiscriminately? If there were several bishops in one little church, the "bishopric" or "episcopate" must have been very different from what it became later. John Wesley's "class leaders" were probably a close analogy to the "bishops" ("overseers") of the Philippian church. For those whom the suggestion might offend, the analogy could be changed to that of "the ruler of the synagogue" in Judaism (Luke 13:14; cf. 4:17, 20). The office of "elder" or "bishop" of the Early Church was indeed, in all likelihood, a carry-over from that of the ruler of the synagogue.

That the office and function of the primitive "ruling elder" was the basis for the enormous development of the "episcopate " of the second century, and increasingly so later, is the probable fact. That there was this enlargement is a simple matter of history, which cannot be denied. Objection, however, must always be taken to the claim that what the " episcopate " developed *into* was identical in all fundamental respects with that which it developed *from*. It is highly probable that the original Christian " ruling elders," with perhaps the added function of " teaching elders," were men who earned their own living, and that the same applied to those elders who were charged with a more extended supervision. In fact, one may surmise that these early " overseers " were men of such economic limitations and of such unpretentious official duties that many a modern bishop who thinks of himself as like unto them, and of them as like unto himself, would flatly refuse the office if it were offered to him with the same conditions that attended the office of " overseer " in, say, Ephesus or Philippi.

Nothing of this is intended as a severe, harsh, or hypercritical judgment. Anything but that. A very strong case may be made for the claim that historically the " episcopate " has proved itself of the *bene esse* of the Church. There have been periods when it is doubtful if the Church could have survived without its integrating influence. The work of Augustine and of Gregory the Great, institutionalists as they were, was epochal. A student of Church history can have nothing but unmitigated contempt for great numbers of individual bishops (he has but to read Coulton!); he can have nothing but profound appreciation of the episcopate *as an institution*. In initiating and developing the office the Church did itself a great service. All that is being claimed here is that, like other forms, it was a *Church device*. What sanction it has is the sanction of that fact. To say that there cannot be a Church without it is to say what is not true. Untold numbers of the followers of Christ have lived their lives, nurtured their faith, and maintained their fellowship with their Lord, without the benefit of this device. They have been content to create and use other devices. In fact, many of them have deliberately abandoned the instrumentality of the episcopate as it came to be, just because they were convinced that it had become a hindrance to the cause of Christ in the world instead of a help. "By their fruits ye shall know them" is not only a sound test of a Christian *disciple:* it is equally a sound test of any Christian form, any Christian institution, any Christian polity. The whole intent of this book is to show that the ultimate issue of the Biblical faith is Christian freedom. The man for whom his faith-relation to Jesus Christ as the self-disclosure of God is the one great fact that profoundly matters is a free man in respect of all else, and all men of like faith with him are equally free. These are the Church, the only Church the New Testament knows as the body of Christ. On this Church Christ laid no other obligation than to be his "witnesses" for the increase of the witnessing body, the Redeemed Community (Luke 24:48; Acts 1:8). How to strengthen the will to witness, how to make the witnessing effective — these are matters for the Church to determine with the sought guidance of the Holy Spirit. The Church, because its faith sets it free, will create its own forms, devise its own instrumentalities, establish its own procedures. But it will not be the helpless victim of its own devisings. What the Church devised the Church can modify, change, abandon, replace. No such devising is of the *esse* of the Church.

Two forms attended the Church from the beginning — baptism and "the breaking of bread." There is no evidence of any uniformity in the *mode* of early Christian baptism. Nothing can be proved from the Greek word *baptizo,* which could mean dip, pour, sprinkle, soak, drench, immerse, wash, and so on. What seems likely is that the candidate stood in or by water, and that water was then splashed, poured, or sprinkled upon him. The ceremonial washings of the Pharisees were sometimes called "baptisms." They were symbols of purification. On the walls of the catacombs are pictures portraying early Christian practices. A picture of a baptism shows the ministrant pouring water upon the head of the candidate. The church at Corinth was sharply divided about the procedure in baptism, a fact which led Paul to write his important passage about his own detached attitude to the ceremony (I Cor. 1:13–17). In the accounts of Paul's missionary journeys, there are only two or three references to baptism (Acts 16:33; 18:8; 19:1–7). The meaning of Gal. 3:27 is somewhat enigmatic: " For as many of you as were baptized into Christ did put on Christ." It could hardly mean, in view of I Cor. 1:13–17, that Paul supposed that baptism *as such* changed pagans into Christians. Only if baptism really were *into* Christ did the baptized *put on* Christ. Baptism by water stood for baptism by the Holy Spirit, this being the form in which Christ was possessed, and if the second did not occur, the first was useless.

The New Testament does, in fact, seem to support the following conclusions: (1) Baptism by water and baptism by the Holy Spirit *could* coincide, but the coincidence was not invariable. (2) There could be baptism by water and still no baptism by the Holy Spirit, as in the case of those of Corinth who, baptized though they were, so wrangled about baptism as to show that the Holy Spirit had never touched them. (3) And there could be baptism by the Holy Spirit where there had been no baptism by water. The *locus classicus* is the story of Cornelius and his household as told in the great missionary chapter, Acts, ch. 10. As Peter, with some reservations, was preaching to this Gentile family, " the Holy Spirit fell on all them that heard the word " (v. 44). The fact amazed Peter and his companions: unbaptized Gentiles were baptized by the Holy Spirit! The water baptism *followed,* but what difference did it make beyond being a sign of admission to the Christian Fellowship? Peter might conceivably have suffered a revulsion of feeling (cf. Gal. 2:11 f.), and refused the water baptism, but would that have rescinded the Spirit baptism? Hardly. No action of man can make invalid an action of God! The Church of the New Testament regarded baptism as a rite of initiation into its fellowship. Whether it automatically guaranteed vital participation in that faith which created the Fellowship was another question. As a matter of fact, it did not do so, and it could not have done so. No rite can assure a faith-relation, and a faith-relation cannot be hindered by the non-occurrence of a rite, or its so-called faulty administration. The only faith that can unite the soul with Christ, and hence with the Church considered in its inwardness, is the soul's own faith.

The bearing of this on the custom of infant baptism is obvious. The inwardness of the Church is answered by its outwardness. Infant baptism means incorporation into the outwardness, but this leaves for a future time to determine whether there is to be incorporation into the inwardness. There are good reasons for infant baptism, but the supposition that salvation is thereby assured to the infant is not one of them. The claim of baptismal regeneration — which means the salvation of one by the prescribed action of another — springs from those processes of self-organization which led to the creation of the hierarchical system and through that of sacramentarianism. It would save much confusion, much false supposition, much Christian lethargy, and would lay upon parents, sponsors, and the Church alike a much more exacting obligation, if the term " infant baptism " were to be abandoned entirely, and replaced with the much more meaningful term, " infant dedication."

The breaking of bread was the second form in use in the Early Church. One speaks of it with great caution and restraint because such deep-seated emotions gather around it. Considering the later history of the form, however, one cannot but be astonished at the sparseness of the New Testament references, and their lack of clarity. The one or two references to " the breaking of bread " in The Acts (chs. 2:42, 46; 20:7) might be to an ordinary common meal participated in by Christians, an illustration of the " all things common " of Acts 2:44, or to a meal specifically designed for observing the Last Supper. It is chiefly to what Paul writes in I Cor. 10:14 to 11:34 that we owe our knowledge of the fact that at least at Corinth there was such a specifically designed meal. But the description indicates little of what the Supper later became in the Church as sacerdotalism and hierarchism were developed. In Corinth, according to Paul, the Church was wont to assemble for a meal commemorating the Last Supper. The members brought their own food and drink, and this led to ostentation and excess, even to disorder. Paul undertook to correct these abuses by reminding them of the utter simplicity of the Last Supper Jesus ate with his disciples, and of the purpose of it. To recover this simplicity and purpose, the Corinthians should satisfy their hunger at home, and then assemble in a becoming way for the commemoration.

We notice (1) that there is no clear statement of the necessity of some official or priestly consecration of the food and drink, and that while the " cup " is " blessed " and the " bread " is broken, each person apparently does this for himself; (2) that there is no clear statement that because at the Last Supper Jesus used bread and wine to convey his instructions, Paul therefore supposed that only bread and wine were to be used at the simplified meal; and (3) that there is no clear statement that the members were not to bring their own food and drink for the simplified meal, since they would find it already provided by some designated persons. What Paul chiefly emphasizes is that when Jesus said, " This is my body," he meant, " This is I." The broken bread meant the shattered life; the outpoured wine meant that the life would be shattered by the shedding of the blood. To eat the bread and drink the wine was to represent participation in Christ as sacrificed. The fruit of such participation is, for Paul, unity. Christ is one; the participants are one; hence the Church is one.

There are two related questions. One of them has to do with the language used by Jesus at the Last Supper. How complicated the textual problem is may be seen in the detailed study by Kenyon and Legge in *The Ministry and the Sacraments* (Edited by Headlam and Dunkerley, pp. 271–287). There are actually two traditional forms of the so-called " language of institution." One is that of Mark, probably the earliest form, and doubtless derived from Peter (Mark 14:22–25). Matthew virtually repeats Mark. The most important difference is the adding of " unto remission of sins " to Mark's " for many." Paul follows the Marcan order, but uses language noticeably different. It would seem that Paul and Mark represent two different traditions, Paul being strongly influenced by Luke. But the Lucan account exists in two forms, a shorter and a longer. Early MSS. divide fairly evenly between them. The shorter Lucan form closely resembles Mark. Where the longer Lucan form differs from Mark is in the points in which it chiefly resembles Paul. Since both Mark and Paul are earlier than Luke,

it is evident that Luke represents an effort to utilize the two oldest forms of the tradition — Mark and Paul. This would seem to give the longer form of Luke a preference over the shorter form, since it adds to the shorter form something which Paul supposed to be lacking from Mark. The nearest we can come to what actually happened at the Last Supper is probably by a combination of Mark and Paul as attempted in Luke. But where are we then? We are then in the position of not being certain that we have an exact verbal account of "the language of institution," while yet the dogmatic sacerdotal view of the Supper — whether it be called the Eucharist or the Mass — *not only assumes that we have but loses much of its force if we have not.*

A second related question has to do with Jesus' intent at the Last Supper. The common supposition is that he was deliberately and consciously instituting a formal sacrament. But was he? The "linguistic illusion" that applies to "church" and "bishop" applies also here. We take to our reading of the New Testament accounts the bias created by that form and theory of the commemoration with which we ourselves are most familiar. We are all sure that what we think and do about it is what Jesus himself intended that we should think and do. It is evident that we cannot all be right, and it is possible that we are all wrong. Yet "the Lord's Table" is the most divisive single factor in the organized Church!

May it not be that we have made out of the Last Supper what Jesus did not intend, and that what he did intend we have missed? "Do this in remembrance of me." Do what? "This is the last time we shall drink wine together as we drink it now. The next time we drink it together will be in *a new way* [the meaning of Greek word *kainon*] in the Kingdom of God" (see Matt. 26:29). Is this perchance Jesus' way of suggesting the transformation of even the commonplaces of life that will come with the Kingdom of God? *The permanent presence of Christ with his people under a new form and in a new way* — is this what Jesus' actions at the Last Supper are intended to express? The disciples will soon lose his physical presence. But that will not mean that he cannot still be with them. The author of the Fourth Gospel, looking back over many years of experience, and even undertaking to correct some misinterpretations, says precisely this in his retelling of the last interview (chs. 13 to 17). " I will not leave you orphans: I come unto you " (John 14:18). Where? Anywhere. When? Anywhen. " This is my body. I will replace it by another body which will be different, but its equivalent. *This* body will pass, and you see me no more. *That* body, invisible, ubiquitous, indestructible, will include you. Because it lives, that is, because I live, ye shall live also." The ordinary round of life, and its ordinary necessities, of which eating and drinking are taken as representative — all this is to be " reminiscent " of Christ, all this is to become an activity of Christ's new " body." So again: " Do this in remembrance of me. Whatever you do, wherever you go, with whomever you are, remember that you are bought with a price, that you belong to me, that you are my body, that you are my witnesses, that you are the only means whereby I can continue to be active in the world." Briefly, in the intent of Jesus the Last Supper was a dramatized representation and anticipation of the Kingdom of God as consisting in the permanent " witness," " togetherness," " unity," of Christ and his people as one body. " *As they were eating*, he took bread, and when he had blessed, he brake it, and gave to them, and said, Take ye: this is my body " (see Mark 14:22). And Paul's comment: " The bread which we break, is it not a communion [a one-with-ness] of the body of Christ? seeing that we who are many, are one bread, one body: for we all partake of the one bread " (I Cor. 10:16, 17). The conclusion is so inevitable: " Whether therefore ye eat, or drink, or whatsoever ye do, do all to the glory of God " (v. 31).

If this be called a forced interpretation, then let it be noted that the three " appearances " of the Risen Christ to his disciples that are described in most detail are all connected with a meal; not with a meal set up for the occasion, but one which would have taken place in any event. They are the self-disclosure to the Emmaus disciples (Luke 24:13 ff.); the self-disclosure to the Eleven while they " sat at meat " (Mark 16:14; Luke 24: 24, 43); and the self-disclosure at the Sea of Tiberias

(John 21:1 ff.). Can it be that these three experiences represent the fundamental meaning of the Last Supper, namely, a representation of the great truth of the presence of Christ with the men of faith in the common round and the daily task, and, by consequence, such an attitude toward the common round and the daily task as that by means of them Christ is declared? And if this is not what the author of the Fourth Gospel is saying in his sixth chapter, in his interpretation and application of the feeding of the five thousand, then what does he say — and mean?

It is possible that what has been said will be taken as implying that a specific formal ceremony for the commemoration of the Last Supper is neither justifiable nor necessary. This is far from being what is intended. The very abuses of "the bread-breaking" that Paul rebuked at Corinth call attention to a persisting element of human nature. It is the element that assures that the actual will rarely answer to the ideal. There is no least doubt that the first Christians met together in each other's houses for prayer and fellowship and the breaking of bread. Each such gathering was an expression of the faith and love that bound the group together. By it they "showed forth the Lord's death." In fact, the occasion became known as a love feast (the *agape*). As the groups grew larger, situations similar to the one at Corinth inevitably arose. Persons joined the Christian movement from mixed motives. The common meal tended to become a festive occasion. Its real purport became obscured. No one house was large enough to accommodate the group. It was necessary either to divide the group or to gather in some "secular" building. At Corinth the difficulty appears to have been met by a process of simplification, and this was doubtless typical. A distinction was made between the common meal at which the satisfaction of hunger was a consideration, and a much simpler occasion, sometimes following the other, sometimes at a separate time, at which only bread and wine were used. At this simpler meal, special prayers of thanksgiving were used; hence the Eucharist (*eucharistia* is the Greek word for thanksgiving). In time, this simpler meal became known as the Lord's Supper. It was more and more distinguished from the *agape,* which tended to disappear, partly because of Roman suspicion of unauthorized "banquets." Meanwhile, the Eucharist, or Lord's Supper, became increasingly formalized. Justin Martyr, in fact (middle of second century), held that the commemoration was not valid unless a "bishop" was present to preside.

We can quite understand this formalizing. Human nature being what it is, the general needs the help of the special. The Christian's very contact with the world tends to modify "the spiritual glow." To keep the whole of life "sacramental," we need to turn aside to an *arranged* sacrament. The pathos is in the fact that the "arranged" sacrament is often set around with so many restrictions that what should be the supreme expression of Christian unity becomes instead the chief means of Christian division.

Paul speaks of the Church as "the body of Christ." He uses other terms, such as "flock," "building," "temple," "habitation of God in the Spirit," but discussion centers chiefly around what he meant by "the body of Christ." Much depends on whether Paul's view of man is Hebraic or Hellenistic. In the Hebraic view, the relation between "the spirit" and "the body" is much more intimate than it is in the Hellenistic view. The Hebraic view is essentially "holistic." The Hellenistic view is essentially "dualistic," to say nothing more. Here and there Paul seems to echo the Hellenistic view, as when he writes, "May your spirit and soul and body be preserved entire" (I Thess. 5:23), but in general he reflects Hebraic "holism." At the same time it should be noted that he uses the expression, "the church, which is his body," or a similar expression, *only a very few times.* It does not occur in Romans (the sense of ch. 12:5 is different). Its occurrence in I Cor., ch. 12, is somewhat ambiguous: the Church is *compared* to a body and its parts. It does not occur in II Corinthians, or in Philippians, or in Galatians, or oddly enough, in the "churchly" Pastoral Epistles. Granting that the thought occurs in I Corinthians, but with the implication that the believer helps to create the "body" (ch. 12:27), the only other definite occurrences of the phrase are in Ephesians and Colossians, and the Pauline authorship of both of these has been questioned! Even in these two epistles, there is some confusion between the Church as "the body of Christ" and the Church as that "body" of which Christ is the "Head" (Eph. 1:22, 23; 4:15, 16; Col. 2:19), much as in I Cor., ch. 12. The conclusion seems justifiable that Paul moves back and forth between two senses of the word "body" as applied to Christ and the Church: one indicates an identity of the Church with Christ; the other indicates a distinction between Christ and the Church similar to that between the head and the remainder of the body, the function of the head being both to continue life in the body and to control and dominate it. Where identity is implied, we are close to Hebraic holism; where difference is implied, we are closer to Hellenistic dualism.

It is possible to protect both emphases by the conception of *organism*. An organism is a distinctive kind of life expressed in a distinctive form. ("Form" is not used in the Aristotelian sense.) There is here a mutuality: each factor is inseparable from the other. The form is the kind of form that such a life naturally produces. The bird nature calls for the bird form: the bird form discloses the bird nature. If the bird nature could be changed, the bird form would change. The relation between each, while bespeaking mutuality, also bespeaks necessity.

Many would like to believe that the conception of organism fits the Church exactly. In fact, the hierarchical and sacramental system requires it. But the conception as held of the Church conceals a fallacy. An organism is under a law of necessity: the relation of the form to the nature could not but be as it is. But whatever form or forms the Church has taken or devised has been an expression of freedom. It has been an expression of freedom because the creative power which is the very *esse* of the Church is faith, and faith is freedom. The bond between Christ and the soul is a bond of faith. It is a bond that can be dissolved, if the soul will. "I live, yet not I, but Christ liveth in me." Christ and I are a unity — not a natural unity, not a necessitated unity, but a faith unity. In this sense, the Church is Christ ("this is my body") and the Church is I ("many members, but one body"). But the Church thus understood is *life;* it is life, however, of a distinctive kind. It is life under a law of freedom. But even free life will function in its own way. It will function as creative of appropriate and expressive forms. It is this functioning of free life in a free way that has given rise to all the forms, all the procedures, all the institutions, of what we know as "the historic Church." This being the case, all these expressions are *relativities, not absolutes.* Their category is not *esse,* but *bene esse.* The *esse* of the Church is Christ-held-in-faith. The *bene esse* is in whatever freely devised instrumentalities best serve the life and purposes of the *esse.* What was freely devised may be as freely modified, and the demand for the modification rests heavily upon the Church today, not for the mere sake of change, but for the sake of its very life as Christ-held-in-faith.

Here we meet the problem of ecumenicity. There is an ecumenicity of the Church as life constituted of Christ-held-in-faith. There is an ecumenicity of the Church as this life expressed in freely devised forms, polities, procedures, and other instrumentalities. The first ecumenicity is inherent in the nature of the faith and its reference. Nothing can prevent it. No decrees of any kind can limit it. Of Christ-held-in-faith comes the Church with the notes of unity, apostolicity, catholicity, and sanctity. Such a Church bears no limiting label of any sort. It is not Roman Catholic; it is not Greek Orthodox; it is not Protestant. Its ecumenicity is in its very existence. I, a Protestant Christian, am of it; you, a Roman Catholic Christian, are of it; he, a Greek Orthodox Christian, is of it. But I am not of it because I am a Protestant; you are not of it because you are a Roman Catholic; he is not of it because he is a Greek Orthodox. Indeed, I could be a Protestant, you a Roman Catholic, he a Greek Orthodox, and none of us be of the Church in its true ecumenicity. This true ecumenicity does not need to be prayed for, or planned for, or made the subject of earnest discussion. It is itself a fact — inevitable, indubitable, indestructible. It is nothing of the will of man: rather, it is of the will of God, of "God-in-Christ." The only relation it has to the will of man is in the fact that participation in it comes of faith, and faith is a free act, and a free act is an act freely willed.

But there is the Church *as life,* and the Church *as form.* The inevitable ecumenicity of the life does not extend to the form. It might do if the relation of the life to the form was intrinsic, inherent, and therefore necessitated, but it is not. Church governments, of whatsoever sort, are devised. Church procedures in worship, of whatsoever sort, are devised. Sacramental ceremonies, of whatever sort, are devised. Even the most awesome of these ceremonies, the Mass, is devised. Anyone who doubts that has but to read the *history* of the Mass, from the days of Gregory the Great, who broached the *idea* of transubstantiation, through the controversy of the ninth and tenth centuries, which was initiated by the famous treatise of Paschasius Radbert, *On the Body and Blood of Christ,* to the perfecting of the appropriate liturgy late in the twelfth century, and the final clarification of transubstantiation as dogma at the Lateran Council of 1215. It is a long story, and to eliminate from it the human element as determinative of both the process and the result is simply impossible.

The real problem of ecumenicity is created by the various devised instrumentalities, especially those having to do with government and procedures. All the Faith and Order conferences, all the conferences on The Ministry and the Sacraments, all gatherings like that of the Amsterdam Assembly, make this perfectly plain. So long as the instrumentalities are held to be intrinsic to the Christian faith, so that without them the faith ceases to be Christian, we shall get nowhere. Even the Amsterdam Assembly could not agree on a statement concerning the Church, and had to be content with accepting and publishing a number of different statements representing different points of view. The complexity of the problem is appalling. While the world burns, the Church, even if it does not fiddle, at least stubbornly resolves to remain nonecumenical, and by that much incapacitates itself for the urgent task of extinguishing the fire.

Meanwhile, the logic of Biblical faith as Christian freedom must continue to be emphasized. It is safe to say that the vast majority of Christian men and women have never been faced with this logic. They have never been faced with the truth about the Bible. They have never been faced with the truth about the historical Church. Christian freedom in Christ means freedom to devise appropriate instrumentalities for serving the cause of Christ; it means freedom in the use of them; it means freedom in judging them as to their continued usefulness; it means freedom to turn aside from the hindering to the devising of the more appropriate. It does not follow that nothing traditional is worth keeping. Mere novelty is no more defensible than mere antiquity. What it does mean is that we must continue to declare that faith is freedom, freedom to be itself, freedom to serve its own necessities, freedom to submit to restraints and freedom not to submit. Whatever hope there may be of the natural ecumenicity of the free Christian faith finding its counterpart in an achieved ecumenicity of free Christian forms depends upon unrelenting insistence on that great truth which Paul declared to the Christians of Galatia, when in their ignorance and simplicity they were preparing to follow the lead of subtle ecclesiastics who would entangle them in a yoke of bondage. What he wrote was simple with the simplicity of the ultimate: " For freedom did Christ set us free."